COACHING ABROAD

How 8 Coaches Got Jobs and Succeeded Worldwide

Blaine McKenna

BENNION KEARNY

About The Author

Blaine McKenna is a UEFA A Licence coach who has travelled the world coaching football. At the beginning, he didn't see a career in the game, due to the lack of opportunities at home. At that stage, he was unaware of the world full of opportunities that existed outside the bubble of his homeland.

Over 11 years ago, that changed when he first coached abroad and saw the amazing opportunities that were out there. He has since coached in North America, Africa, Oceania, Asia and Europe. It has changed his life.

Blaine wanted to use the power of social media to share this message with coaches who aren't getting the opportunities they deserve at home. He has helped coaches get jobs around the world and his goal is to continue helping coaches bring their football dreams to life!

Twitter: @BlaineMcKenna77

Instagram: @bmck77

Acknowledgements

To my Mum, Dad and Sister, without you, none of this would have been possible. Thanks for always encouraging me to chase my dreams, no matter how far I ventured from home.

A huge thanks to the magnificent coaches who provided great insights for this book. You went into a level of detail that all great coaches do. To my brilliant publisher, James, thanks for your excellent guidance and support. You always kept me on the right path.

Thanks to all the incredible coaches, staff and players I've worked with around the world, you've had a huge impact on me as a coach and more importantly as a person. Thanks to you for reading and the many people on social media who have interacted and sent lovely messages over the years. It was you superstars who inspired me to write this book!

Foreword: A Day in the Life*

I only recently found out the inner workings of a 'based on a true story' movie.

One of the time-saving techniques is to tell a longer story over a shorter period – so I'm going to tell you about some 'highlights' of my two years living and coaching in Tanzania as if it were one day.

I woke up at 6am in a nice two-bedroom apartment in the upmarket Masaki Peninsula area of Dar es Salaam. This is where most of the nice hotels, embassies, and wealthy foreign businesspeople live. I used to sleep with the blackout curtains slightly open as there was nothing better than waking up to the natural sunlight, rather than a blaring alarm! The sun rose between 6 and 6:30 every morning, and it was always pitch black by 6:30pm. A local coach said their 12 hours of darkness and 12 hours of light was a "gift from God".

The sponsor of our academy paid for my accommodation – a whopping $2,000 dollars per month. I include this detail and those above about the upmarket region of the city, not to brag, because it was never lost on me just how fortunate I was. The difference in living conditions between the 'haves' and the 'have nots' was startling.

As I drive from the peninsula towards our academy in the middle of the city, things dramatically change environmentally. Traffic bursts the roadways as soon as you hit the main transport artery through Dar. I would have to leave home for the 15-minute drive before 6:20am – any later and that 15 minutes could turn into 2-3 hours! If I ever did run late, it was easier to cut my losses and work from home and start the journey after 9am.

Being a foreigner and a 'mzungu' (a white man), driving alone through the city was as heartbreaking as it was dangerous. A typical commute would involve dozens of the poorest people on earth pleading with me and anyone else on the road for money or food. A lack of social services meant that kids, the homeless, and the disabled all trickled the route in an attempt to survive another day. To many others in their cars, these people were invisible, not due to a lack of sympathy, but due to the commonality of it. It was so visible that people didn't see it anymore.

I could give these people a meal every day on that commute and do it all again tomorrow. The problem wouldn't cease. There was one old lady who would camp on the junction leading to the academy. She had what I assumed were a couple of barely-clothed grandkids in her care on the roadside. I would give her money every day. A colleague of mine actually told me to stop as "she would begin to expect it". Probably one of the most degrading, heartless things I heard there.

I took myself into this 'discomfort zone' for one reason – football!

Once through the gates of our academy, things changed. The dreary, run-down city landscape was replaced by the site of a glistening, brand new floodlit 3G pitch, purpose-built clubhouse, and various other sporting amenities. It was an oasis in the desert.

As Technical Director of an independent Academy, there was a huge responsibility to develop the next crop of elite football in the country. Nowhere else, even the Football Federation, had the scale of resources or expertise that we did. Our plan was clear. Like a pyramid, we would run programmes for young players up and down the ability and age structure. If the best of the best were at the tip of the pyramid, we knew we had to serve the rest of it better – "the broader the base, the higher the tip". The more kids we could get playing at the base, the more and better players would emerge at the top.

Across the day, our coaches would run various programmes for school children, homeless kids, girls, and the disabled (who were both severely under-served in sport there). If you were a youth in the city – of which there were millions – you could access coaching almost every day of the week, something I became very proud of. In terms of success stories, we had two players come through our 'street kids' programme, through our academy, and into the national team. It was literally life-changing.

As we headed towards our early-evening dusk, our academy players would arrive to train and play. Whilst UK-based academy players arrive with mum and dad, these boys arrived independently. Few of them will have eaten any more than a portion of rice during the day. One player arrived crippled with malaria, but insisted that he could play (our doctor took control of that one!). The 'grit' was at another level to most western players – football may be their best chance of a comfortable life.

Games, under the lights, would see hundreds, often thousands, of locals come to attend along the perimeter fences. We became many people's evening entertainment! And, in one of those bizarre customs that you find in some countries, games were halted by a flag – and not that of a linesman! Before sunset, it was custom to take the national flag down from its flagpole. We literally had to pause in the middle of a game to observe and respect the tradition. It didn't matter if you were through on goal, or in the middle of a cup tie, everything stopped for a minute or two to observe the gesture!

Although, with maybe the exception of Mbwana Samatta, you've probably not heard of too many Tanzanian footballers, but I promise you, these kids could play! They do what western kids no longer do –

they play for hours every day. On the streets, on the beaches, barefoot. They could handle a ball so our programme became about teaching them the game. How to apply their excellent technique in game situations. Simply put, *tactics*.

Thousands came for our initial assessments for entry into the academy – this meant everything to them. This was a chance not only to play football, but to scramble their way out of squalor. Of the final 40 selected, between 12 and 16 years old, 80% of them didn't even go to school. During the day, they grafted making petty earnings for their family. The boots we had for them (direct from Adidas) had to be stored at the academy as the potential for them to be stolen or sold was too high. We lost one Under-16 boy when he just stopped turning up. Having asked around, he had left – on foot – for South Africa, sneaking across several national borders to get a job drug-running on the streets of Johannesburg. Something that was apparently quite common. Ironically, I saw his name on a South African Academy website some years later, and interestingly, he was still playing as an Under-16!

Age was a funny thing in that part of the world. We had one boy attend academy assessments for our Under-16s on a Monday. He was sent away as local coaches knew him as being too old. He returned the next day for the Under-15 trials! One of our midfielders was selected for a place with the prestigious Aspire Academy in Qatar, only to be too old. His 'agent' came to tell me that they would be paying someone in a local government office to get a new birth certificate, changing his year of birth from 1999 to 2000!

All in a day's work!

The drive home at night, at the end of a football-filled day, was also fun. The glass in my wing-mirrors was routinely stolen and sold at the local market. Police would stop me from time to time and if the business card of their Chief-of-Police didn't persuade them to let me go, I'd usually have to pay an "agreed cash fine, without a receipt" for whatever phantom misdemeanour I was pulled over for!

Coaching abroad not only leaves your football-fix sorted, it never leaves you short of a true story!

Ray Power

Table of Contents

Coach Introductions

Let's introduce you to the eight coaches who kindly shared their stories, insights, and experiences throughout this book. The coaches have worked at various levels of the game, are at different stages of their careers, and have had successes and setbacks that we can all learn from.

Scott Cooper has been Head Coach of two national teams in the Caribbean and was Technical Director and Head Coach of the Philippines National Team. He has worked at top clubs in Thailand and coached in the AFC Champions League and World Cup Qualifiers.

Sam Bensley is an English coach who has worked at professional academies in England, the New York Red Bulls, a grassroots club in China, and the Hong Kong Football Association. He has worked from grassroots to youth national teams and senior football.

Michael Yau is an English coach who has worked from the youngest grassroots teams in England and China, up to the first team of Shenzhen FC in the Chinese Super League. He was there during the boom of Chinese football, working alongside top players and coaches.

Steve Darby is an English coach who has worked in 12 countries. He has worked at professional clubs in England, Malaysia, Singapore, India, and Bahrain. Steve has also worked for several National Associations such as Bahrain, Vietnam, Australia, Fiji, Thailand, and Laos.

Cederique Tulleners is a Belgian coach. He has coached at academy level in Belgium, camps in America and Africa, from grassroots to professional League Two in China, Federation level in Lithuania, and professional clubs in Belgium and the United Arab Emirates.

Colum Curtis is a Northern Irish coach who has coached Youth National Teams in Northern Ireland, done camps in the USA, grassroots in China, and worked in professional clubs in Cambodia as first team Assistant and Head Coach.

I am **Blaine McKenna** from Northern Ireland. I have coached in 11 countries on five continents, working from grassroots to Academy Director at a topflight Thai League club, and working individually with international players and Head Coaches.

Simon McMenemy is a British Head Coach who has worked at professional clubs in the Philippines, Vietnam, and Indonesia. He has also been Head Coach of the Philippines and Indonesian National Teams. Let's find out how it all started for Simon in the Philippines…

Chapter 1. Simon's Journey: From the 11th Tier to National Team Head Coach

In July 2010, Simon McMenemy was Assistant Manager at Worthing FC and working full-time for an insurance company. Six months later, he would change Philippines football forever.

Previously, in December 2008, Simon was working for Nike and was player-manager at Haywards Heath Town FC. During a game, disaster struck as he broke his leg, which led to him losing his job at Nike. To make things even worse, his partner Sarah also lost her job.

2009 was the hardest year of Simon's life. He couldn't get a job in football, or any other industry, to make ends meet. Employers outside the game knew he wasn't a long-term solution as he would always return to football. Ultimately, Simon was out of work for nine months that year and sat in bed for three months with his broken leg.

After many setbacks, Simon finally got offered a job. It was in insurance rather than football, but it was enough to fund his football passion until he could get back into the game full-time. He was grateful for the job, but he spent the entire day staring out of the window thinking about football. He also took on a part-time role as Assistant Manager at Worthing FC. Then, fate intervened.

In July 2010, Simon received a Facebook message – out of the blue – from Simon Greatwich. Greatwich had been coached by Simon at a local U18 team and told him that the Philippines had lost their British Head Coach. He encouraged Simon to apply for the job.

Simon didn't think he had the credentials. He was a UEFA B coach working as an Assistant at Step 7 of Non-League, which is the 11th tier of English football. Greatwich, however, thought he had a chance and said he would recommend him to the decision-makers.

Simon sent his CV which included filming Nike videos with Ronaldinho, Cesc Fabregas, and Carlos Tevez. He thought there was no chance it would happen, and when he told Sarah he had applied to become Head Coach of the Philippines, she laughed and they both forgot about it soon after.

Impossible Dream

Simon was at work one day when the phone rang. It was the General Manager of the Philippines National Team. He wanted to have a chat with Simon about his philosophy and thoughts on football. Simon gave it his all but still didn't believe it was possible.

Two days later, the General Manager called back and offered Simon the job. He had to be in Manila in 10 days. Simon was in complete shock... he was the new Philippines Head Coach. He had never even been to the Philippines!

I was on top of the world. I was travelling to a new country to coach football. I was massively excited, but genuinely had no idea what was in store.

Simon didn't know what it took to be a National Team Head Coach but he was never going to turn it down.

When you get asked, "Do you want to be a National Team Head Coach?" you don't think about it. You say, "Yes of course I do." No one asked me if I could do the job or if I had the confidence to get on a plane and do it. I said yes and then I'd work the rest out... because those chances don't come around often.

Simon went into the office of the Managing Director of his insurance company and told him he had to step down as he was now a National Team Head Coach. The Managing Director congratulated him and asked about his salary. Simon was so shocked he forgot to ask. They opened a bottle of champagne to celebrate.

Simon went home to tell Sarah and she started crying. He consoled her, and they sat down and discussed how to make it work.

Philippines Head Coach

Ten days later, Simon arrived at Manila airport, and it was absolute chaos.

Landing at Manila Airport was crazy. I was wheeling my trolley out and it dawned on me that I had no idea who was picking me up. I didn't have a number to call, my phone didn't work and I didn't have any local money. I was there with my cases hoping that someone would pick me up.

I walked out of the building and the heat hit me. I'm thinking, what if this was a joke? I don't have a return ticket. What happens if no one picks me up? What happens if they've changed their mind? What am I going to do? I was genuinely worried.

At that moment, a man tapped me on the shoulder and said, "Hey, coach, I'm Ace from the National Team."

Ace (National Team coordinator) took Simon straight to the training ground to watch a session where the Philippines-based players were preparing for an upcoming tournament. After the session, he went back to the hotel and it was terrible. He couldn't sleep that night and was all over the place with jet lag.

The team had training the next day, which was Simon's first session in charge as the Philippines Head Coach. It was a big moment for him, but as soon as the session started, he completely relaxed.

The session was all about football, which is something he knows. Getting thrown in at the deep end was a blessing in disguise for Simon.

I didn't have a long run up to the flight. I wasn't there for a month thinking, Oh my God, I'm going to the Philippines, what on earth am I going to do? Can I do the job? I just got on the plane and went. It worked out well because it was so fast. It didn't give me time to think. If I thought about it, I might have chickened out.

Severe Doubts

Simon had three weeks of training before the 2010 Long Teng Cup in Taiwan. The Philippines were using the tournament to prepare for the ASEAN Football Federation (AFF) Championship qualifiers in Laos.

The AFF Championship was known as the Suzuki Cup. It's a major tournament in South East Asia and the Philippines had only qualified twice in their history. Simon had a massive job on his hands.

The team arrived safely in Taiwan. Their first game was against Hong Kong's U23 Team, who were preparing for the Asian Games.

The rain was torrential and the pitch was flooded. The game went ahead regardless, as it was live on television. Both teams were trying, but it was impossible to play football in such conditions.

As the conditions got worse, Simon stood up and started shouting at the officials. The conditions were ridiculous and someone was going to get hurt. Simon's first fixture as Philippines Head Coach got abandoned. He had berated the referee to such an extent that he stopped the game early.

The game was rescheduled for the following day, and the team lost 4-2 to Hong Kong U23, which made Simon question himself.

I thought… this is above me. I don't know if I can do this. I was very new to professional football and I'm standing in a stadium in Taiwan. What the hell is going on here?

But you remind yourself that you know football. I need to understand the accent and how it's played here. But I know football. I'm here for a reason. And I can coach; I know I can coach.

The Philippines drew their next game 1-1 against Chinese Taipei, scoring a 93rd minute equaliser. The final game of the Cup saw the team beat Macau 5-1, and they finished 3rd overall, with Hong Kong U23 topping the group.

After the tournament, Simon had ten days to prepare the team for the Suzuki Cup qualifiers in Laos.

One Goal is Enough

The results at the Long Teng Cup made Simon question himself, but he had to hide this self-doubt to convince people he was the right man for the job. The foreign-based players still hadn't arrived, but the preparation games were helping Simon assess the local players.

Simon researched the previous coach's approach and watched the team's games on video. He didn't want to change much as there was no time with the foreign-based players arriving merely days before the qualifiers. Simon tweaked things a little but kept it simple.

The Philippines were in a qualifying group with Cambodia, Laos, and Timor-Leste. They got off to a great start, winning their first game 5-0 against Timor-Leste, and Simon was encouraging the team to play out from the back, press high, and win the ball close to the opponent's goal. It worked, with Ian Araneta bagging a hat-trick.

They weren't getting carried away, though, as Timor-Leste was one of the weaker teams, and Simon knew he would have to change tactics and be more defensive against the other teams. If they played open against Laos and Cambodia, they would have no chance of qualifying.

The next game against Laos was a much tougher test. The Philippines found themselves 2-0 down at half-time, which was a big blow to their hopes of qualifying. Phil Younghusband managed to make it 2-1 from the penalty spot in the 76th minute. This gave them hope, but it was fading as they headed into added time 2-1 down.

But Simon's side kept pushing and snatched a 94th-minute equaliser through former Chelsea academy player James Younghusband.

Neil Etheridge launched a ball into their area – route one football – and Jimmy Younghusband is a foot taller than anyone else on the pitch. He's gone up with the keeper, nodded it past him in the 94th minute, and it's gone in.

With the draw against Laos, another draw – against Cambodia – in the final game would be enough to secure qualification. The Philippines started the game poorly, with Cambodia creating chances and rattling the frame of the goal twice. The Cambodians were up for it as they needed a win to guarantee qualification. They were level on points with the Philippines but they had an inferior goal difference.

The Philippines managed to keep them out, though, and almost scored a late winner. The game finished 0-0, which meant the Philippines had secured Suzuki Cup qualification for only the third time in their history. Simon was struggling to keep his emotions in check throughout the tournament.

I'd be crying on the bus, on the way to games. I'm thinking, Jesus Christ, my Dad's watching this game. I'm in the Philippines playing against Laos. And I'm getting messages before the game from my friends at work who've got the game open on their laptops. Everyone's crowded around watching the Philippines versus Cambodia because they know the guy on the sideline.

Simon felt they had a lot of luck in their qualifying games, but the Laos coach thought their 94th-minute equaliser was more than lucky.

The Laos coach, David Booth – who I'm good friends with now – swears to this day there was something wrong about how his goalkeeper approached that. He's never done it before. He's quite a good goalkeeper and never comes off his line. He came out to punch but didn't get anywhere near it. We didn't care. Without that goal, we wouldn't have qualified, but we were through.

Timor-Leste's performance against Laos in the final game also raised questions. Laos had to win the game by three goals to qualify on goal difference.

You got this feeling the Timor-Leste players weren't trying. They were letting guys run past and score. We were sitting in the stands watching it, and we were looking at each other. "What's going on here? They didn't play like that against us." We won 5-0 against Timor-Leste, but they worked hard. It was a very different performance against Laos.

Laos won 6-1 against Timor-Leste to top the group, with the Philippines 2nd and Cambodia 3rd. All three teams were level on five points and were separated only by goal difference.

The Philippines were through to the finals of the Suzuki Cup, and that 94th-minute goal against Laos was enough to give Simon an incredible opportunity to make a name for himself. If he could get a couple of results on the big stage at the Suzuki Cup, it would set him up for a career in the region. He dreamed and told himself he could do it, but he still had a lot to prove.

Team Divide

During the qualifiers, there was conflict between the local and foreign-based players. Most of the foreign-based players had grown up in

England and had British and Filipino passports. One of the locals would tell Simon if he was conversing with the foreigners more than the locals during team talks.

The local guys weren't tackling the bigger, stronger foreigners out of respect. We started making rules. You can only have two foreign guys at a table at any one time. If you had more, then everyone at the table does press-ups.

He got the captain on board to get everyone on the same level, which had a positive effect.

I pulled the captain to one side; he was a bit of a legend in football there. I said, "I need you to work with me here," and explained to him, "I'm going to take the piss out of you all the time. You're going to be my number one target. I'm doing it for the right reasons. I need to bring this team together. I need guys to be comfortable laughing at you. I need everyone to be on the same level."

The Filipino players raised in England were a big help for Simon.

What helped was that every unit within the team had a British influence. I had Neil Etheridge (Ex-Premier League) in goal who was barking orders at everybody. Rob Gier, who used to be at Wimbledon in central defence. He organised his line. Chris Greatwich, in centre midfield, was organising the midfield. Phil Younghusband, a former Chelsea striker, was organising the other striker.

I wasn't coaching Phil anything. I was getting him organised and motivated. The same with Chris and Rob. I was asking them to listen. "If we're going to do this, you've got to buy in, and help me out. You've got to be four Assistant Coaches on the pitch. Let's get organised; let's not get beat." It gave me more time to focus on working with the local Filipino players who didn't have the same sort of knowledge.

Simon organised team-building activities to bring the local and foreign players together. After qualifying, they all went to a nightclub in the hotel and Neil Etheridge put his card behind the bar to pay for everything.

It brought everyone together, and they were joking on the plane home. This helped performances moving forward.

Miracle of Hanoi

After qualifying, the Philippines had one month to prepare for the Suzuki Cup. The team flew to Thailand to play a final warm-up game before going to Vietnam. The game wasn't ideal preparation as they got beaten 8-0 by a second division Thai team, Nakhon Pathom.

The Philippines were in a tough group with Myanmar, Singapore, and Vietnam. There wasn't any pressure going into the games; Singapore had won two of the previous three Suzuki Cups, and Vietnam was the reigning champions. It looked like an impossible task for a team that had never qualified for the knock-out rounds.

Simon faced the press along with the other Head Coaches. Everyone was discussing how many goals Singapore and Vietnam would score against the Philippines. It wasn't whether they would win… but by how many.

It annoyed Simon, but it also motivated him to prove everyone wrong. He had limited time with the players, but he wasn't worried about the opposition.

The biggest strength I had during the whole stint with the Philippines National Team was my naivety. I'd never been anywhere near that level before. I went into every game going, "Let's try and win it."

I didn't even do that much research on the opponents. That helped because it didn't scare me. I wasn't like, Oh Jesus, we've never beaten Vietnam before in our history. I didn't know.

I had a look at their previous games to assess their shape and formation. I was like, "Okay, this is what we're going to try and do." I didn't go that in-depth. Not as much as I do now that's for sure. If I had thought about it, I wouldn't have done the job. I would shit myself and be on a plane home.

The Philippines' first group game was against Singapore in Hanoi. Singapore had the better chances in the first half. Etheridge made a few good saves, and Anton del Rosario cleared one off the line. The Philippines managed to reach half-time at 0-0.

After the break, the Philippines had chances, but Singapore finally broke the deadlock in the 65th minute through Aleksandar Duric. They then missed opportunities to make it two, but one goal looked to be enough as they headed for added time. That was until Chris Greatwich (Simon Greatwich's brother) stepped up to score a 93rd-minute equaliser and snatch a shock 1-1 draw. What a start for the Philippines!

Their next game wasn't going to be any easier as they were facing the Suzuki Cup champions, Vietnam, in front of 40,000 expectant home fans in Hanoi.

The Philippines hit the post with an early chance before Vietnam fought back, forcing Etheridge into a good save, and Vietnam then fired a free-kick wide after Etheridge handled outside his box. It was the Philippines, however, who took a shock lead through a Chris Greatwich header in the 38th minute.

After scoring, they defended for their lives! Etheridge made some great saves, and Vietnam couldn't break them down. The Philippines managed to break – on the counter – to seal the win in the 79th minute. Phil Younghusband slotted it home to secure a historic 2-0 victory.

The Vietnam manager, Henrique Calisto, refused to shake Simon's hand. He accused them of being overly defensive. Simon didn't care as it was a huge moment for him and the country.

It was the first time the Philippines had ever beaten Vietnam and was a massive step towards qualifying. The game is fondly remembered by Filipino football fans as the "Miracle of Hanoi".

The Philippines needed at least a draw in their final game against Myanmar to progress out of the group. Myanmar was the perfect opponent. They were bottom of the group with no points and nothing to play for.

Despite this, Myanmar started well, creating a few chances. The Philippines grew into the game and began taking control. They hit the frame of the goal three times, but the 0-0 draw was ultimately enough.

The Philippines had qualified for the Suzuki Cup semi-finals for the first time in their history!

Finishing the group with 5 points was an incredible achievement. No one expected the team to take any points from Singapore or Vietnam. Never mind qualifying for the knock-out rounds in second place.

During the tournament, Simon had doubted himself as a National Team Head Coach. He didn't believe he could succeed in front of 40,000 fans. He thought this role would be short term and he'd go back to a development role in England. Despite his self-doubt, his side managed to overcome all odds and win in front of 40,000, making history in the process.

90,000 Fans

Before the semi-finals against Indonesia, Simon cried his eyes out. He couldn't put into words the feelings he had experienced over the six months he had been in charge. Going from Worthing to the Philippines Head Coach and semi-finals of the Suzuki Cup, he wasn't ready for it, and he had to suck up his emotions constantly. He was so caught up by the experience and the support he had from people at home.

Simon was intimidated by the games as he didn't have the experience. He was telling players who played at a much higher level what to do, and it affected how he spoke to people.

How do you prepare for something like that? When you go to Indonesia, one of the most populous countries on earth, with football the number one sport. You're playing their national team in the semi-final of an international competition. You walk into the stadium. It's a huge amount of stimulus from all angles; the noise, smell, feeling, and atmosphere.

That's Championship Manager, yet I'm in the stadium. Not sitting at home winning the FA Cup with Worthing. I'm playing Championship Manager in real life. This is a dream; this isn't happening.

The two legs against Indonesia were played in Jakarta due to the Philippines not having an AFF-approved stadium. The semi-final first leg was played in front of 90,000 passionate fans in the Bung Karno stadium. On the way to the stadium, the Indonesian fans were rocking the Philippines bus, and they had police onboard to protect them.

The game was a close affair with both teams creating chances. Indonesia scored in the 32nd minute after a defensive mix-up, which left Gonzales free to head into the empty goal. Both teams continued creating chances, but Indonesia held on to win the first leg 1-0.

During the game, the Philippines players and staff couldn't hear each other talk, such was the noise of the fans in the stadium. It's an experience all coaches dream of.

My naivety helped in that I'd never been here before. It's like a 17-year-old playing for the senior team for the first time. I was fearless. I wasn't worried but I would be now. It got emotional, oh my God, this is something incredibly special. This is somewhere people dream of being and I need to give this everything I've got.

The second leg was three days later in front of 90,000 fans at the Bung Karno once again. Indonesia had the better of the first half, with the Philippines unable to create any clear-cut chances. The game got heated with players coming together after an altercation that saw Chris Greatwich booked. Gonzales scored for Indonesia two minutes before half-time to put them 2-0 up on aggregate.

The Philippines grew into the game, however, and created some chances in the second half, but it wasn't enough. Greatwich got sent off for a second yellow after a lunging tackle three minutes before the final whistle. It was a disappointing finish, but what an experience to play in front of 90,000 passionate fans.

It was the perfect atmosphere to end what had been an emotional rollercoaster for Simon and the team.

To this day, nothing's come close to that. The Bung Karno, it's a bit like the Bernabeu. You're underneath the pitch. You can hear the rumbling, the noise, and the dust falling from where the fans are. There's a staircase you walk up onto the pitch. They open this huge trapdoor and you walk up the steps into this cauldron of sheer noise. It hits you like a punch.

They made history by reaching the semi-finals and changed Philippines football forever. It was the most amazing experience of Simon's career.

It was life-changing. After that, I was immediately experienced. I've been in a stadium with ninety thousand fans all wanting to kill me. It was phenomenal.

We did a lap of honour, and everyone was shouting and clapping. Neil Etheridge was half-naked; he was only left in his pants. All of his kit had gone back into the crowd because they were going mental. It was a crazy, crazy time. It's a dream of every football fan to play Championship Manager for real.

New Opportunities

When the team returned to the Philippines, they received a heroes' welcome at Manila airport. Many people were there to greet them and the media wanted photos and interviews. Since that fateful tournament in 2010, Philippines football has changed, with a professional league forming and the winners qualifying for the Asian Champions League.

After their success, Filipino football was cast into the spotlight. Simon thought he would get his contract extended after doing so well, but it didn't turn out that way.

People didn't expect us to do as well as we'd done. All of a sudden, they're talking about building a professional league in the Philippines. They started importing players from all over the place. Sadly, it cost me the job because I was a no-name coach who happened to be lucky.

Simon got the Head Coach job through Facebook and found out he lost it on Facebook, too. A journalist told him the Philippines General Manager held a press conference announcing their new German Head Coach.

The German Football Federation offered a lot of money and support in return for a German National Team Head Coach. I ended up losing the job because we'd been successful, not because we failed.

They claimed Simon didn't have the right qualifications or experience. Simon felt this wasn't true as AFC and FIFA said it wasn't a problem and he had shown his capability in the Suzuki Cup. But success in the tournament had put Simon's name on the map, nonetheless, and he started attracting attention from clubs.

Suddenly, my phone started ringing with different agents trying to get in touch. I'd never spoken to agents before and had no idea how to approach it. I was getting offered this and getting offered that. I ended up going back to Vietnam, and it launched my career.

Losing the Philippines Head Coach job was a sad end to an incredible six-month journey from Worthing to Manila. A journey that saw him become the youngest National Team Head Coach in the world at 32 years of age. It was, however, the perfect springboard for Simon to start his career as a top-level Head Coach in South East Asia.

Chapter 2. Education Essentials

The importance of coaching licences and university degrees are hotly debated in coaching circles. Let's find out how these qualifications have impacted the coaches' journeys.

Coaching Licences

Coaching licences don't guarantee great coaching, but they do present opportunities to:

- Network and learn from professional coaches and ex-professional players.
- Learn and discuss with knowledgeable course tutors.
- Display competence and get assessment feedback.
- Cover a range of topics such as sports science and leadership, with top guest speakers.
- Access higher-level jobs.

They're a small but vital piece of the puzzle if you have ambitions of coaching at a high level.

Top Level Insights

The best part of coaching licences is the people you meet on the courses. Colum Curtis and I had a high calibre group on the UEFA A course in Northern Ireland.

We had ex-pros who had won European Cups and Premier Leagues; managers in the Championship and amateur leagues.

Paul Warne was very good. He was talking about his chairman ringing him after games in the English Championship. These conversations give you a broader idea of the football world.

Such courses also open your mind to different beliefs and approaches. Colum learned a lot from the debates during the course.

It tells you that there are no wrong and right answers. There were 60 people in a room arguing about who calls the line in a back 4 when we need to get up. A Premier League centre back was saying, "If I'm playing at Old Trafford, do you think my left back's going to call the line?"

I was in the car with Ricardo Carvalho, and I asked him what he thought. He said, "I always call the line."

On the course, we watched Tiago Mendes coach a session on 4-4-2 defending in a low block; a session he often did under Diego Simeone as a player and Assistant at Atlético Madrid. It must have worked as they won La Liga, the Europa League, and got to the Champions League final twice!

Tiago was brilliant. He spoke to everyone and was telling fascinating stories about playing for Jose Mourinho and Simeone. The ex-professionals were telling eye-opening stories they wouldn't dare say to the media.

There were ten former Premier League players on our course and we also watched five former Premier League players doing their UEFA B assessments. It was fascinating observing them and listening to their insights.

We also had a range of excellent tutors to complement what we were learning from each other. We had guest speakers like Michael Caulfield, who is a fantastic presenter and has worked with Premier League players and teams. Simon Davies was the Head of Coaching at Manchester City and gave a fascinating insight into their approach and Pep Guardiola's expectations.

It was a great experience learning about coaching from those who have worked at the highest levels of the game.

Networking

You learn from the people you meet, but it also creates opportunities – if you can make an impression. I met Colum on a youth certificate course, and we had long chats about coaching. A few years later, he brought me to China to work alongside him.

Scotsman Ian Cathro, meanwhile, made an impression on Nuno Espírito Santo at a coaching course in Scotland. This led to spells working with Nuno at Valencia, Wolverhampton Wanderers, and Tottenham Hotspur. Going from Dundee United's Academy to working at first team level at La Liga and Premier League clubs transformed his career.

It may not happen for everyone, but it shows you what is possible if you impress people on coaching courses.

How to impress on coaching courses:

- Be outgoing and talk to everyone. Have lots of individual chats with different people on the way to venues and during breaks.
- Do your research on other participants to improve the quality of your conversations and to find things you have in common.

- Speak up in group discussions to ask questions and share your ideas and experiences.
- Step up to volunteer for practicals or presentations.
- Be well prepared for assessments. These are key moments to show your work.
- Get to know people, share your ideas, and create connections.
- Get people's contact details to stay in touch.

You never know what it will lead to.

Assessments

The feedback you receive from assessments is valuable, and Colum believes it's worth putting yourself 'out there' to get it.

The assessment feedback was always good, as it gives you confidence. I was a nervous wreck before my level 2 assessment. Now if they ask anyone to do a session, I'll happily do it.

Colum also saw that *everyone* gets nervous before assessments, regardless of their profile.

Some of the pros have played FA Cup finals at Wembley, and there's only a couple of us watching, and they're panicking.

Job Requirements

Clubs are often required by their league, FA, or confederation to have staff with a certain licence to enter competitions. In the top league in Thailand, for example, I needed an A licence to be Academy Director.

I had a UEFA B at the time but informed the club I would be starting my UEFA A that year. On paper, I was first team Assistant, and the Pro licence first team Assistant was Academy Director. This could have held me back, but I was able to secure a place on the UEFA A course that season.

Colum Curtis needed his Pro licence once he qualified for the AFC Cup in Cambodia. He had a UEFA A licence at the time but managed to secure a place on the UEFA Pro licence that season. You can get special permission to coach in competitions when you provide evidence that you're working towards the required licence, as Scott Cooper did with the Philippines National Team.

It isn't always that straightforward for coaches, though. The Philippines claimed they didn't offer Simon McMenemy a new contract because he didn't have the required licence. Naturally, there may have been other reasons… but it can only strengthen your position having the required licence.

There are ways around not having the right licence, but it's best to *get qualified* to the required level and keep your licences valid, so you don't miss out on any opportunities.

Unique Journey

Some people rush through their coaching licences. Michael Yau believes you need time to embed the learning before moving on to the next course.

Sometimes, we're too quick to get rid of courses, and we don't apply any of the things that we learned. The coaches that have taken on the knowledge, applied it on the field, and refined their work – get better as a result.

Colum also believes you should take your time.

On the level 2, there was a guy who wasn't ready. He said about coming back in the summer, but he needed more time on the grass, coaching. There's no rush.

There is a balance to be attained – where you need to reach a certain level – if you want to get a good full-time job in football. Sam Bensley realised this and got to UEFA B to increase his opportunities.

You can't get some jobs without having a certain licence. You've got to push yourself to do it. I got myself up to B licence.

Once Sam got his UEFA B licence, he took six years before doing his A licence. It wasn't a necessity for getting jobs at that stage. This changed once he joined the Hong Kong FA. He decided the A licence would benefit his work with the Youth National Teams.

Sam mentioned that cost is a big consideration but if you can afford it then it's worth it.

If you can afford it and you've got the team required to do it, then why not? Because it's going to open more doors than it closes.

If you need a certain licence to get a job, then go for it. Getting into the right coaching environment will be the best learning tool. If it's not essential for getting the next job and you're not ready, then take your time. Maximise the value of the courses by revisiting the information and applying it.

As with any journey in life, it's down to the individual and their aspirations. Cederique believes it's important to pave your own path as a coach.

You need to find a balance. Should you go a little faster or take a slower pace? It depends on the coach. Every coach has their own pathway.

Cederique is right; progress depends on what level *you* want to work at, and where *you* are in your development as a coach.

Don't rush the journey.

It took me ten years to get from level 1 to UEFA A. In the beginning, I was in a mad rush to do every qualification possible. With experience, I've come to realise expertise is built over years and there are no shortcuts. Be patient and work out what timeline is right for you; good opportunities will come with planning, high-quality work, and time.

Drawbacks

We have highlighted the positive aspects of courses, but some downsides need consideration:

- Courses are expensive, can be time-consuming, and may involve time off work.
- It can be hard to get accepted onto courses in certain countries.
- The information is not delivered with your coaching environment in mind. You need to adapt it to the experience, level, and style that works with your group.
- A large volume of information gets delivered in a short timeframe. This makes it hard to go into detail or revisit information.
- With limited time, course leaders can't always adopt the best teaching practices, hold many interactive discussions, or cater to individual coach's needs.
- The technical and tactical are often prioritised over other important areas.
- There is less individual technical detail on the higher-level courses. They're aimed at the 11v11 game and not youth formats.
- Psychology information is limited at the beginning. It only increases once you progress to higher licences.
- The assessment criteria can be quite rigid. It won't always match how you would coach in your environment.
- Some course tutors may not have a great coaching record in the game. Whether this affects their ability as coach educators is debatable.

(These drawbacks were collated from the experiences of the coaches in this book.)

Coaching Licence courses are improving all the time. Assessments may now take place in the coaches' environments, which is more realistic.

There are also more youth pathway courses for those working with younger players.

Learning on the job, from other coaches, and personal reflection often provide the best lessons. Coaching courses supplement your learning and are a necessity for working at higher levels. The courses will continue improving and – in my view – the benefits far outweigh the drawbacks.

Moving Abroad

If you plan to move abroad, it's important to have a clear strategy for your education.

Flights, courses, and accommodation costs are often expensive. Travelling across time zones is tiring and courses may include 12-hour days. The courses can also eat into your holidays, which are already limited for coaches.

Video assessments are becoming more common for coaches living abroad. This is great if you have enough players available to do the assessment where you live. If you don't, then it can be challenging.

You may need to do an intensive course which often takes place during the off season. The dates can clash with foreign leagues which will mean you either can't do it, or you will need to leave your team during the season.

Your boss may not support your courses financially or grant you leave. Scott, for example, couldn't get time off to do courses. He recommends getting allowances in your contract to obtain new licences and revalidate existing ones.

Any coach in contract negotiations should push to get permission to do licenses. I know a lot of coaches that have failed with that, and have not been allowed to go on courses.

You can't always predict what the future holds. I wasn't ready to start my UEFA A before going abroad full-time. I also didn't anticipate becoming an Academy Director two years later.

You don't always know what will happen, but planning helps! Figure out what qualifications you'll need for future roles and how you'll get them.

Course Rejections

Every year, we hear stories of coaches having their coaching licence applications rejected. Sam knows how tough it can be to get onto courses in England.

Many coaches in England are frustrated. They've repeatedly applied for the A licence year after year and cannot get in.

Sam believes coaches should have the opportunity to do courses in their own country.

If I've grown up in England and I want to work in an English Academy. I should have the chance to work underneath my FA.

If I looked at it from the English FA point of view, I would want to run more courses to get more A licence coaches. That's going to raise the top-level of coaching in our country. It would be interesting to hear why that isn't the case.

I am sure many people would echo Sam's thoughts.

Foreign Countries

Doing your licence with a different Football Association is an option. I know coaches who have done courses in countries including Northern Ireland, Republic of Ireland, Wales, Scotland, Spain, Germany, Malaysia, Philippines, Brunei, Hong Kong, USA, Singapore, and Serbia.

There are opportunities out there. Sam has noticed coaches getting onto courses in different parts of the United Kingdom.

The door has opened a little in Northern Ireland, Scotland, and Wales to get onto A licence courses there.

There are opportunities elsewhere in Europe too. Scott did his licences in Serbia after creating contacts there during his online studies at the University of Belgrade. The course was in English and Scott found it to be a valuable experience.

I like how their coach education works, and the way they think about the game. It was also quicker for me to get through because there was a long waiting list at home.

Jonny Pipes did his UEFA B licence with the German Football Association (DFB). He searched online – how to find a UEFA B course abroad – and found a company that organised it there. The course was delivered in English and Jonny loved it.

It's my favourite coaching course so far. The English and German UEFA B courses have very different focuses and ideas surrounding the content. It was refreshing to learn a completely new take on coaching, while also taking in everything culturally from the way they experience and feel about football.

It can be tough for coaches to get onto courses in foreign countries, however, since locals get priority, courses are in demand, and not all courses are delivered in English.

AFC Courses

Michael worked for a Chinese Super League club but decided to do his Asian Football Confederation (AFC) B licence in Singapore. He recommends doing licences with AFC if you are working in Asia.

Some say there's a difference between the content and credibility of UEFA and AFC licences but it allows you to meet the locals. They share practical experiences that help you understand the environment you're working in. You also start to understand more about how the local coaches think.

The courses are delivered differently. It's a good experience.

Sam did his AFC A licence in Hong Kong. Working for the Hong Kong Football Association made it easier for Sam to secure a place, and the course was in English. He also found it to be a positive experience.

The Japanese instructor was hugely beneficial. Japan is by far the most developed country in football terms in Asia; particularly in the way it develops coaches and grassroots players. I did a study visit in Japan and the level of players is unbelievable, even at the grassroots level.

The environment they create with the parents and coaches is fantastic.

Doing courses in a different region of the world gives you a new way of thinking. Sam learned a lot about the Japanese approach to development.

The physical stature of Japanese people as a whole is a bit smaller. They're not physically strong when compared to their European or African counterparts. The Japanese FA came up with a way of using what they've got to their advantage.

The training they deliver for their players and coaches is far more technique-based. When they get to senior level, they can't rely on going toe to toe with Belgium from a physical point of view. The players must play in tight spaces, work combinations, and create 2v1 situations. They can't go 1v1.

This was a very different approach from what Sam had experienced when working and doing his UEFA B in England.

In England, we encourage players to be very creative, good on the ball, and dominant in 1v1 situations. We have the players who can handle that at senior level. Whereas Japan had a different perspective, which was interesting to learn from.

Being able to pick up different ideas is invaluable and informs your work in the region.

Challenges

Sam experienced problems moving home as his AFC A licence wasn't accepted in England.

It took me 18 months to get through my AFC A licence course and it was extremely intense. I came back to England and it's not seen as equal to the UEFA A course. This means I would need to do a second A licence to reach that level. It's frustrating because you have worked at the level required.

Sam would recommend doing your licence in the region you plan to work long-term.

It would depend on the long-term goal… if the coach knows what that is. If the coach makes connections in Thailand, and sees themselves living there long-term, then why not? You can look for courses in Asia that deliver English-speaking courses – like in Malaysia.

But if your goal was to work in professional European academies, you need a UEFA licence, and you need to stay in Europe.

Scott agrees and will do both the AFC and UEFA Pro licence courses. He chose to do the AFC Pro Licence first as it was quicker and a requirement for his job.

I was waiting on the UEFA Pro list in Serbia and Moldova because my UEFA licences are through Serbia. I wanted to do the UEFA Pro, but it takes too much time to complete. It is quite extensive compared to the AFC one.

You can't get a job in Europe with the AFC Pro, you have to have the UEFA Pro, so I'm going to have to do both. I want to do the AFC Instructor licence course too. I've got a teaching degree, a Masters, and PhD, and being an instructor might be an option one day.

Do Your Research

Reach out to different FAs and coaches who have done courses abroad. Gather as much information as possible regarding the entry requirements and course details to find the course which is best financially, time- and career-wise.

Most importantly, if you suffer rejection, don't give up!

An English coach got rejected on the course of a neighbouring Football Association. Instead of feeling sorry for himself, he wrote a heartfelt letter. His home association wasn't allowing him onto the next licence to progress his career, and it was also proving impossible for him to get on courses elsewhere. They listened and accepted him onto the next course.

University Education

You don't need a degree to coach at grassroots, professional, or federation level, but it can:

- Give you a deeper understanding of coaching-related topics.

- Teach you to analyse things critically, such that no views, methods, or studies are perfect.

- Open up career opportunities in other areas of sport.

- Enable you to become a specialist in an area that offers opportunities at higher levels of the game.

- Create opportunities to coach and lecture at colleges or universities.

- Lead to post-graduate or doctorate-level study in an area of your choice.

- Allow you to network with students and lecturers.

- Provide opportunities in professional and community clubs through university partnerships.

- Include a placement year that offers opportunities for experience at home or abroad.

- Help you get an employment visa in countries that require a bachelor's degree.

Knowledge

Degrees are not essential, but they can increase knowledge and opportunities. Sam believes a sports science or coaching degree gives you a deeper understanding of coaching.

With coaching licences, you look at things on the surface. At university, you are looking in depth. You cover topics like coach-athlete relationships, coaching styles, sports science, nutrition, and mental wellbeing.

There's all this stuff underneath that impacts the quality of the session and your development as a coach. It's really important.

Degrees give you a more rounded understanding of coaching and sports science. Applying this knowledge helps you become a better coach. It's also crucial for broadening knowledge when managing multi-disciplinary teams.

Coaching Abroad

Universities provide opportunities to coach at home or abroad during the summer or a placement year. Sam thinks this experience is positive.

Sports courses that include a one-year stint abroad can be beneficial. That means, when you finish your degree, you have had that experience abroad. That puts you above those who haven't. It requires someone to have a very clear picture of what they're going to do.

The year out can give you that experience and can set you up for future roles.

Drawbacks

There are many positives to doing a University degree, but there are also some negatives.

- Degrees can be expensive with large sums due each year.
- A full-time undergraduate degree can take 3 or 4 years.
- There is limited time on the grass and learning in the office compared with a full-time coaching job.
- The information might not always be relevant to your coaching context.
- A lot of the information is heavily theoretical and not as practical. It needs to be tested to see how it works in practice.
- Scientific journals use academic language, which is harder to understand and transfer into practice.

Experience

Two of the coaches we interviewed don't have degrees. Colum believes some graduates don't have the required experience when leaving university.

Coaches may be doing sports coaching degrees, but they need to get out coaching. Staff at Premier League clubs have told me they've got guys coming out with degrees and they wouldn't trust them to run a session.

That's not the degree itself but rather their lack of coaching experience. It's important doing a degree somewhere that you can coach a lot. It's *applying* knowledge and *reflecting* on experiences that make you a better coach.

A part-time degree is a possibility but it takes longer. It may be worth it if you are already in a position to secure a full-time coaching role to get that experience built up. Others may not be ready for a full-time coaching role, of course, and need time to build up their coaching experiences part-time while studying full-time. Colum is studying for a part-time online psychology degree alongside his full-time coaching role. It's not easy balancing the two, but it's been well worth it for Colum.

Michael feels a degree is important but getting experience alongside it is key.

Having a sports science degree acts as a very good foundation. But you need to get experience to discover which things from a degree are practical. This is the most important thing.

A useful academic approach:

1. Study lots of relevant information.
2. Apply it in practice.
3. Reflect.
4. Try again.

If you apply what you have learned at university, you'll leave with a lot more than a piece of paper. Think *beyond* using information to write essays or pass exams. Use it to inform your practice, as this is what makes you a better coach.

Some coaches will tell you that degrees are important, but they aren't always required for jobs. Coaches such as Jurgen Klopp, Jose Mourinho, and Julian Nagelsmann have sports degrees but many others don't. Degrees are valuable for those who have the time and finances available.

Learning Never Stops

It doesn't matter where you live in the world. You can do degrees or a range of courses online to educate yourself. Different ideas emerge regularly, and there are still multiple areas that courses won't cover. Develop a plan to keep learning. Focus on areas that are crucial in coaching, ones you are not so knowledgeable about, or that you want to specialise in.

We are fortunate to have virtually unlimited information available at our fingertips. This presents us with opportunities beyond what we learn on licences and degrees. Coaches have benefitted from networking, books, learning from different sports/industries, social media, podcasts, webinars, and online courses. The key is being open-minded while keeping a critical eye. This helps you filter information that is useful while discarding what isn't.

All the coaches featured in this book have a hunger to continually improve themselves. Having a clear plan to further your education and understanding you are on a unique journey is key. *Invest* in your education, and you will open up new opportunities and a brighter future.

Chapter 3. Scott's Journey: From the Caribbean to the Champions League

Scott Cooper started coaching in a United States indoor soccer league. The owner was planning to start an indoor team in the UK, and he wanted to get Scott involved. It didn't happen, but the owner placed Scott into the first team of an English third division side instead.

There was going to be a world indoor soccer league team. The American guy came to me because he was going to put two teams in the UK. He said, "I know you've coached, and you're from the UK."

I agreed to do it, but it never came off. At the same time, he bought Chester City Football Club. I ended up at Chester as the second Assistant Coach to Dave Fogg, Gary Shelton, and Kevin Ratcliffe.

Caribbean Connection

Scott connected with two Trinidadian players at Chester City in 1999. This opened the door to his first Head Coach role in the Caribbean.

The real Head Coaching experience started in Anguilla, which was a cool little island. There were two Trinidadian players at Chester City. I got to know them, and one of them said there's a Caribbean team looking for a coach. I spoke with them on the phone and they invited me over.

Scott had studied at the University of South Florida and went to the Caribbean on tour.

I'd been there on a tour in 1988 with a British college team. I got to know Caribbean people. I knew people in Trinidad and Tobago at the Jack Warner training site. It was the CONCACAF headquarters at the time. I kept in touch with them.

This helped me get more familiarised with the CONCACAF region. I never expected to go there and coach. I'm not sure if I even wanted to. When I met them, it was a luxurious, and relaxed lifestyle coaching football.

It was a great environment for Scott to learn his trade as a Head Coach.

It was a beautiful and very affluent island. The facilities were good. It had a very good FA, a national stadium, and two or three other stadiums. There was a 10-team Premier League, and all the players lived on the island. They trained with their club teams twice a week and the national team twice a week. I was seeing them all the time which was great.

Scott's connections also landed him a beachfront mansion to live in during his time in Anguilla.

It's a small world. A good friend of ours in Leicester owned property in Anguilla. I ended up living in this massive mansion on the beach. The Anguilla federation said, "Oh, we're supposed to pay for your accommodation. Why are you living in this place? Who do you know? Who owns this?" They couldn't understand.

There wasn't any pressure on results or rankings, which gave Scott the freedom to develop his way of working.

There was nothing said about winning or moving up the FIFA rankings. We had some pretty good games within the islands. We beat our local national team rivals, Saint Martin.

Scott was still learning the ropes at that stage, but the local people made his job much easier.

I didn't know what I was doing as a coach but I was learning whatever I could. Everybody was receptive to me and it was a nice, stress-free way to start your coaching career.

I'd go out for dinner and meet a lot of people. Sepp Blatter came over. I'm still in touch with the FA President and his wife. They always say I'm their son.

After three years in Anguilla, Scott moved to become Head Coach of Montserrat. He stayed on the Caribbean island for three years before having a second spell as Anguilla Head Coach. Scott enjoyed his apprenticeship in the Caribbean but he felt ready to move back to England to pursue a career in the professional game.

Thai Connections

A friend connected Scott with Jon Rudkin, who was Leicester City's Academy Manager at the time, before later becoming the club's Director of Football.

I'd known him for a while, and he asked me to come in before and I couldn't. He came back a second time, and I went in. It was a great move because it was a fantastic club.

Scott was coaching Leicester City's U15 Academy squad, alongside the England Independent Schools Football Association U15 team. Leicester City's owners were Thai which gave Scott the opportunity to coach a talented Thai team.

I was head of an International Youth Programme. The owner said they were going to bring a group of the top Thai youth players to stay with us for six months.

The owner of Buriram United, one of Thailand's biggest clubs, came to watch and liked what Scott was doing. He presented Scott with an opportunity that would change his life in 2013.

The owners of Leicester were close friends with Buriram United owner Newin Chidchob. Newin came over to visit the players and watch the training sessions. The team performed extraordinarily well against other academies. We played 11 matches and won every game – which was remarkable.

The owner was impressed. He said, "We want to take this guy over to help with our academy, and he can do some work with the first team." That was how I got the move to Buriram.

Buriram United

Scott had the perfect transition into Thai football. He could settle in without the pressure of coming in as the new first team Head Coach.

Once I was there, I got to know the owner and his wife. I could take a look around without any pressure. It was a nice way for me to grow into Asian football.

No one could be as fortunate as that. You start growing into it while you're at Leicester by coaching Thai players and getting to know about their culture. We constantly spoke with the players about the Thai league and the teams. I knew a lot before I even got there.

The first job at hand was to improve Buriram United's academy structure.

I went straight into the academy to get the training and pathway structured. We focused on discipline, punctuality, the types of sessions, the coaches, and what they were doing. Before, it would have been ad hoc. We pulled it together and created an academy handbook.

Scott was also working with the first team and the Thai Head Coach. He learned a lot from being around that environment and watching Coach Tak.

I liked the way he broke the sessions into small segments of preparation for games. I'd never seen that before. We're going to do 5x8 minute 11v11s with this context. Breaking it into seven or eight segments worked well for Thai players.

He was also composed in his management. He was not a shouter or a screamer. Sometimes I'm a little too hard on players and that's where we were different. He was a bit more composed and reserved. You always wondered what he was thinking, which in a way is intimidating itself.

Taking Charge

Scott soon took on more first team responsibilities once Coach Tak became unwell.

I was working with the first team almost straight away, doing a few sessions as an Assistant. It got to the point where I was doing a lot of the tactical stuff and the team meetings. Then Coach Tak stepped down for medical reasons and I took over.

It was about eight games into the season that coach Tak's illness got the better of him. He went on to coach Bangkok Glass for a bit and then sadly passed away. Coach Tak was a nice guy and a good coach.

Scott had severe doubts about taking over as Head Coach. It's a huge responsibility to manage one of Thailand's biggest clubs in front of 30,000 fans.

I had massive self-doubt. I'd been at Chester, done some jobs in the US, and some small national teams. But you look at the Buriram Stadium – it's a carbon copy of the King Power stadium at Leicester – and it was full every week.

You can enjoy it more when you're an Assistant. But once you become Head Coach you think, this is on me now! Through prayer and talking to myself, I found a way to step up and be confident.

Scott already had a good understanding of the culture and how things worked, which made life a little easier.

I never had a strategy going in. I came from a Thai ownership group in Leicester and left it for a Thai ownership group at the best club in Thailand. It was the wealthiest, most organised, and had the best facilities. I also had the transition from Assistant to Head Coach.

I'd already got an insight into how the club worked and a guide on the ownership. I got used to how players were signed and the culture. This gave me time to figure out what could and couldn't work, and to get a read on everything. I also had an owner that knows his football and is passionate. He was at every training session, which isn't normal for a lot of owners.

Being able to sit back and assess things before taking the hot seat was a luxury few coaches get.

I was lucky. Some coaches land smack-bang in the middle of Asia as Head Coach without any transition. That's where you get into the issues. You don't know the culture or the owner.

Scott had to adapt and deliver his messages differently to ensure none of the players "lost face". Being embarrassed in front of the group is a huge issue in Thai culture.

I'd got to know how a Thai football mind worked. When I got to Thailand, I started doing a lot of individual meetings with players. I never embarrassed a player in front of the group, unless I felt the player is on his way out and was being disrespectful. Then I don't mind giving him everything because we won't accept that.

New Approach

Scott's first game in charge was an eye-opener.

We played 4-4-2 against Osotspa that day, I will never forget it. We started well. Then I got to see how Thai football can get stretched in the last 20 minutes, and it alarmed me. The team had always been in a back four at that stage. We moved to a back three, which became synonymous with Buriram's style for years.

Buriram had a quality group of players at the time, which helped Scott's transition into his new role.

I was lucky because there were players like Osmar, a top-quality centre back. We also had Carmelo, Javier Patino and Kai Hirano. We had top Thai players like Theerathon and Adisak. Suchao was our inspirational captain.

The team was good, but Scott identified some areas that needed work. He was continually learning and adding new ideas to the team.

The motivation of the team was high, but the preparation wasn't. It was standard to what I'd been seeing, but it wasn't even 20% of what it became. I started learning, seeing things early, and tightening them up. We spoke about different aspects of the game, including the pacing of the game and what's expected.

One of Scott's key aims was to stop the game becoming stretched. This was something he worked on a lot during training, video sessions, and team talks.

I constantly showed players evidence of it happening in other league games. We highlighted it as an area to exploit, through fitness and offensive and defensive transitions. We worked on this with and without the ball in training sessions to reiterate how key it was.

We made sure from back to front that the team always remained connected. During games I'd be more expressive during the minutes after. I'd also remind the players again at half-time what I expected, and how it can win the game or kill it off.

Scott put his stamp on things and the players bought into it. He had already built good relationships which helped.

The players got to know me as an Assistant first. They believed in what I was doing and enjoyed the training sessions. We increased the tactical aspects of the team. We adapted and improved the quality of the possession in a 3-5-2, and what we were expecting from each position in and out of possession. We also got stuck into set pieces.

They would do the tactical meeting for the next game at the beginning of the week. This gave the team a clear focus in every session so they were 100% prepared on match day.

The meetings were one of the things we did, which the owner and players liked. We would play on a Saturday, and the players would be in on Sunday for the recovery session. Monday was a day off. Tuesday we would have a tactical meeting about the next game, and they'd see what the training plan was for the week.

We'd look at the video analysis to assess what we can do tactically, and then we'd start applying it during the week. That's something I stuck with because it felt like we focused all week on what we needed to do in that game. It was almost like fight camp. Some people say you need a day or two to take your mind off it. We never did that and it worked well.

This approach saw the team pick up results which eased the self-doubt and pressure on Scott.

If I had two or three bad results from the start, they would have sacked me, but we got the results. We were third, and we took them to the top of the league. We kept building on this 3-5-2 system, which the owner bought into.

Things that were happening in training were paying off. Players were saying complimentary things about me and the sessions in the media. The owner was happy. The first month, I won coach of the month.

It was the perfect club for Scott to grow into the role of Head Coach in South East Asia. Scott realises how fortunate he was that everything fell into place.

Of course, you've got to do the work and back it up. But there was a lot of fortune there, too.

Champions League

Buriram United were the underdogs in a tough AFC Champions League group.

I took over midway through the AFC Champions League campaign. We had a tough group with Vegalta Sendai, JS Sainty, and FC Seoul.

Under Coach Tak, the team managed to finish second, ahead of JS Sainty on goal difference. FC Seoul won the group but second place was enough to see Buriram progress to the last 16.

Scott's first game in charge was the last 16 tie at home against Uzbeki side Bunyodkor. Buriram took a 1-0 lead through Jujeen in the 17th minute, then Bunyodkor equalised through Taran right before half-time. Buriram United regained the lead with 15 minutes remaining through Samre and held on to secure a 2-1 first-leg win.

This gave them a slight advantage as they headed to Uzbekistan a week later. Bunyodkor had a vital away goal which meant a 1-0 victory would be enough for them to progress. Buriram managed to get a 0-0 draw, however, which secured a place in the quarter-finals.

Then, Buriram faced the Iranian side Esteghlal with the first leg away. What an atmosphere awaited the Thai side as they entered the Azadi stadium in front of 96,000 exuberant fans. Esteghlal scored an early goal through Heydari in the second minute and managed to win the game 1-0. Despite the defeat, Scott fancied their chances at home in the second leg.

Thai League

Buriram's excellent league form saw them go top of the table.

We played Army United, who were a decent team. Mano Polking was their coach after leaving the Thailand national team. It was right after we'd beaten Bunyodkor. We could have been fatigued and had a hangover from the Champions League, but we beat them 3-0 at home. That result put us top of the league.

Carmelo and Osmar scored in the first half, followed by a 65th-minute effort from Jujeen. This was enough to see off Army at the Chang Arena in Buriram.

Their hard work on the training ground paid off as Buriram subsequently beat Chonburi away. It was a day that made everyone believe they could achieve something special that season.

The best result we had in the league was Chonburi away. At that stage, it was Muangthong, Chonburi, and Buriram. Buriram was only level-pegging with those guys at that stage. Chonburi and Muangthong were big clubs.

We won 4-1 in Chonburi and everything we prepared for – tactically – came off. What we'd expected from them and what we wanted to do. It was that day the players started believing that we could do something special that year.

Goals from Srisai, Patino, Samre, and Carmelo gave Buriram victory at Chonburi Stadium. Scott believes the great away record was down to the team's preparation.

It was mental strength. The preparation was early and we gave clear and concise instructions. We talked about preferring 2-0 to 4-1. There was an emphasis on denying anything, no matter what the score was; we were just going to keep denying teams.

The team's set pieces were striking fear into their opponents.

It came to a point where teams were starting to panic when set pieces were given. Teams were changing their game. Defenders with the ball bouncing around their chest at the back post were trying to hook it back up the pitch. They should have put it out for a corner but they were fearful of what it would lead to.

You could hear coaches and players saying, "Don't foul, don't foul." I said to the players, once you get into that state of mind, we've got you. The belief in our set pieces was so high that it felt like we would score. Something would happen every set piece.

Scott recognised they had a big advantage over opponents. They had great delivery from Theerathon's left foot and players who were excellent in the air.

We had Theerathon's delivery, which was as good as anything you had in Asia at the time. We had Patino, Osmar, Tanasak, Suree, and Surat Sukha who could all head a ball.

We backed it up with pressing and the way we played in possession. We always played two up front and ran in behind teams. We put the pressure on; we turned them around. It got to the point that it didn't matter whether we were home or away, that's what was going to happen.

The club's owner, Newin Chidchob, was a big influence in Thailand as a former politician. He was also the Chang International Circuit President, who brought the Moto GP to Buriram. One night he called Scott for an important meeting before an away game.

It was 10pm the night before Buriram United played Police in the FA Cup. Newin Chidchob is a deadly serious guy – ex-politician – and he calls me out and says he needs to speak to me. I went out to the poolside for a serious meeting.

I sat down at the table, and he says to me, "Coach, I have got some information on Police for tomorrow night." I asked, "What is it?" "I've got information that Police have changed formation." "OK, what is it?"

We'd been planning on the formation all week. I thought, maybe we'll have to do a meeting in the morning. He looked at me and said, "They've changed it to 911." Which I thought was very funny, coming from him.

Brink of Success

Scott had a good relationship with the owner but had to leave towards the end of the season. It was an unfortunate time to go... with the team on the brink of winning the treble.

There was no international school around Buriram so I couldn't stay. They said, "We can send your kids to a boarding school." But it's not something we wanted to do. They were saying, "We can help with the school in Bangkok [390km away]. You could be here and back." But I didn't want to be without my family.

My family came and it was OK for a month or two but the problem was education. I've got three kids, and I didn't want to be separated from them. I said, "I can resign if you want me to." He was saying, "Don't do this because you've got a future here." But for me, my family always comes first.

Scott's family moved to Bangkok so their children could go to an international school there.

It came to an end before the season finished. My family had already moved to Bangkok and we agreed to part ways. I have to go home at night and see my family. It's the way I am.

It was a sad way for it to finish, but I'd never expected to be there that long. I was going to come in to help the academy. I didn't realise I'd stay and become the Head Coach.

Scott said his departure had nothing to do with his relationship with the owner.

People thought there was a fall out between the owner and me, which isn't true. The owner and I had a good relationship. After I left, we signed seven players from Buriram on loan because they helped us out. We played them in the league and everything was fine. I still see him now and his wife always comes over to chat.

Spanish coach, Alejandro Menendez, took over for the remaining games. He had coached Real Madrid's B team and Racing Santander but didn't get off to the best of starts.

The week after I left, they lost to Rayong in the League Cup, which was a shock. I didn't want to watch it. Someone called me and said, "Did you see the result?" "Oh, wow."

Scott wished the team luck before the Champions League quarter-final second leg. He believed they could overturn the 1-0 deficit at home.

I messaged the General Manager and players, saying, "All the best." There were no hard feelings.

They lost 2-1 to Esteghlal at home. I was gutted for them when they got knocked out because I felt like we could win. We lost in Esteghlal; we conceded after 30 seconds of the quarter-final... it was a freak cross. Their scorer stumbled before crossing it, and it was one of those bloopers that drifted into the top corner. They didn't do much after that. I felt they could turn it around in Buriram and get to the semis.

They went out of the League Cup, and the Champions League within that next week. It wasn't a great start.

The new coach managed to steady the ship, however, and got the team across the line in the league and won the FA Cup. This victory saw the club complete a historic treble.

The league position was already strong. We'd already won the charity shield and they won the FA Cup and the Thai League. I was pleased for the players and the club. They won everything with the same system, formation, and set pieces. My Assistant was still with them. I got messages from the players that I've kept to this day. I took great pride in that.

Scott left after 29 games, during which they won 23 and lost only once. It was an outstanding first season as a Head Coach in Asia.

We knocked out the favourites, Bunyodkor. That season Buriram was ranked number seven in Asia. It was a huge accomplishment. I'm not sure we'll see a Thai club getting back to the quarter-final stage of the AFC Champions League for a while.

We had such a good spirit and system that we trusted. Our only defeat all season was Esteghlal in the quarter-finals away from home; a 1-0 loss.

It was a combination of players buying into what we were doing and increasing their tactical awareness. Alongside being focused and prepared.

There were never any hard feelings from either side after his departure. Scott did a great job there and had good relationships with the fans and everyone at the club.

Every time I went back to Buriram, I got a massive reception from the fans. The ownership always went out of their way to look after me. Two to three years afterwards, they were still playing with the back three that had been put in place. It was unfortunate that it couldn't have carried on for a while. I could have been there for two to four years had it been right for my family.

Scott's record and Champions League performances generated interest from across the region. Scott left with his reputation enhanced and ready for his next challenge.

Chapter 4. Five Pathways into the Professional Game

There is great debate about the opportunities presented to ex-professional players when they're starting out as coaches. It used to be almost impossible to coach at the top level without being a top player. This has changed in recent times, with more and more coaches and support staff breaking into the game without playing professionally. The coaches will discuss the pros and cons of not having had illustrious playing careers and the five pathways into the professional game.

The Top Level

Colum Curtis feels knowing what players are experiencing is beneficial for an ex-professional player turned coach.

If you've played at the top level, you know what players are feeling and going through.

Cederique Tulleners also believes playing at a high level improves your game understanding.

You see the game at a higher level and have a better tactical understanding.

You can learn from experiencing different situations on the pitch, but coaches need to be capable of communicating these ideas effectively. Sam Bensley feels being exposed to top coaches can be a huge advantage for learning the skills required to be a coach.

I've never walked out in front of 60,000 to play for my national team. I also haven't been exposed to high-level coaches. If I'd been in that environment, with my coaching hat on, the amount I would have learned and been exposed to would have helped massively.

Some players may not have played for great coaches and Colum thinks those who have may not reflect on their coach's skillset and decisions.

Some professional players don't think about the game in that way.

Despite this, Sam thinks being in the game for many years helps professional players build a valuable network.

The connections I'd get from playing 400 professional games are going to help far more than what I've had without a professional playing career.

A strong network in the professional game is one of the biggest advantages for coaches who were ex-professionals. It presents more opportunities and can help coaches progress quicker.

Starting Early

Starting early is an advantage for coaches without a professional playing career. Colum feels it can take years for ex-professionals to catch up.

I'm 31 and this is my 14th season in coaching. Some professionals play until they're 35 or 36. They'll be 50 by the time they've had as much time on the grass as me and made the mistakes and learned from them.

Working with different age groups has been beneficial for Cederique.

Your pedagogical skills to connect with players are sometimes more advanced than professional players. If you have no experience working with players – you can have the best knowledge in your head – but you don't know how to transfer it to the group. How you speak, present, and deliver training sessions is what makes the difference.

Sam had the freedom to develop his approach in the less pressurised grassroots environment.

I started coaching at 17 and I could do what I wanted to experiment. I had the opportunity to get things wrong, come up with new ideas, and build a solid foundation.

Starting in youth football presents a great opportunity to learn and develop yourself. Top ex-professionals get fast-tracked through their coaching licences and may go straight into first team jobs. Some will not be afforded the freedom or time they need to develop as coaches.

The pressure to deliver results makes it difficult to experiment and learn from your mistakes. Some ex-players have excelled as coaches but others have struggled. When it goes wrong in the senior professional game, most coaches never get a second chance to get it right.

There are no shortcuts when you don't have a high profile in the game. This means you have to work at your craft and go above and beyond to climb the ladder. Once you reach a certain level you will be competing with former professional players for jobs, so you need to stand out. Cederique has experienced this first-hand.

I had to work from the bottom up to the level that I am now. Every day I work hard to improve and become better. You have to make sure that you are ahead of other people if you're going to reach that level.

The skills developed during a professional playing career can hugely benefit coaches but it requires more to succeed. Coaches need to design sessions, training schedules, decision making processes and have many other responsibilities that a professional playing career won't prepare you for.

Grassroots football has given the coaches without professional playing careers a head start and the freedom to develop. They found a way of working without the pressures you'd face at professional clubs where you must get immediate results. It has provided a great grounding and can be a pathway into professional football, as we'll discuss.

When it comes to ex-professionals and those who didn't have professional playing careers, one isn't better than the other. It depends on the individual. It's all about each person maximising their experiences, utilising their strengths, and adapting their ideas to fit the environment they're in. If they're successful, then no one will question their playing background. We now live at a time when playing pedigree is no longer a barrier to working in the professional game!

Standing Out

No matter what your playing background is, you'll need to stand out. Many coaches will be going through the same coaching licence pathway as you. This means it's the *experiences you gain* that help you stand out from the crowd. They should build your quality of work, relationships, and a track record that proves what you're capable of.

The experiences you're accumulating need to be a stepping stone to your future goal. Find out the requirements for the role you want by searching for the job description online, checking the LinkedIn profile of people in the position, finding online interviews which outline a coach's journey to the role, or reaching out to experienced football people online.

Key questions when selecting a voluntary or paid position:

1. Is this experience relevant to the goal you want to achieve?
2. What is the age, level, and motivation of those you'll be coaching?
3. How many hours of experience will you get per week?
4. Will there be responsibilities off the pitch that help you develop a wider skillset?
5. Will there be opportunities for promotion?
6. Can you learn from the people you'll be working alongside?
7. Will the organisation provide any educational opportunities?
8. Do their philosophy and values fit with yours?
9. Will you be given the resources needed to succeed in the role?
10. Does the organisation have a good reputation in the game?

You've got to make the most of opportunities when they come. Show your willingness when you go into a club to maximise the value of your experience. Colum has always been willing to work hard and try new things.

I never say no to anything. Even if I didn't know how to do it, I'd go and find out.

Other ways to make an impression:

1. Arrive before the designated arrival time.
2. Always dress professionally.
3. Be enthusiastic, positive, and set a good example.
4. Set up well in advance of sessions beginning, so that you can welcome players on arrival.
5. Be prepared to deliver high-quality sessions.
6. Help tidy up, and do what needs to be done after sessions.
7. Show curiosity by asking coaches questions, and asking players and coaches for feedback.
8. Build strong relationships with players and coaches.
9. Share your ideas and add value to everyone at the organisation.
10. Help out with things that need to be done off the pitch, when you can.
11. Work hard off the pitch by studying, reflecting, and continually trying to improve.
12. Observe other sessions and matches at the club and locally when you are free.

It might not always be possible but try taking a few ideas from above to show your commitment. It may lead to further opportunities.

Michael Yau has always given coaching his all, and it's led to opportunities for him.

The most important thing is being the best that you can be every day. You have a direction and focus on becoming a professional coach. What qualifications and experience do you need? You find out and start to prepare.

I've never said I have to go this particular way. I focus on doing the work to the best of my ability. If my ability gets recognised, I'm going to get opportunities.

A young coach made an impression on Colum, so he brought him in when he started an academy.

A coach came with a sports coaching degree and level 1. But most importantly he had an open mindset. He wanted to learn about everything and he was always asking questions. He started conducting interviews and had a well-rounded knowledge of building a grassroots club. He was very switched on and good with people.

Try to get as much experience as possible. This may require giving a lot of time up for free to gain that initial experience. Colum recommends reaching out to clubs.

If someone wanted to be a football coach, I'd say go and batter everyone's door down and start coaching and volunteering your time. I've put headstones in place for a funeral director, and I've delivered Chinese Takeaways and Pizzas. I've done all sorts of jobs so I can coach.

There can't be many professions like coaching where you have to do *so much* for free and invest in so many qualifications before earning a decent living. You've got to find ways to get by while gaining the experience and qualifications required to get the job you want. Some coaches have to work at multiple clubs to work full-time in football. Others have to combine it with a full-time or part-time job in another industry.

Although the experience is key… it's the quality that really matters. Is it experience that will set you up for future roles? Are you reflecting on your experiences and setting action plans to improve? You may have five years of experience, but without reflecting and improving, it will be the same year repeated five times!

Climbing the Ladder

It's tough getting into professional clubs without a professional playing background or having connections, but there are five pathways you can take. These are proven pathways that have helped the coaches in this book break into professional football around the world.

Five ways to start climbing the ladder:

1. Start at a grassroots club and show your value to the staff at professional clubs to earn a move.
2. Start in the community programme or academy of a professional club and work your way up.
3. Start as part of the first team staff before being promoted to Head Coach.
4. Start as an Assistant or Head Coach in a smaller professional team or league and earn a move to a bigger team.
5. Start as an Assistant or Head Coach in a lower league and get your team promoted to a higher league.

Grassroots Springboard

Grassroots is where most coaches who don't have links to professional clubs begin. Coaching at grassroots at home or abroad can be a great place to develop as we've discussed. You can show your capabilities and start developing connections in professional clubs.

Identify the locations with the best opportunities at home or abroad. Five coaches who feature in this book identified that Chinese football was growing. A lot of money was being invested, which meant coaches were in demand. They decided to move there in grassroots roles to start their careers in Asia.

Many coaches have good careers in grassroots abroad. There are schools and grassroots clubs worldwide that offer full-time coaching jobs. Many coaches are happy to work there to develop themselves and the next generation. Finding the right organisation and location can provide coaches with more stability than the professional game, and a good lifestyle.

Coaches can also use grassroots as a gateway to the professional game. Five coaches at our grassroots club in Beijing got into professional football in Asia. Michael felt grassroots was a great way for him to start in China.

The entry qualifications didn't need to be that high as you're coming to a country where football was developing and still in its infancy.

Some coaches look down on grassroots jobs when looking to make the move abroad. Not knowing anyone or being outside the country makes it difficult to get into professional clubs. How can anyone hire you if they don't know you or your work?

It wasn't possible to break into professional teams from the coaches' homelands, as they didn't know anyone. Moving to work at grassroots is great for learning the culture, language, and developing a network.

Being in the country is the best way to learn how football works there. You can figure out the football system, league, players, and what approach works best. This gives you a huge advantage when applying for jobs. Michael has spent over six years working for a Chinese Super League club and has seen what clubs are looking for.

You need to have an entry-level to come into the country. You might have an A licence, a Pro licence, or a Master's in sports science. But that doesn't mean it's going to present you with a professional job.

At the professional level, clubs are looking for well-qualified and experienced coaches. Especially in the continent they're working in. In China, they're looking for coaches that have had experience working there because Chinese football is unique. If you haven't experienced it, it's going to be a bit of a shock to the system!

Get into the country, understand the culture, connect with people and show your value. You'll be amazed at what opportunities arise.

Application

When applying for roles, you must have the *relevant* qualifications and experience. If you want to work at first team level, then coaching at youth level may help you to develop as a coach initially. But, you will need experience with senior players before a higher-level club will hire you.

The reverse also applies as Colum had countless unsuitable coaches apply for a youth role. They were overqualified(!) and only had senior-level experience.

The guys applying for jobs in China knew part of the job was grassroots. They still applied despite being UEFA Pro licence coaches working in third division senior teams.

Many coaches wanted to come to China to break into Chinese Super League clubs, and grassroots clubs were wary. Colum recommends tailoring your CV and cover letter to what the job role entails.

Your CV gets you an interview, and then your interview gets you the job. I would recommend catering your CV to what they require. I remember reading one-page CVs that were nothing fancy, but they had what we needed... so they're getting an interview.

Sam looks at what employers are asking for. He then explains – in detail – exactly how he achieved these requirements in previous roles. This shows he has looked at what the club requires, and that he wants the job.

Keep your CV concise and make it look appealing. It needs to be easy to read to help you stand out from the hundreds of CVs that recruiters receive. My CV included a link to my website so people could find testimonials, media links, blogs, pictures/videos, and my career profile. Colum always looked for experience when going through CVs.

Firstly, I'd always look at experience. How many years have they been coaching? What age groups have they been coaching? It shows a level of competency.

Colum hired some less-experienced coaches. He knew they would develop with the number of coaching hours they would get in China.

There was one lad who came over to China with a first-class honours degree out of University. They said take him. You know that off the pitch his planning was going to be meticulous and punctual, which are all very important. They're young guys. If they blast out two years coaching 15/16 sessions a week with different levels and player ages, they can only benefit.

It's important to think about the individual behind the application. Colum hired lower-level coaches if they came across better in the interview.

Especially abroad, some people see the licencing, whereas I wouldn't. If level 2 was the minimum licence requirement for a visa, I'd check the level 2. Sometimes I've hired a level 2 coach over an A licence coach because of how they interviewed. They sent videos of their sessions. The big thing for me is their interaction with players.

Professional Clubs

Many coaches have benefitted from working in community programmes or academies at professional clubs. An increasing number of academy coaches are progressing into first teams in the top leagues and around the world. Clubs want first team coaches who can develop players, and academies are a great breeding ground for such coaches.

Scott Cooper went from Leicester City's Academy to Buriram United's first team in Thailand. Sam, meanwhile, has worked at the academies of a range of English professional clubs. This looked good on his CV and offered good environments for him to develop. He feels this helped him land the job at the Hong Kong Football Association. Sam knows how hard it can be to get into the academies of professional clubs in England due to their requirements.

You need a UEFA B license and youth module three to get a part-time job in an academy in England. To get a full-time job, you need the AYA (Advanced Youth Award), and to get the AYA you need to work in an academy.

It's extremely difficult to get in at the beginning. You may need to go in part-time for two or three years – to prove yourself – before getting a full-time role. Doing this with the AYA on the side isn't easy.

Sam recommends thinking outside the box to get your big break in an academy.

Coaches who want to get into a professional academy in England complain it's a closed shop. You've got to try and think of a way around it. A lot of clubs are doing more outreach within the grassroots community. If grassroots coaches can find a way to tap into that, they'll be making a bridge to the academy.

Find creative ways to get your name known in the places you want to end up. Sam says you could arrange friendly games with a professional academy once or twice a year.

Once you start taking your team to play at the academy, they know your face and name. The academy coaches are going to be watching: how you coach, the way your team plays, and how you deal with different situations.

It may help – further down the line – when they are looking for a part-time coach. It's a long shot, but if it's your end goal then you need to find a way. How can you break it down and work towards building those bridges?

Getting noticed through your practice is the best approach. Other ways include meeting people on courses or social media. Get creative in finding a way to make a breakthrough to the level you aspire to reach.

It's not only professional clubs that can impress, but youth national teams too. Colum was working with the youth national teams in the Irish Football Association. He worked alongside UEFA Pro licence coaches, which was great for his development. This experience added to his profile when going for an Assistant role in Cambodia.

Assistant Benefits

Everyone wants to be a Director or Head Coach but being an Assistant can be great for working at a higher level, learning from an experienced coach, or propelling yourself into a Head Coach position or an Assistant role at a bigger club, if you impress.

Worry less about the title and more about how it will take you towards your goals. Without a large profile, being an Assistant can be your best way into a professional team.

If you can impress a Head Coach and develop a relationship, they can take you with them wherever they go. This is what Serbian coach Ramadani Rezidrdan-Kiza (Kiza) did by impressing Scott Cooper. Kiza was at Ubon United when Scott arrived, and Scott asked him to be his Assistant in his next two roles. Kiza brings a skillset that complements Scott's, and they trust one another.

You look for loyalty and someone willing to give you their strong opinion behind closed doors. We argue like cat and dog about things. Sometimes it's me being softer and him being aggressive. He pushes players hard, and they respond well to him.

Players like him. Off the pitch, he'll have a quiet word with the players saying, "Scott will need to see this, this, and this." We have a long history of trust and working together. We know each other well, and we know what we're looking for. I know what he does well, and how it complements how I work. It works for us.

Colum's salary was low in his role as first team Assistant in Cambodia. He did it to prove his worth and planned to stay as an Assistant for a few years before becoming a Head Coach.

Show that hunger and desire. I worked for very little in my first club in Cambodia. I knew my qualities on the pitch as a coach and the way I can develop relationships with players. I was hoping it would earn a bigger contract and a bit more stability. Turns out it didn't but that's football. A couple of days later, I got a phone call and another job was there.

Colum couldn't agree on terms to renew his contract as Assistant. He had to move on and got a good contract as Head Coach at another club. That Assistant role allowed Colum to make an impression and to learn about the culture and league. Colum feels coming in as Head Coach in Cambodia without knowing the league or having a large profile is difficult.

I can't see someone coming straight in as a Head Coach. I was coming from Svay Rieng and I knew every player in the Visakha team. I had analysed them and knew their strengths and weaknesses. This helped me massively in the interview process and when recommending potential signings.

Michael is well aware the best jobs don't get advertised. He feels connecting with a Head Coach with a good profile is your best option.

Professional level in China is going to be difficult unless you're coming with a Head Coach as part of their staff. If you're coming by yourself, then it's going to be challenging because these jobs are not going to be advertised. There's going to have to be a very strong link for that opportunity to materialise.

This shows the importance of networking. Having someone inside a club who trusts you and knows the quality of your work is vital. The best jobs don't always get advertised, especially abroad. Even when they do, having someone the recruiter trusts recommending you is priceless.

Applying alongside hundreds of coaches, without a connection, is like buying a lottery ticket. It's too big a risk taking an unknown coach. Recruiters would much rather hire someone they know and trust. It might not be the best recruitment strategy, but it's the reality in football.

Standing Out and Adding Value

If you are knowledgeable in an area the Head Coach is not, that can be a great selling point for you. This may make them keen to talk to you and allow you into their environment as you add value. Get yourself in the door, make an impression, and they may want to work with you long-term.

Use your situation to your advantage and develop a skillset to supplement a Head Coach. You could be an analyst, fitness coach, translator, individual coach, set piece coach, or mental skills coach. It can be any related role that impresses a Head Coach and earns a place in their team. Michael believes you can add to what a Head Coach is doing.

If you've not been a professional player, you may be coming from a theoretical background. You'll have a lot of theories underpinning your methods. Therefore, if you're working with those that have played, you can complement their work.

When I was in Thailand, the Head Coach let me work with first team players due to my sport psychology background. The owner also asked me to do presentations for the first team. People recommended my work which led to working with other Head Coaches and international players.

Michael learned Mandarin and was an analyst, which got him into a Chinese Super League club. Technical coaching is Kiza's strength, which complements how Scott likes to work.

Kiza isn't a carbon copy of me. He likes the technical aspects of the session and I like the more tactical aspects.

Kiza also had a medical degree and a passion for sport science. He would do the fitness work with the players, which was an extra skillset he brought to the team.

Clubs with bigger budgets will usually have more staff which creates additional specialist roles. Clubs with smaller budgets don't have as many roles available as they have fewer members of staff. A different skillset from a Head Coach can get you in the door as an Assistant.

Knowing the game, coaching methodology, and having an additional skillset is key. It may be analysis, sport science, or how to use technology, software, or data. Look at the trends or gaps in provision and predict where the industry is going. My research showed sport psychology was underutilised, but it was growing. I also loved the subject and studied it for my Master's degree.

Find a topic you are passionate to master and one which will open up career opportunities moving forward. Build your expertise by researching and practising your methods. *Record* the results using stats or testimonials from the people you work with. It's a great way of showing the value of your skillset.

Find ways to communicate your ideas with Head Coaches and professional clubs. Gaining entry to higher-level environments allows you to learn and gain experience. It could be a stepping stone to earning promotions with a Head Coach, moving to a bigger club as an Assistant, or becoming a Head Coach yourself.

Head Coach

Most Head Coaches won't get into clubs in high-level leagues when starting out. Your initial opportunity may come at a big team in a less-developed footballing nation, a small team in a less-known topflight league, or a lower-level team in a country with a good league pyramid.

They're great for gaining experience, showing your work, and working towards the licence you need. Colum started as Head Coach in a strong club in a smaller league which was good for his win percentage. Simon McMenemy worked for a low salary in his first job as Philippines Head Coach.

If you're wanting to get a job because you need money, your first job is going to be very difficult to find. Considering the Philippines job, for example, I was incredibly lucky to get it over Facebook; I knew some of the players.

When I look back at what that job gave me financially – I was in the job for six months, the most successful Head Coach they've ever had, and we got to the semi-finals of the Suzuki Cup – I got paid three thousand dollars and a bonus of a thousand dollars. That was it. Four grand in total for six months of work.

That success was enough to propel Simon on to earn good contracts elsewhere. Simon says getting that experience is essential for progressing your career.

The best advice I can give is to forget about the money with that first job. If someone offers you 50 quid to go and coach a team full-time, look at it. Understand what the club is, and what it could do for you. Go and get it on your CV. You might not like it. You might have to struggle and sell everything you own to do it. But if you are that keen to get on the ladder, go in and get the experience. It allows you to make contacts, and for people to see your work.

Simon says work for experience and the rewards will come. If you ask for too much too soon, you will get nowhere.

Work for the experience because that's crucial. If you're good, the money will come. Getting your foot in the door leads to other things.

If you're going around saying, "You've got to pay me five grand a month", no one's going to take you off the back of a youth team that you had in Sussex once. It's never going to happen.

You've got to be realistic as coaching at professional academies may not get you jobs in top leagues abroad. Get yourself in the country you want to be in, and climb your way up.

Scott Cooper went into an ambitious third division team in Thailand. He managed to get back-to-back promotions to the topflight. It was a risky strategy for Scott, but it was the right club for him and it brought him back to the top league in Thailand.

Going into a lower-level club and growing with the club can be a good way to progress to higher levels. Although, it won't always work out as Cederique found. He went into a club intending to earn promotion. Unfortunately, the club had financial problems, which didn't make it possible. It's easier said than done. It requires doing your research to ensure the club can help you achieve your goals.

Progressing to higher levels will only happen for a select few; those who can find the right club and have the drive, resilience, and quality of work needed to progress. There is no easy route into the top leagues!

Create Travel Nets

Networks are location-specific. You can have an amazing network in your hometown, but that won't help you get a job in other cities; unless someone in your hometown has connections, of course, which won't always be the case.

Choose a country or city you would like to work in, and search for clubs in the area. You can type the club's name into LinkedIn to connect with the staff who work there. Find the club's email on their website or reach out to them on social media.

Holidays aren't only for sightseeing. Jamel Wojtczak had a short holiday during his time in Beijing. Instead of going to Tokyo or Hong Kong, the English coach took off to Inner Mongolia to meet Cederique. He built relationships at the full-time academy, which earned him a move there. Cederique has always been a great networker himself. He even used his wedding as a chance to meet coaches.

I got married in Malta and met Malta's Head Coach. For my wife, it was not fantastic. But for me, you can build a good network and take advantage of all sides.

The more countries where you lay nets, the more opportunities you will have. Not only in that country but in other countries, depending on the network of the person you're connecting with. According to Cederique, travelling to different countries helps you see things differently.

In Belgium, we always look from this side; in England, they look from their side. If you gather more countries, cultures, and people with different backgrounds, you can see more angles. This gives you a different view – not 100% different – but an alternative way of seeing football.

Travelling is great as it enables you to:

1. Assess current and future opportunities in different countries.
2. Build new relationships and improve existing ones with individuals and clubs.
3. Show contacts and clubs you are serious about working there.
4. Observe the staff, facilities, and day-to-day work.
5. Gain new perspectives on the culture and lifestyle there.
6. Enjoy the sights and beauty the region has to offer.

Adding a face and personality to your profile adds credibility and trust. This is important as you can't always see the opportunities online. There's also no better insight than talking to the locals or expats face to face.

People don't take it seriously when they're contacted by someone on the other side of the world. Time is precious and attention spans are limited. People won't always take the time to read an introductory email from someone they don't know. The moment they're sitting face to face is when they will take you seriously.

Cederique has flown many miles to build new relationships.

I invested a lot of time and money flying to Beijing to meet people without expecting to get a job. People asked me, "Why did you go there? Did you go to negotiate your contract?" I said, "No, I went to meet people." "Ah, they paid everything for you to go there?" "No." "Oh, so why did you go if they don't offer you a job." "If they don't know me, and I don't invest my time, why would they offer me a job?" You need to invest in yourself: time, money, and travel without the expectation of a job. Speak face to face with people and see what is possible.

Colum recommends doing what he did and landing in a city you want to live in.

Save up a few quid and land in a capital city with your qualifications, relevant experience, and go for it. If you don't get a job, then you can go back home. You won't get a job sitting talking about it.

Michael was in China to meet the club before joining.

I had the big advantage that I met the employers face to face which allowed them to understand more about me. They said that because they had met me in person, I had a real advantage over the other candidates.

If you're going to get a job abroad, you need to first go to the country you want to work. You need to understand the culture and the people. You have to build that relationship with the employer. You need to know them, and they need to know you. Sometimes, you go to do things blindly, and that's not good. Others may like that adventure, but I want to go there and see what it's like before deciding.

You can't always take people's word for it during conversations online. People can sell the dream during interviews, but it may not live up to your expectations on arrival. You should witness the day-to-day setup before making a decision, if you can.

Travelling before applying also gives you a feel for the location and the cost and quality of life there. I have landed in one or two places and within hours known that *it is not* a place I would like to live. Save yourself time and hassle, plus enjoy a holiday. Going into this depth with your research is an investment; but it can save you a year of struggle if the role is not what you signed up for. Picking a beautiful location can also make for a great holiday when doing your research.

The coaches in this book used any advantages they had, and were proactive. Getting into professional football isn't easy, as it's a bottleneck with coaches wanting to reach the top. You've got to assess which pathway works best *for you*. It may be at home or abroad but choosing the right pathway will ensure your career is heading in the right direction.

Chapter 5. Cederique's Journey: Inner Mongolia- Where's that?

Cederique Tulleners is an ambitious coach from Belgium. His coaching journey started like many others, due to a love for Football Manager.

I played Football Manager for many hours when I was younger. Even at a young age, I was intrigued about coaching but I was still hoping to become a professional player. When I got older, I knew it wasn't possible so I decided to focus on coaching.

Belgium

Cederique started volunteering at grassroots to see if coaching was the career for him. He fell in love with it and progressed into a part-time role at the academy of a professional first division club. It was a great experience but Cederique's dream was to work in football full-time, which wasn't possible in Belgium.

I was trying to find a way to become a full-time coach. In Belgium, there were no full-time youth coaches at that time. I had to find a different way, and for me, that was going abroad.

Cederique thought his age and lack of experience abroad would make it hard to get jobs.

It was difficult because I was only 22. I was working in a professional academy in Belgium, as an U14 and U12 coach. I saw some adverts for coaching abroad. I thought, there are so many coaches around the world, why would they choose me?

Cederique tried to create experiences that would make him attractive to clubs.

I was looking for ways to gain experience abroad. I organised camps in England for Belgian players. A Belgian organisation sent me to Cameroon for two weeks to deliver coaching clinics and I also went to America twice for summer camps. These experiences proved I was able to work abroad amongst different cultures. Even though I didn't have the biggest CV, it showed I was adaptable. At a young age, you are similar to everyone else, so you must do something to stand out.

Cederique's experiences abroad grew his network which led to more opportunities coming his way.

One of the Dutch guys in America asked if I was interested in a job in China. I sent them my CV, did the interview, and got the job. I also had the chance to go full-time in America but I chose China. I had already spent two summers in America and I knew what to expect there. In China, I had no clue. I wanted to see what it's like working there. I thought, if I didn't like it, I can always go back to Belgium.

Beijing, China

Cederique flew to Beijing to get his break in full-time coaching.

I had to choose whether to finish my university studies and coach part-time in a professional academy, or go to Beijing and coach full-time at grassroots. I chose Beijing and was there for 11 months.

Working in China was a great experience for Cederique.

One of the biggest pros is it shows that you can work abroad. It puts you in contact with people who have the same mindset. Some of my colleagues wanted to work at a high level, but others were there to see the world which is OK – these people have networks. Many coaches from our grassroots club are now working at higher levels. It was good working with them and it was a stepping stone to a better job.

As Cederique's contract was nearing its end, he was in talks with a professional academy in Beijing.

I checked the facility of Dayu FC and agreed to sign for the club. My girlfriend was living in Belgium and we decided she'd move to join me in Beijing. Everything was good as I entered the final six weeks with my grassroots club.

Cederique's new job was cast into sudden doubt only weeks before he was due to start.

The director called me. "Hey Cederique, we have a small problem, but it's nothing to worry about." I said, "What's the problem?" He said, "The investor doesn't want to pay anymore." "Oh, that's not a small problem," I said. He responded, "Ok, ok, we have four weeks. Don't worry I will find a solution." I was concerned but what could I do? I just had to wait.

Great news arrived the week before his contract began as they found new investment. Little did Cederique know the ramifications this investment would have on his life.

One week before I was due to start, the director said to me, "Good news, Cederique, we found some investors from Inner Mongolia." That's fantastic news. I was ready to do my work visa when the director sent me flight tickets. I thought to myself, flight tickets? That's strange. I was already in Beijing. I called him, "Are we going to a training camp?" He said, "No. We have investors from Inner Mongolia." I said, "I don't care where the money comes from. What are we going to do there?" He replied, "Our investors are from Inner Mongolia so we will move there."

Such is football that you agree to join a club in Beijing and end up moving to a place you've never heard of a few weeks later!

I signed a contract for Beijing and suddenly I was moving to Inner Mongolia. I didn't even know where it was. I had never heard of it. The director said, "Don't worry, Cederique, it's only five hundred kilometres from Beijing so you can get there quickly. It'll feel like home."

Inner Mongolia, China

Dayu FC was playing in the professional youth competitions in China. Their investors decided to move to Guangzhou to invest in another club. This left Cederique's new team desperately looking for investment.

Dayu FC was playing tournaments around China to find new investors. At the same time, a club outside the capital of Inner Mongolia was building eight fields. They got money from the government and in the middle of nowhere, they built a top training facility.

The government officials wanted to see the club's team but they didn't have one. The President called his friends — who were over thirty-five and had beer bellies — and they started playing friendly matches with the government. The government officials said, "This is nice but I want to see your real team." The club said, "This is our real team." The government was in shock. They had invested so much money into this club and they didn't even have a team.

The Inner Mongolian club needed a new team urgently.

They hosted a tournament at their facility in Inner Mongolia to find a team to buy. The team I was joining won the tournament so they bought the team. Long story short: one team had the players, but no money. The other team had the facility and the money but no players. It was a match made in heaven. Only in China would this be possible!

A coach Cederique had brought to his camps in England years earlier had connections at Dayu FC.

He said I will put you in contact with one of the coaches and something may be possible. A couple of months later, they called me after a coach left. They asked if I'd be interested in coming to the club. We started negotiating and discussing the team and structure.

Cederique believes being in China was the key to getting the job.

If I wasn't already in China, there was no chance that I could have got the job at Dayu FC. Being in Belgium and needing to speak to people on the phone would have made it more difficult. I was inside the country to network and meet people face to face which was my biggest advantage.

It was a great move for Cederique to work at a professional academy with full-time players.

Dayu FC was in the professional leagues of China. The club had two goals. One was to develop young players and sell them. The other was to get the players ready for when they reached China League Three.

Tough Task

This was no easy task with the team isolated in Inner Mongolia. They were without strong local competition and the professional youth games were infrequent.

We couldn't play many matches on a high level, especially in the first year because the league system was different. Every six weeks, you flew to a Chinese FA tournament to play there for two weeks, you flew home, and then six to eight weeks later you flew somewhere else. This was a challenge. All our boys were 17 or 18 and we played against local adult and university teams, but it was not the same as competing with professional teams.

The club would organise an annual tournament and fly clubs in from around the world.

We had top teams like Palmeiras, Sao Paulo, Standard Liege, Czech teams, a Russian team, and the North Korean national team. We tried to play in other big tournaments and friendly matches against the likes of the Mongolia National Team. We also went to the Czech Republic for a month-long training camp and played against professional teams.

Cederique enjoyed competing in the Chinese FA tournaments.

You were playing against the top Chinese teams. Some teams had foreign staff and we shared experiences, discussed football, and connected with them.

It wasn't always a pleasant experience with one Chinese FA tournament being a disaster for Cederique's team.

We were training for eight weeks to go to a CFA tournament. We arrived and suddenly they said there was one team too many and that our team couldn't participate. One week later, they called and said, "We have organised a new tournament to test the VAR system with the U19 teams. Your team must compete there because they didn't in the last tournament." So, they compensated us and we were using the VAR system for the first time in China with all the top referees.

The people running the Inner Mongolian club didn't have much experience in football which made life difficult for Cederique.

Some of the decisions they made were irrational and it was very difficult for us to understand one another.

The Inner Mongolian club's management wanted to increase their standing with the Government and the Chinese Football Association. To achieve this, they decided to host a big event.

They arranged with the Brazilian FA to do a Brazilian football camp in Inner Mongolia for four weeks. There would be tournaments, coaches from Brazil, coach educators, and the World Cup winner Edmilson would come. We had the facilities to attract a lot of players with our accommodation and pitches. It would be fantastic and they expected players from all over Inner Mongolia to come.

The camp didn't hit the heights they expected.

A few days before the Brazilians arrived, I heard almost no players had signed up and they hadn't even advertised it. On the first day, there were seven kids and they had the Brazilian coaches plus Edmilson. The club called me saying, "Maybe the Brazilian coaches can train our academy teams." The Brazilians came to give all the training and coach education, but all they had to do was train our academy teams. They only had to work for one hour or two hours a day, and that was it.

They also didn't invite any coaches for the coach education. There were five coaches from the club and five from outside. They made the academy players come to bulk up the numbers. The Brazilians knew they weren't coaches – they were Chinese kids who didn't understand English.

After two years of developing the Dayu FC squad, Cederique's team was sold to a bigger club. The Dayu FC manager gave Cederique two options to choose his next position.

We had a partnership with two clubs and the manager of Dayu FC sold the team to Beijing Sports University (BSU) Qinhuangdao. The manager said, "I can put you in this BSU U19 team or I can put you in League Two as Assistant Manager – which would you prefer?" I immediately responded, "I want to be with the first team!"

Cederique had made a good impression which helped him make the break into senior professional football.

My manager became my agent which helped. You build a relationship and deliver good work. He knows if I put Cederique in this club… I know what he can do. There are some things Cederique still needs to improve but if I take a random guy from abroad, it's always a gamble.

Things worked out well for Cederique and Dayu FC. But the club back in Inner Mongolia was still struggling to justify the government's huge investment.

The Dayu FC side of the story was successful because they were able to sell the team and some of the players played in League One for BSU. For the Inner Mongolian club itself, they were still facing the same struggles they had at the beginning.

Sichuan, China

Cederique's first foray into senior football with League Two side Sichuan Jiuniu wasn't easy. Cederique and the new Head Coach arrived mid-season and were tasked with saving the club from relegation.

We came in mid-season because the team was struggling and they wanted a foreign coach. Not getting relegated was the main goal and to get some good results to create more positivity around the team. We had a very young team and a couple of older players. The club wanted to develop and sell the young players to make money.

The coaching staff had to hit the ground running.

We had two training sessions before our first league game. It's always very difficult to take over in the middle of the season. You cannot implement your tactics or vision immediately because you don't have a pre-season of six weeks to eight weeks to train it. It needs to go step by step. If we could have done it from the start of the season, we would have got better results. But this is something you know when you sign.

Despite the challenges, it was amazing for Cederique to play against a former Real Madrid Head Coach and to feel the fans' passion.

We played in the cup quarter-final against Dalian Yifang who had Bernd Schuster as their Head Coach. It was fantastic playing games in big stadiums. We played Hunan away in our first game. The flight took three hours but we still had 50 fans travel to watch. These guys were driving for two days straight to watch the game. We drew 1-1, so thankfully we didn't lose. Seeing the passion of the fans was special. After three home games, we moved to a smaller stadium. The stadium was full with 12,000 fans. There were fireworks and they were singing the whole time. It was a great atmosphere.

The team needed police protection getting onto the bus after games.

We lost and after the game we walked to the bus. There were fans as far as the eye could see. I thought, oh my God, they're angry. They want to kill us. I don't know what's going on here. There were two lines of police and we needed to walk through them to get to the bus. When we walked outside, they started singing and had big banners saying, "We love you." The fans were trying to touch you and were letting off fireworks. It was crazy.

This is the reason you're working in football… to experience these emotions. The same thing happened at the end of the season after we had lost two or three home games in a row. There was a police escort to protect us when we were walking to the bus.

The coaching staff met the club's expectations of keeping the team up and creating a feel-good factor around the team.

The club's expectations were met and we also understood why they wanted us to win. The more we won, the more they could ask for when they sold the club, which they eventually did.

Sadly, doing a good job didn't convince the new owners; they got rid of all the foreign staff.

After eight months, the club was sold. When they were in the process of selling the club they said, "We want to keep you." Then the day they sold the club, they informed us that they wanted to work with Chinese and not foreign staff. That was a very low moment, but that's football.

After leaving Sichuan, a guy approached Cederique online and encouraged him to move to Xiamen for an exciting project. The aim was to get the club promoted into the professional leagues in China. Unfortunately, promises from the club weren't met and the project quickly ran out of funds.

I was Head Coach in the Chinese Members Champions League for five months until the club dissolved due to financial problems.

After leaving Xiamen, Cederique went home and was doing video analysis for the Belgian FA as he waited for his next move.

Lithuania

Cederique was approached about a project in Lithuania by the Belgian FA. FK Vilnius wanted a Belgian coach and Cederique agreed to join.

I joined a good project as head of U15 to U19 and Head Coach of U17. I was involved with the academy's coach education, building the structure, and working with the players. We had a lot of national team players in the academy.

Shortly after signing, the lack of stability in football reared its ugly head again.

After six months, it became clear that the cost of running the club was higher than expected. They could no longer afford my salary and we found a mutual agreement to finish the contract.

Cederique had already met the Technical Director of the Lithuanian Federation who was a fellow Belgian. He liked Cederique's work and gave him a job at the federation.

I invited him for coffee. We spoke, and after a couple of months he said, "Maybe you can help me with something." I helped him, he saw I can deliver good work and two months later he asked me to join the federation.

Working for the Lithuanian Football Federation was a great opportunity for Cederique. Already being in Lithuania and having worked at a good level in Asia boosted his profile.

The experience in Asia, working at a good level, was a big influence for the federation to take somebody like me.

Cederique was involved in youth national team games, including one against his own country.

When we played Belgium with the woman's national team, hearing my national anthem during the game gave me goosebumps.

The women's national team performed well during his time there.

We won the Baltic Cup, which was quite a big tournament in that region. They hadn't won it for over ten years. It was a big achievement for Women's Football. We went to play a women's cup in Armenia and we won that too. We were developing the players, but we also showed that we could win at our level. We couldn't win against the top countries yet. But you could see that if we worked well, we could win.

Cederique found you can make a real difference in a Federation.

When we did webinars, we reached all the academies at once. Working in a club is great but if you're a Head Coach, you can only reach 18 or 25 players. If you are Academy Director, you can only reach the players and coaches inside your academy. The reach is much smaller.

It's also harder to make decisions in big organisations.

The bigger the organisation gets, the more bureaucratic it becomes. If you're a Head Coach, you decide what we'll do today and everyone follows. If you're an Academy Director, you need to speak to other departments and the board because the changes are long-term. At the federation, I needed to work with other departments so it took more time to make changes. But when we made a change, it had a bigger impact.

Having a managerial role inside a Federation has set Cederique up for the future.

I had no chance of becoming a Technical Director at my age without a UEFA Pro License. I got inside a Federation and had a managerial role with the women. I was doing the same work a Technical Director does which was a fantastic experience.

During his time at the Lithuanian Federation, Cederique got a call from a Belgian coach he had met on his UEFA B course.

He was working as head of recruitment for United World who have five clubs. We had never worked together or had much contact. We spoke about my philosophy and he said, "Are you interested in working in Dubai?" I was in Lithuania and my wife had a good job there. I was very excited but I wanted to check with my wife. I called her, and she said, "You can go to Dubai? Why did you even call me? Call them back now and say yes!" I called them and from there we made it official.

Dubai, United Arab Emirates

It was an exciting project for Cederique to work for an organisation that owned five clubs around the world.

United World's five clubs included Sheffield United in England, Beerschot in Belgium, Chateauroux in France, Kerala United in India, and Al-Hilal in Dubai. Al-Hilal and Kerala were feeder clubs for the European teams. In Al-Hilal, we had ten professional players. We signed them from Africa and South America to develop and send them to our clubs in Europe.

Cederique had great facilities to work with.

We used the training ground of a team who had the best facilities in division one. They trained in the afternoon so we trained in the morning. We had a small stadium, three grass fields, one artificial field, a gym, swimming pool, and the hotel all onsite. It was in the desert but it was quiet. The grass fields were one of the best in the UAE. I had an Assistant Coach, a physio, then two team managers and that's it. It was basic but it was enough to deliver good work.

The five United World clubs met to discuss philosophy but Cederique had the freedom to do it his way at Al-Hilal.

We had a lot of meetings between the five clubs to discuss philosophy, how we work, and how to share ideas. I was always in communication with the head of recruitment for the five clubs. But it didn't directly impact the club or how I operated on the field.

The team played in the UAE second division and expectations were clear heading into the season.

They wanted to get the players ready to go to Europe. If we won, fantastic. If we didn't win, it's okay. But once you are in football and you have good players, everybody wants to win.

Cederique spent hours watching player videos to build a team that could compete.

I started in July and we began training at the end of August. Alongside the head of recruitment, and scouts, we watched so many games to select the best ten players we could to build the team.

The team was made up of 10 professional players and the rest were amateur.

We had ten professional players from Brazil, Ghana, Ivory Coast, and Senegal who we selected from videos. They got a contract with housing and then the other amateur players were already living in Dubai. We had over 300 players sign up for the trials. Around 80 to 100 players attended each trial and it was difficult to see who stood out because there was so much to watch. We managed to build a very competitive team between the professional and amateur players.

When the players arrived for pre-season, it was clear plenty of work needed to be done to get them to the level required for Europe.

I realised immediately they weren't used to the European training style. They were talented players but I had to teach them how to train because they were not used to this way of thinking. Some players didn't have a good tactical understanding so the first couple of weeks were very intense. But after that, you build expectations and good habits for the season so everything went more smoothly. It takes time to create your identity and get used to the training sessions. When they can understand and learn from you, it's easy to get them hooked on your training methods.

The season got off to a disastrous start after suffering from registration problems.

In one game, we had no defenders and had to play midfielders at the back. It was really difficult. I stayed positive because if I started complaining then the players would complain more. They felt like the coach is helping us, and it's difficult for him. It created a good bond with the team. They felt like, we don't want to play as defenders but we'll do it and we'll fight.

The registration problems cost them points early on but Cederique drove the team to close the gap on the top two promotion places.

Methodical Approach

Cederique's days were busy as a Head Coach in the UAE third tier.

I'd wake up at 6am and get to the training ground at 7am. At 8 am we had a team meeting before training started at 8.30 am and we'd finish training around 10-10.30 am. After training, we'd have a debrief with the staff on most days.

Twice a week we'd have the gym so I'd stay until 3 or 4 pm. In between then I'd plan the training session for the next day and prepare the analysis presentation. When there was no gym, I'd go home to eat and start working on the preparation for training the next day. I'd also analyse our team's matches and our opponents if I could find it. A typical day started early and was always very busy.

Al-Hilal trained five times a week, had one game day and one day off. Cederique held team meetings before every training session to get the players up to speed.

Every day, there was a meeting; sometimes it was only 10 minutes, sometimes 45 minutes. At the beginning of the season, we were speaking about training, methodology, identity and style of play, so the meetings were longer. They needed to understand why we were doing things. Most of the time, I used animations showing actions in the game to build understanding.

The second half of the season was more about the details of what we're coaching and not about why you need to stand in a certain position. Normally, after half a year, they already know this. It was more about details, whereas in the beginning it was about teaching them the tactical basics.

Cederique also held video analysis twice a week to review and preview games.

The hotel where the players stayed was next to the training ground. We had a meeting room there with a big screen and projector. If we played on Saturday, then Monday or Tuesday, we had a video analysis session to review the game. On Thursday or Friday, we did analysis to preview our upcoming opponents. For games, I used the

Subbuteo field as we didn't have a projector at the stadium. I liked Subbuteo because it shows the body position. You can ask players, "Why is your back like this?"

Managing players from a range of countries isn't easy, but Cederique's ability to speak multiple languages helped.

I had the advantage that I was able to communicate in English and French. A lot of the team was French-speaking. If I was not able to communicate in French, it would have been more difficult to get my message across. Some members of the club would get frustrated with the French-speaking players because of how they talk. When I'd speak to them, I'd find they are not saying anything bad. They speak very loudly, but that's just how they are.

I had one guy from Brazil who only spoke Portuguese. By the end, he spoke a little bit of English, but we had a very good connection. I couldn't communicate in his language but I used Google translate and communicated non-verbally with him.

Cederique's team was up against Fursan Hispania FC, who were owned by former Real Madrid player Michel Salgado.

Our league was difficult because you had Fursan FC and our team who were very professional. Then you had a couple of somewhat professional teams, and then you had two or three teams... I'm sorry but I cannot say it in a better way, they were amateur. That's why many players wanted to come to our club and Mr. Salgado's because they saw a different culture. Our clubs set the example for how things should be done. Over time, if they took some ideas from our clubs, the level of football in Dubai would grow.

Season Review

Cederique was happy with how the season went.

We finished third – one point behind second place. It was a good season. The team and the individuals grew a lot. I was very happy.

Three players went to France on trial but unfortunately didn't sign; two players did sign for second division teams in Belgium and Portugal, though. The amateur players also played their part.

If we only played with the amateur players, we would have been mid-table. We were lucky to have some very good amateur players who were trying to showcase themselves inside the UAE and internationally. We made video compilations and spoke with their agents. One amateur player signed for a UAE division one team midseason.

Although he was happy with third place, Cederique believes they deserved second place.

I was happy with third. Of course, I wanted to be first but second place would have been fair. If we had no problems with registration at the beginning, then we would have had seven, eight, or nine more points.

The top two teams got promoted with Michel Salgado's Fursan FC winning the league.

Our team had more quality and potential but Fursan FC was more experienced and more balanced with players at similar levels. They were a very good team and we were the only team to beat them all season.

The team's principles of pressing aggressively and attacking football were tested against Fursan FC.

We didn't change our approach as we have principles. Fursan were strong so we often did a medium press rather than a high press but the principles and pressing triggers remained the same. The biggest issue was getting a red card after 15 minutes. We had to change a bit but we showed a strong mindset... the players had to run a lot. Our principles were less visible due to having one player less and playing a strong opponent. It wasn't always good football but the win against Fursan was enjoyable.

Cederique was also proud of their friendly performances against a top UAE team and foreign teams who were in Dubai on training camps.

We beat Ghanaian champions Kotoko and lost to Al Ain 3-1, but they were UAE champions and two divisions up. We also lost 2-0 to Mumbai City who was in the Asian Champions League. We did well in all matches against tough opposition. If we had more experience to give the final pass, we would have been better. But we showed we were a young team full of talented players. I was very proud of the team.

After leaving the UAE, Cederique signed for another of United World's clubs. He joined second-tier Belgium team Beerschot as U23 Head Coach and Assistant Coach of the first team. These experiences have put Cederique in a great position to succeed and point towards a bright future in the game.

Chapter 6. The Power of Networking and Social Media

Having the skillset required to build a strong network is priceless. Sam wishes he'd been taught how to do it earlier.

The most important piece of advice – and I wish somebody had told me before – is to meet and network with as many people as possible.

It helps you on the job by developing good relationships with your colleagues and creating a positive and efficient working environment. Cederique also uses it as an opportunity to improve performance by observing people, exchanging ideas, and tapping into their expertise.

Speaking with coaches and discussing philosophies, tactics, and ways of working... it educates you as a person and a coach.

A wide network also helps you recruit better players and coaches to improve an organisation at all levels. Sam developed a wider network by working at different clubs.

I was fortunate, through university, to work at multiple clubs in the Northwest of England. I did analysis for Wigan and coaching for Blackburn and Morecambe. I also went down to Fleetwood Town. Working at those clubs allowed me to meet different people, including first team managers. All those connections help.

Experiencing different environments is a good learning tool, but it's also vital for developing a wide network at different levels of the game. Once you get yourself into a professional environment, people will start reaching out to you. Working at higher levels and roles raises your credibility. More people will want to connect as they think you can add value and help them.

Most coaches in this book got their best jobs through networking. Your network can provide direction and future opportunities by giving advice, referrals, and job opportunities. This is how Michael got his break in the Chinese Super League.

I've got a friend that works in the Chinese Football Association. We studied together in the UK, and he recommended me to the club.

Colum kept in touch with staff at the Irish Football Association when he was in China. This regular communication was vital for Colum getting a job when he returned to Belfast.

With the elite programme, I was always on the phone asking are any positions available. One opened up, and the first two weeks I went up, and said you don't have to pay me... just let me coach. After that, I was in.

You might not reach the people you want, initially, but that shouldn't stop you. You may be able to reach them through another person. Start lower down the chain to build relationships and showcase your work. Once they get to know you, they may open doors higher up the chain. Keep working your way up until you reach the people who can create the biggest opportunities for you. In the modern era, there is always a way to reach people!

Connection Quality

It only takes one person to reach your dream job. For this to happen, you need to develop a strong connection. Cederique gets frustrated by people asking for jobs without building a connection first.

LinkedIn is the worst. They send you a message, "Hey, I'm looking for a job. Can you give me one?" I don't know you or what your qualities are. There's no job opening now. Why would I even consider hiring you? It's very important to build a connection and get to know people first. If they're a good person, it has a big influence, and you'll want to help them.

Sam feels it takes a lot of work and reflection to become good at networking.

You have to understand their personality and how you can build a connection. When you're building up your career, you have to think about how you're going to do it and plan it out.

This is why getting to know people – and what makes them tick – is massive for connecting. Sam knows it only takes one connection.

You may have a hundred connections, and it could be one that helps you get something. When I first started coaching, I wish I had some guidance on courses or through my degree. All those soft skills that, if you don't learn in the formal environment, you have to learn as life goes on. Studying how to develop relationships with people will help you long-term.

Get to know people by finding out the types of information and conversations they enjoy and the things you have in common. Knowing their values, goals, strengths, and areas they want to improve can help you find ways to connect. Ask what platforms they prefer communicating on, whether they like face to face, calls, texts, or voice notes and what time of day is best to chat. The better you know someone, the easier it is to have meaningful conversations and add value. It allows you to cater to their needs and create stronger connections. Connecting with the right people opens the door to better opportunities.

Adding Value

You need to add value for others to consider you part of their network. It takes more than exchanging a few messages before people are going to go out of their way to help you. Add value by sharing information or connecting them with a valued contact. You have lots to offer, so find ways to benefit those in your network.

A Head of Academy at an English League One club contacted me, saying he was going to Asia. I reached out to Sam Bensley, and he welcomed him to present to the Hong Kong FA staff. Adding value by creating opportunities strengthens bonds and leads to opportunities. Cederique highlights the importance of having a network that values your work. This will make them more likely to connect you to opportunities.

Have a network of people who want to help you – not only because they like you or think you're funny – but because they know your qualities. It's very important.

Football is more about *who* you know than *what* you know at times. This can cause frustration as it doesn't seem fair. Instead of getting frustrated, put that time into developing your network. Having a strong network helps you overcome the job lottery and access higher level jobs.

Helping Others

Doing good deeds for others is powerful as it makes you feel good, inspires people to do good deeds for others, and is a future investment – as people may want to repay the favour. *Invest time in the right people* and you will reap the rewards. This may be the most important tip of all, and is how I got my job in the Thai topflight. A friend recommended a physio reach out to me for feedback on his A licence coursework. I took the time to read through all his session plans and provided detailed feedback. He responded with his thoughts and thanked me for helping.

One year later, the physio called me to say he had recommended me to his club in the Thai topflight. A few weeks later, I was greeted at the airport by the physio and the president's son to start my new role. This was a massive opportunity I wouldn't have got without taking the time to help him. Helping others without expecting anything in return is one of the best investments. Good deeds live long in the memory. People who help others will have a queue of people waiting to help in their hour of need.

You won't get very far if all you do is take from people, and only reach out when you're in need. Have a list of contacts who you value as people, and who can help with your goals. Stay in regular contact and message them on their birthday, when significant events happen in their life, or when a shared interest pops up. You can pass on information they will find beneficial, an event they may like to attend, or when a suitable job opportunity appears. It can be anything that may interest or be an opportunity that adds value. You can also engage with their social media posts. Regular communication helps to develop a relationship and shows you care about them as a person. You'll reap the rewards once you have invested time in the relationship and shown your qualities.

Connecting Across Levels

It can be challenging developing connections with high-level people when you're not in a high-profile position. You may not have anything in common or be able to add much value to people at the top. Get creative in finding ways to connect. It could be setting up a weekly 5-a-side for influential football lovers in the area, or offering them something linked to their favourite hobby. If you can't add value through your knowledge or experiences, then run events with people who can. Setting up online or local events with high level operators could be a great way for everyone to promote themselves whilst helping the community.

You can also connect with high-level people you can't add much value to by showing passion and commitment. You may remind them of a younger version of themselves. It also highlights your potential, and reassures them that any time they invest in you won't be wasted.

It's not only about reaching people higher up the pyramid but connecting with people at all levels. It's important to be open-minded as you can learn from anyone, regardless of whether they're a UEFA Pro or a level 1 coach. Helping those starting out grows the game and gives them the confidence to reach out to others. Give time to those with potential as they may rise to a high level which could create opportunities for you. It's much easier to connect with people early in their journey. Once they rise, their time will be at a premium, and they will have lots of people wanting their attention. Connecting early in their journey strengthens your bond, and they'll want to repay you.

Networking Opportunities

Every day, we're provided with opportunities to network. Build strong relationships at work and show your qualities. Go to coaching conferences and courses to get your face known. Interact during the group sessions and share your message and beliefs with others. Get people's contact details and social media handles to keep in touch. Arrange to meet different coaches for a coffee and catch up. Go to watch games and observe sessions to show your commitment and willingness to learn and meet people. The key is developing a strong network and being creative with ways to get yourself into jobs. Connecting with others and showing the quality of your work is essential for progressing in the game.

Social Media

Social Media has given a voice to the coaches in the shadows and gives us access to coaches who are realistic role models. Coaching wasn't given the respect it deserves, and was not seen as a real career, when I was starting out. I could only see coaches in full-time jobs at the highest level on TV, which was unrealistic for most people. There weren't many full-time coaching jobs where I lived or role models with realistic journeys to follow. My main goal was to change that – using the power of social media – by showing coaches that you can make a full-time career out of coaching and travel the world.

Social media enables you to share your message with thousands of people every day. Sam believes it's a great way to extend your reach and network.

One of the best ways to network is through social media. For coaches coming through, that's one way to extend their reach. Follow and communicate with coaches who are well-connected and post quality educational content.

Social media can be a great learning tool, but it is important to filter information as it won't all be high quality or useful. Cederique thinks social media can help you get jobs, but it won't help coaches at the top level.

Social media can be beneficial for your career but not for the top jobs. Mourinho will not get his job through social media, even though he put his CV on Instagram. There are lots of jobs at grassroots or good academies that are looking for coaches. Putting yourself out there on social media makes it easier to be visible. If you're stuck in the forest, nobody will find you, and there's no chance you will get a job.

Simon got offered a job in the Maldives by a club owner via Direct Message (DM) on Twitter.

He tweeted me saying, "Can I send you a DM?" I looked at it. The Maldives? I don't know who this guy is. But he wanted to talk football and was the owner of a club. I said, "Yeah, ok."

The first thing he said wasn't, "Hello coach, how are you?" He said, "Coach, would you come to New Radiant sports club in the Maldives?" I said, "Ok, can we talk about details?" He replied, "Well, the salary is not very good but I know you, I have followed your career. You don't need to send me a CV." I flew there a week later, and helped them through their AFC campaign.

Simon also got the Philippines job on Facebook after making an impression on a player he coached. This worked out well for Simon, but you need to be careful as there are a lot of scammers online.

Share Your Ideas

Some people have lots of followers but don't reap any rewards from it. How can you impress people if you don't post or show what you do? Identify your target audience, and what content they engage with. Get involved in discussions and join coaching groups. People will see your ideas and may follow you if they find value in what you're sharing.

You can learn without posting, but you can't impress or get opportunities. Use the platforms to showcase your ideas and work. Post highlights from what you've been working on that week or when you get a new job. Show the courses, qualifications or books you have completed with a review of their impact. You can take pictures and videos to provide evidence of your work and to generate interest. Colum posts pictures with the trophies he's won as Head Coach.

It's self-promotion as well. If you go to my Instagram, it's me holding a load of trophies. Hopefully, an owner clicks on it one day and thinks, he seems to be winning a lot, so we'll hire him. In Asia, that's possible. It depends how clubs do their research. I've heard of players who have changed their Wikipedia stats and got big contracts.

If you post high-quality content, your followers will grow and more people will want to connect with you. I've been offered jobs based only on what I post and helping those who reach out. Some of these people have never seen me work, which shows the value of posting good content and creating a positive image. You might not always get lots of engagement, but you never know *who* is watching. Colum advises being active on social media as it could lead to job opportunities.

Be active, give feedback, and get into groups. You don't know who is on it. People might be hiring and have seen someone's posts and they're in line with their values and principles. They might ask what the coach's situation is and if they would be interested in coming.

Be Visible

Post regularly to appear in people's views with quality content. It helps you stick in your audience's mind, and it will give them a clearer idea of who you are and your message. It also adds trust and credibility if they get to know your beliefs and what you have achieved.

Trust is also built by coming across as a good person, and your followers seeing people they know engaging with you. This accelerates the networking process as, when you reach out, your followers feel like they know you already. Having a professional-looking profile picture adds credibility. Add your qualifications, who you've worked for, plus your achievements into your biography. It's the first thing your profile visitors see, so make sure to create a good first impression. Have links for people to find your website and other social media accounts, too. Your posts need to be well-written to engage your audience and all visuals need to be high quality.

Analyse Data

Social media gives you access to data that shows how your posts are performing. Keep an eye after posting to watch the performance of your posts, and spot any mistakes or comments. Track your posts and what content is getting the most engagement. Focus on that (if it's a message you believe in), as it will provide the greatest growth. Keep an eye on accounts that post similar content and get good engagement. It may be tactical reports, session ideas, visuals, snappy summaries, or detailed threads. See what works for them and how you can learn from it.

Tracking the time you spend on social media apps can make for alarming reading. Small visits add up to a lot over time! The key is ensuring you spend more time creating content and networking than you do scrolling through with no intention. Time invested in creating content, learning, and connecting with others will reap rewards, whereas memes and aimless scrolling will not.

Engage with others

Collaborate with others by doing interviews, podcasts, or creating content for their page. Work on projects together to grow your connections and reach new audiences. *Share your content for free* with large accounts in your target area. Like and share their posts to support and add insightful comments to attract new followers. This helps get your name and story in front of new people.

Take the time to respond to every thoughtful message or comment you receive on social media. Doing so develops a connection, and that person may become a supporter of your work. As your profile grows, so will the number of messages you receive. It's important to take the time to give back when you can.

Say *yes* to requests. If people reach out and ask you to do an interview or a podcast, do it. No matter how big or small their reach is. I did a podcast for two guys in a large country. Afterwards, I had the Technical Director of the federation contact me, as well as a national team player.

You never know what opportunities can come from putting your ideas out there!

Reach Out

Keep in regular contact with your network. A professional player shared their highlights on their Instagram story and I reacted with the fire emoji. He responded by saying a teammate had recommended me, and he'd been thinking about contacting me. We set up a call the next day, which was the start of a long-term working relationship.

I've sent plenty of messages and got no response. It didn't do me any harm. Some players and athletes I have reached out to were great, and we've kept in touch. Having a strong social media profile can create countless opportunities. Follow the people you want to connect with, and they may follow back, if they like what they see. Mutual connections, a good following, good content, or being in the same region, may earn a follow back. This can be the start of your connection over time, once they see your posts and understand your message. There are a host of people on social media who can help progress your career. Identify ones who may be useful and reach out to them. What's the worst that could happen? It may lead to big opportunities!

People worth reaching out to

Reach out to job holders, experts, mentors, and connectors.

1. **Job Holders:** People in the position you'd like to reach can provide a great case study to follow. You can find out how they got to where they are today and the advice they have for someone starting their journey. It's also a useful contact in the industry as they'll know other people in similar roles, and when vacancies may come up. They would also be a good reference if you can prove your suitability for the role. You can also discover their journey through LinkedIn and online interviews. Reach out to people in their network to ask about their journey and how you can connect with them.
2. **Experts:** Surround yourself with people who are more knowledgeable than you. Find top coaches from different sports or coaching academics you can learn from. Buy their books, listen to their podcasts, or talk to them directly. You can also learn loads from observing them in practice and asking questions.
3. **Mentors:** Finding a knowledgeable and experienced mentor can fast-track your development. Asking them to watch your sessions and provide feedback can help uncover blind spots. This allows you to show your capability in practice which can lead to a good

reference. Soaking up their experience teaches you a lot and ensures you don't make the same mistakes they did.

4. **Connectors:** People with a large network can connect you with a recruiter or job. This could be a player, coach, agent, or any well-connected person in the game. Finding someone who will share their network can open doors. Before they will do this, you have to show your passion, credibility, and earn their trust. Their name is on the line if they recommend you, so you've got to prove your worth.

Online Messages

Reaching out is a skill that takes time to master. If you believe a person could add value to your network, then there will be a lot of others thinking the same. Put yourself in their shoes. What type of message would *you* like if you are receiving multiple messages every day from strangers? The best three-step approach is to make it personal, ask for advice, and to offer an escape.

The best messages start with a brief positive note on how the person you are reaching out to has impacted you. Complimenting them creates warmth towards you. If you don't know them then do your research. Use their name and say something specific about them. This shows you're not sending a mass message they can ignore. Mention something you have in common to create a connection right away.

Follow the above with a short note on what you are working on to provide context and ask for advice. This could be advice on how to progress your career or a project you are working on. You are reaching out to them as they are the expert. Never make a sales pitch right away, as that turns people off.

Close the message with an appreciation of how busy they are, and that it's no problem if they can't do what you're asking. This makes it feel like there is no pressure. When people come across too strongly, we tend to switch off and not respond.

Never start a message to someone you have never spoken to by only saying hello or asking how they are. You need to *earn* a response and start building context and a connection from the first message. They are busy people and most don't have time for small talk with strangers. Keep it short, *never* try to sell anything, and don't be too forceful. It's the difference between connecting and being ignored.

Be Careful

Cederique feels some coaches don't use social media in the best way.

Some coaches oversell themselves on social media. They try too much and it feels unnatural. You see something, and you think, what is this? They write something to get attention. You need to find a good balance. What you put online... will be online forever. Think about it and the idea behind it.

You need to be brave to put yourself out there as there will be people waiting in the shadows to bring you down. Often, they will not share anything and are only there to critique others. Be wary of these people, and do not give their posts any oxygen by reacting badly to them. It can take years to build your reputation and credibility, but it only takes *one post to destroy it*. Be careful what you put on social media as it will come back to haunt you. It may affect you immediately or further down the line. Never post anything you wouldn't want your family or boss to read!

Be Prepared

In the beginning, you won't get much engagement. But the good news about social media is you don't need to be a big name to get a good following and benefit. All it takes is a plan to analyse the data and create an action plan to keep improving your content. When you start using social media correctly, it will become a valuable tool.

Networking is essential for career progression. You may excel on the job but poor networking limits the opportunities to maximise your potential. When you become a skilled networker, you never know when an opportunity will arise. The key is to keep developing yourself, so you're ready when the opportunity comes.

Agents: The Good, the Bad, and the Ugly

Agents are a hot topic in football circles. They can be a useful asset when networking but the coaches in this book have had mixed experiences, as you can imagine!

Sam has not benefitted from using agents.

I've had some experience with agents but never positive. I'm not particularly attractive to an agent because I'm not a big enough name. If I do engage an agent, they're going to be a very average one because they're working with someone like me. There's no real benefit from having them, but that's my experience.

Dealing with lower profile coaches with smaller salaries results in lower financial rewards. Cederique says agents will find you once you reach a certain level.

When you are a coach at a high level, with a big salary, the agents will come by themselves. They will be very happy to work with you and take 10% or 20 thousand euros or more. They will try to find you a position as quickly as possible.

Cederique doesn't see much benefit for those at the start of their careers.

Most agents aren't interested in coaches who are starting out and aren't earning big money. I wouldn't focus too much on getting an agent at the outset. If you're in contact with someone and you feel that they can help you, you should do it. But, in general, there are few agents for coaches not working at higher levels.

Higher Profile

Scott Cooper, Steve Darby, and Simon McMenemy have good profiles in South East Asia which attract agents. Despite this Simon hasn't found many good ones.

I'm still to find a good one that I'd want to sign with. You're relying on them to have contacts around the world, and a lot of the time, they don't. They're good in a certain region, league, or a few clubs and they move players. But they don't have the contacts to know there's a job available in Greece or Norway.

Simon never signs exclusively with an agent.

As a coach, I'm not sure it's a good idea to sign exclusively with agents. What I tend to do is say that I'll sign with you, but I'm not signing exclusively. I'll have 12-15 agents that have me on their books. This gives me a full spread of the world's football leagues as opposed to relying on one.

Simon often has a better network than the agent but still needs their help.

Half the time, I've got better contacts than the agents I'm working with. I know more people around the world, but you need agents to grease the wheels and make things happen. They do the stuff you don't have time to do, or which you can't because you're not in the country.

Simon feels it's harder for agents to get jobs for coaches.

For a coach, there's only one job per club, whereas for players, there are thirty for every club. It's a very different thing using agents for coaching. You're so reliant on their contacts and the club believing the agent's credible and doing a good job.

Scott Cooper found the right agent and stuck with him.

My agent's got the connections and is a good friend. You need an agent that's got your best interests at heart and won't place you in a job for the sake of it. He takes care of your media profile and gives financial advice. He looks after legal matters or looking for houses. If somebody else came in, he wouldn't stand in my way. Everyone goes through ups and downs, so you need the right person. You're better off with a long-term one rather than chopping and changing.

Mixed Experiences

Steve Darby has seen the good and bad of agents over the years.

Most agents I have met are criminals and treat players appallingly. They are quite often willing to pay bribes. I have dealt with a few genuine ones who have been honest and taken 5% for getting a contract. In some cases, they have taken 50%.

Colum has also come across some toxic agents.

I know an agent of a player I tried to sign. The player wanted to come and the agent asked for three months' worth of the player's salary. Ultimately, he sent the player to a lesser club and has taken the money. It can be a nasty business.

Thankfully, Colum has had a much more positive experience with his agent.

My agent's been brilliant. He's got 15-20 years of experience in Asia and the Gulf. As a professional football manager, you don't always know your worth. My agent got me more than what I thought I was worth. He read over my contract to make sure I was protected and sent it to his lawyer. He checks in on you. If I wanted to move somewhere, he'd be on the ball for me. If I needed players with a particular profile, he'd help me get the players I need.

Colum believes your values need to align when choosing an agent.

Make sure an agent's values align with yours. My agent knows the type of club I want to join, the way I want to work, and my beliefs and values as a person.

This shows both sides of the story. Agents may not be as useful for smaller profile coaches, but they can still add value to Head Coaches starting out, as Colum outlined. There are scammers out there. Never trust anyone asking you to pay money upfront, or wanting to take a large percentage of your salary. Sometimes, you may have to pay for a flight which the club may repay at the end of your contract, but I have never paid money directly to an individual upfront.

Be wary of agents unless you know *someone credible* who has worked with them and recommends them. Colum was able to find his agent through a first team player he worked with. Also, look online for positive and negative media reports or websites which present evidence and testimonials of their work. You can check their social media pages to see what they post and if they interact with anyone you know. Use LinkedIn to find people they have worked with or reach out to people in their country who know them. Talking to agents and searching online is useful, but it won't always give you the full picture.

Research is Key

Simon got offered a job in Vietnam, and was sold the dream by an agent.

I didn't get the full picture. I searched for the club, looking through Wikipedia and general news enquiries. I was sold the club by an agent who told me that they had just won the league. He said they had lots of national team players in the squad – which on Wikipedia they did – and they're competing again. What I didn't know was I was the third coach that season and all but one of their national team players had been sold. They were struggling towards the bottom of the league.

It's key to find out not only about the playing squad, but also how the club is run behind the scenes. Simon had to find out the hard way.

I would love to have known more about other personnel as well, because that was a difficult situation. A lot was going on behind the scenes that made the performances on the pitch really difficult. A lot of financial issues and putting pressure on national team players not to go home, and player contracts were threatened if they went to play for their national teams. Despite what FIFA allow.

It was mission impossible for Simon when he arrived, and his agent did a runner after he received his money.

That's the hardest environment I've walked into. I thought I knew what was going on there, and I was quite confident. They were reshaping, but at least I've got good players to work with. Sadly, that wasn't the case. The club had been stripped by the time I got there, and the agent had done a good job of selling it. He disappeared after he got his 10% and I never spoke to him again.

This shows the importance of doing your research and getting multiple perspectives. Talk to people at the club, previous staff, and unbiased people in the country who know the club. When Simon went into Bhayangkara in Indonesia, he had known the Technical Director for years. This gave him a better idea of what was going on at the club, and he knew he would get looked after. It's not only safer for recruiters to hire people they know and trust, but it also reduces the risk for coaches joining clubs where they have strong relationships.

Scammers

A guy reached out to me saying he wanted me to deliver camps in different countries around the world. One week we'd be in Korea, the next Japan, followed by spells in Australia and New Zealand. He would pay a good salary, airfare, hotels, and everything between. The players would wear GPS and the best players would have the opportunity to trial in Europe. The project had already launched and I knew a former English Championship Assistant Manager who was involved. He had already done a camp, got paid on time, and said everything was above board. Alarm bells started ringing, however, when he was using my friend's picture on the website when he hadn't been involved.

News then broke about this guy and all his previous scams. It turns out he had set up academies in other countries, taken the money from those who signed up, and disappeared. He also left coaches who were due salaries that hadn't been paid. There was a range of unsavoury episodes he had been involved in. There are countless stories of people getting scammed so you need to be wary and watch out for any abnormal signs.

Job Sites

Job sites have made jobs more visible. This is great, but it may make it more difficult to get jobs as they're now viewed by thousands of people online and may have hundreds of applicants. The reality is, if my first job (with Arsenal Soccer School in Kuwait) had been on a job site, I may not have got it. I found it as a coach working there (who I followed) tweeted about it from a small account. It thankfully hadn't been shared widely on a subscription job site or by someone with a large following.

It becomes a lottery when looking in the same places as everyone else. A lot of applicants will have similar profiles and it's hard for recruiters to filter through hundreds of applications. Job sites can provide CV and career mentoring services to help you stand out. Cederique believes if you don't have a strong network, then a job site can work for you.

In the beginning – if you have no network and don't know people abroad – this is the easiest way to find a job abroad and get in contact with clubs.

Sam recommends following the job sites on social media and getting a subscription.

Do your research and have a few websites that you check regularly when looking for a job. Follow them on Twitter and they will pop up.

Job sites are great for clubs as they will dip into a large pool of candidates. Coaches can also benefit and get jobs from these sites, especially jobs that fewer people apply for and coaches with standout CVs. The issue with large sites is it's much harder to succeed amongst a large pool of coaches. Applying for jobs that aren't posted by large accounts reduces the competition. It's a huge advantage as most jobs nowadays are widely shared on social media.

The more experienced and the larger your network becomes, however, the less you will need to rely on job sites. As we've said, *the best jobs don't get advertised* and when they do, you usually need to be connected to someone on the inside. Building up your profile and network over time will create the most opportunities for you.

Chapter 7. Blaine's Journey: A Global Adventure

Football has always been my biggest passion. As a teenager, I failed as a player and I didn't believe coaching was a real career, which left me questioning my prospects in the game. Little did I know where the game would take me, and the global adventure that lay ahead.

North America

Everything changed during my first year at university, when I saw an advert for a summer coaching job in America. I applied and ended up spending eight weeks coaching in America and Canada that summer.

We were living with host families and delivering camps in different towns each week. I went everywhere from New York City to Montreal and many places in-between. A family I stayed with in Connecticut organised a helicopter tour of New York City, which was surreal. Some people in Montreal only spoke French, and I had to recall the French I learnt back in school... which was fun.

We were coaching a range of age groups and abilities in a different culture, and I found this hugely beneficial. I asked a boy called Joey to tackle someone and the next thing I know, he wiped out another lad with an American Football tackle. It was an awesome tackle! It was also a great lesson in understanding culture and having a common language.

It was an eye-opening experience career-wise as – before going to North America – I didn't believe coaching was a real career. This all changed when I saw the opportunities in North America, and a lot of European coaches in full-time roles there.

It was also the first time I had travelled outside Europe, which was exciting in itself. This gave me the travel bug, plus the belief that although there weren't many coaching jobs at home... there was a big world out there full of opportunities!

After returning from North America, I was energised, and set myself the goal of coaching in five countries and becoming Academy Director at a professional club abroad. I had no idea how to do it at that stage, with only a small network in Northern Ireland and North America. As my Master's degree was coming to an end, I started searching for jobs.

Kuwait

I got offered one with Arsenal Soccer School in Kuwait but it was almost over before it began. Two months before I was due to leave, a mosque got blown up in Kuwait by a suicide bomber. Twenty-seven people were killed and 227 injured. People feared for my life and said I wouldn't be safe there. This was mostly due to media propaganda at the time – but I wouldn't let that stop me as I set off for Kuwait two days after presenting my Master's research.

I was the U14 Head Coach but also coached a range of age groups. All the players I coached were Kuwaiti but almost all spoke perfect English.

We had no girls in our programme, and there weren't many females playing there due to cultural barriers. I set up a girls-only programme which saw 15 girls come to our soccer school. After I left, the girl's team grew. They hired more female coaches and travelled to play tournaments around the Middle East. It was great seeing barriers being broken down and watching Kuwaiti girls fall in love with the game.

On the player register, you'd see the name Al-Sabah, which meant you'd be coaching members of the family who rule Kuwait. A lot of Kuwaiti children were raised by nannies who are foreigners the family hired, and you would see two brothers walking from the car followed by a nanny, each carrying their bags and drinks.

Some children who were raised by nannies could get away with anything they wanted. A lot of the players were great, but some weren't. One time, I saw a child hit their nanny, which we had to step in and address. Seeing how the children were raised and how it impacted their development was a valuable lesson. Learning how to manage their behaviour and finding ways to get the most from sessions was a great challenge.

Our pitch was based at a university. At my university in Belfast, the students were driving their mum's Peugeot 206. In Kuwait, they were driving Ferraris, Lamborghinis, and Corvettes. Being on campus and seeing how they dressed and behaved was a great cultural experience.

Men and boys would greet each other by going cheek to cheek. I saw one of our U18 players at the mall, and he leaned in towards me. I thought he was going to tell me a secret, but he went cheek to cheek with me. An Egyptian referee would always try to do the same.

Pork and alcohol were illegal, which meant there wasn't much nightlife. I rarely saw foreigners around, and the locals would go to shisha cafes to socialise. All the cultural differences, and hearing locals explain their culture, was fascinating.

Being in Kuwait allowed me to travel around the Middle East to visit Bahrain, Dubai, and Oman. I had a great time there and met some wonderful people. The cultural lessons and managing behaviour made Kuwait the perfect place to start my first full-time stint abroad.

Beijing, China

During my time in Kuwait, I saw an opportunity to work in China. It was a coach and coach educator position in Beijing. Part of the role was delivering coach education for Premier Skills – a partnership between the Premier League and British Council. It was an exciting time with Chinese football on the rise, and lots of money being pumped into the game.

The experience with Arsenal Soccer Schools, and knowing Colum Curtis – who was leading the recruitment – helped me get the job. Over time, I've found that each move became easier as I had proven my capability to do what was required. It also allowed me to meet new people in each role which increased my network and opened new doors.

Moving to Beijing was a much bigger culture shock than Kuwait. In Kuwait, most of the staff in shops were foreign so spoke good English. In Beijing, we lived outside the city centre where few people spoke English, and the shops and way of life were completely different.

I was trying to ask for directions on my first day in Beijing, and no one spoke English. It wasn't possible to use Google Maps on my phone as Google was banned. It was a tough transition. But this was my problem, not theirs. We should never move to a new country and expect everyone to speak English and make us feel comfortable.

Beijing was a tremendous learning environment. We had 16 full-time coaches from four countries. I was based at an international school, and whilst this involved coaching a mix of nationalities, they all spoke English. I had a Chinese driver who couldn't speak English but he took me to the school every day. I was lucky as coaches who were in the other districts had to get a taxi. They would print a map to show the taxi driver where to go. When the driver didn't understand what was on the map, it was difficult to navigate as most didn't speak English.

Language Barrier

Beijing was the first place that I worked with a translator. One translator was called Kevin, and although he was a great guy, we didn't get off to the best start. Kevin was sitting between Sam Bensley and me as our driver was taking us to the pitch. I was trying to talk to him but he had no idea what I was saying, due to my strong accent. To make things worse, he fell asleep in the car, and his head kept falling onto my shoulder.

During the session, I told him, "Our set-up is good. We don't have to pick up any cones to transition between exercises." I turned around, and the next thing I saw was all the children running around picking up the cones. I had to set the whole session up again, but it was my fault for being unclear. Every session got better as he began to understand me and we got used to working together. He is a top guy, and we still keep in touch.

Cultural Lessons

We ran a youth league in Beijing. Sam was responsible for managing it, but we all helped out with the organisation and running it. A boy in my league team was the son of Sun Jihai, who played over 100 games for Manchester City. He was playing for Beijing Renhe at the time and would come to some games; he was the quietest parent on the touchline.

We got to the pitch early one day, and there was a baseball session on. The coach was punishing eight-year-olds by making them sprint after mistakes. Some youngsters ran to their parents crying. The parents sat there and didn't say anything to the coach. I couldn't believe what I was seeing.

I saw some coaches being quite hard on the young players, which meant they weren't as expressive on the pitch. They didn't want to take players on, or break lines with passes, as their coach would shout if it didn't come off. At times, it was very evident how the environment created by the coach affected the players' bravery on the ball. Other coaches were great with the children, though, and created positive environments.

Saving face is a big deal in Chinese culture, which I found out the hard way. We were hosting our Nike Junior Cup event, which over 1,000 youth players attended over a weekend. I was running a section of games, and a boy was on the pitch with a water bottle during a game. I told Hugh (my translator) to tell him to set it at the side quickly and get back to playing.

When the game ended, I was noting down the scores when an elderly Chinese man walked up to me and aggressively smashed the clipboard out of my hand. The clipboard fell, and my first reaction was to grab his shoulders to restrain him as he came forward. All the parents and children were in shock. I pointed to the exit and told Hugh to tell him to leave. He refused as he couldn't back down and lose face. We had to get security, but it was a long time until he left.

I asked Hugh what had happened. The man thought Hugh was telling his grandson that he was not allowed to drink water. A few weeks later, we were at the pitch, and the same man was shouting hurry up in Chinese as it looked like rain was coming. The session started and ended at fixed times, so there was nothing I could do to speed things up. There's just no pleasing some people!

Local Schools

We went into local schools to deliver coach education which was a big challenge, but we did get some fantastic lunches out of it.

The Chinese PE teachers were not keen on young foreigners coming in and telling them what to do. This was partly due to the age hierarchy, with people preferring to be taught by their elders, but our sessions also made them feel uncomfortable. We liked lots of actions, people moving, and fewer lines. They preferred lines and order, which are easier to control.

We were only there as President Xi Jinping was pushing football. The schools wanted to follow his lead and create good football programmes.

There were at least 40 students per class, which wasn't easy. We split the pitch into four and had 10 students per section. The schools had lots of balls, so the students were getting plenty of actions. They loved the sessions, though, which brought the teachers around to our way of working.

We were assessing one teacher, and he was doing a great job with lots of students on a ball and everyone involved. Then the thunder and rain came. He took the students under a covered area and started playing 11v11, shirts versus skins. The other 18 plus students were standing watching. He had the same equipment and enough space available, but he panicked and reverted to what he'd always done.

Beijing was a fascinating place to live with the temples and Great Wall of China. I was also able to visit places like Hong Kong, Shanghai, Hangzhou, Japan, and Korea.

It was an outstanding experience culturally; I learnt a lot from the other coaches, and I made friends for life.

Malawi

After leaving China I contacted an academy in Malawi after seeing a post they made on Twitter. They were keen for me to fly out to Malawi for a month to deliver sessions and coach education. At the time, the academy was called Chigoli, but has since changed its name to Ascent Soccer.

Ascent Soccer is changing lives in Malawi and Uganda. They scout around the country to find the best players, then bring them in to house them, educate them, deliver character development programmes, and provide a football development programme. The goal is to improve players' education, to get them to a level where they can get football scholarships to study in North America.

I stayed with George, their amazing co-founder. The girls and boys were a pleasure to work with, and Thom – who was the Head Coach – acted as a translator for me. It was a real eye-opener on how every country has its unique challenges. We asked the boys and girls how they felt after a trial session and – through Thom – they said how 'heavy' they felt. They'd never been so well fed before playing, nor played in football boots before. It was also the first time they'd played on grass, or left their home town which was 3.5 hours away.

Getting into an academy like Ascent would be life-changing for the children. Not all children in Malawi have birth certificates, and on some of the documents they handed in you could see the dates had been changed to make them appear younger. They believed this would increase their chances of getting selected.

Education

The coach education plan that I had delivered in China needed to be adapted. Most coaches in Malawi only had one or two balls for their sessions. We got on the bus and went to an Ascent satellite academy to observe a coach who had taken my course.

I was told he was usually late and not well prepared. This time, however, he came early and handed me his session plan. He was delivering one of the sessions I had shown him, and it was nice to see the impact a short education programme had in that session. I just hope it continued long after I left.

Going into the local schools was heart-breaking. A maths teacher called me into his classroom where 100 children were sitting on the floor with one teacher. A large number didn't have pens or paper. If they couldn't afford them, they would go without as the school couldn't provide them. Despite all this, the kids were so happy and would sing and dance. It put all those little life problems into perspective.

The passion for football was clear to see. I attended a local game next to the beach and Lake Malawi in Senga Bay. There was no grass or lines on the pitch, but the crowd was packed. There were hundreds of people and they formed the outline of the pitch.

Any time a goal was scored, there would be a pitch invasion, and there was singing and dancing throughout the game. This was what the academy players would do at the side of the pitch when they were supporting the other teams. It was a unique experience. Being in Malawi was a real lesson on being adaptable and culturally aware. These examples demonstrate how you will have to deal with things you'll never have even thought about before.

Ubon Ratchathani, Thailand

I moved to Thailand to become Academy Director of a topflight Thai League club. I had full control of running a professional academy at the age of 25, which is a rare opportunity. There were nerves as I thought about the big challenge ahead, but I met the Head Coach, Scott Cooper, and he put me at ease right away. He told me to get settled *off the pitch* before I worried about anything else.

The President's son arranged a meeting to introduce me to the parents and players. They gave me a warm welcome, and it was so exciting to start the job I had been visualising since my days at university. But it didn't start as the dream job I had envisioned… after arriving, I soon realised I had been hired as a quick fix by the President's son.

Our club had an agreement with another team to let their 17-year-olds play in our Thai Youth League team. The President's son had fallen out with the U17 Head Coach, who subsequently left, which led to the majority of the U17 players also leaving. Their response was to put the U15 players into the U17 team. The season was already three games in when I arrived. I watched the U17 team train the day before a game and saw 40 mixed-age players training together with one coach. I was also informed the U12 team were training more than the first team.

The U17 team played a Thai Youth League game the following day, and I could see big problems right away. They had lost 6-1 the week before, and they set up in a very low block. They played long, aimless balls towards a fast centre forward every time they won it. The centre back was playing as a sweeper and was so deep that he was almost on the keeper's toes. The Head Coach departed at half-time to do a U8 training session and left the physio to lead the team. The U17s lost the game, and it is not much of an understatement to say that things clearly weren't right.

I went to greet the parents after the game. I hadn't met many of them as they chose not to come to my arrival meeting. They were venting through the President's son, who was translating. They were unhappy about the defensive style of play, and that the previous coach had left.

All situations I had no idea of when I accepted the role. It wasn't the great arrival I had hoped for.

Tough Start

I had to coach the U17 Thai Youth League team as the parents were so unhappy. My first game in charge was the following week against Buriram United – one of the biggest clubs in Thailand. What are the chances?

Buriram United hold trials across the entire country and thousands of players turn up. They select the best ones and house, educate, and train them in Buriram. Our squad of 16 was made up of two 14-year-olds, eight 15-year-olds, four 16-year-olds, and two 17-year-olds. All our players were from the Ubon region as we had no accommodation facilities at that stage.

We had five training sessions during the week leading up to the Buriram game. That was enough time to learn the players' names, which isn't always easy in a foreign country. But it would take more than a few days to implement a new style of play and change their current habits.

We were playing in a big provincial stadium in Buriram. Soon, after kick-off, we took a shock 1-0 lead scoring a great goal. The goalkeeper rolled the ball out to the left back, who played forward into the winger, who played inside to the centre midfielder. He opened up and played a lovely diagonal pass behind the defence for our striker, who had pulled wide. He ran onto the ball and lobbed it over the advancing goalkeeper.

It wasn't a sign of things to come as Buriram began to overrun us. Their physical advantage and quality were too much for us to handle. Our Assistant Coach wanted to keep the team on the pitch and berate them after the game.

We had a group of 15-year-olds from Ubon playing against the best 17-year-olds in the country, and the mismanagement of players – being in the wrong age group – was the problem; it wasn't the players' fault. A 17-year-old and 14-year-old decided to leave the club after that game.

It was tough getting out of bed the next day. I had big self-doubts. How could I convince people that my approach was right when our team had been hammered 9-1? I had to get up and face it as I went to watch the U12 team play, and then the U8s training.

No Quick Fix

There wasn't much we could do to balance the teams in the short term. The season had started and we couldn't register any new players at that time. We had to wait until the season was over to fix things properly, although we had a window – mid-season – to register new players and we took on a few. You can't recruit a whole new team at that time, though.

We improved the development programme for players by introducing video analysis and psychology sessions. Players also watched the first team play with sheets to analyse the player in their position. We created individual development plans and held unit meetings before games to reinforce key points and let players ask questions.

We made training more game-based and realistic. We asked the players questions, gave them choices, and got them to reflect on their performances. We introduced this approach gradually over several months as it was all new to them. The feedback we received was that the players enjoyed the process and performances improved.

It was a turbulent period trying to keep everyone on board while results were up and down. We put in a great performance against second-place Nakhon Ratchasima to get a draw at home. We also put in a much better performance against Buriram United at home, even though they came away with the victory.

We were competitive in all games against teams two years older than us who had players from across the country who lived, studied, and trained together. We won some, drew some, but we lost more than we won which made life difficult. Our individual and collective improvements in performance were enough to get some people onside. Others only judged our success on the scorelines.

It Takes Time

The situation was tough but we had a great opportunity to make a difference. The academy was only a year old, which left so much room for growth. The only reason I survived the first season was due to the President's son being raised in New Zealand. He believed in my approach, which was different from previous Thai coaches. He also knew how difficult the situation was and gave me full control to do everything I wanted.

This was key as he was very powerful in the club and the region due to his father. This gave me the power to do things inside the club and in the community. His backing bought me time and, eight months in, we were able to get the players into the right age groups. Results improved immediately, which saw us take big strides forward. Our methodology started coming together. This enabled us to get everyone in the academy onside.

We also got the coaches we wanted and a good translator, which made my life *much easier*. We held trials that attracted 548 players from across Thailand to improve our teams. The original U17 team had been picked during a local tournament in Ubon, which limited the talent pool. There wasn't much funding or opportunity for players in our region. The best players would go to sports schools or clubs in Bangkok as they had the money to house, educate, and train players. We needed to find a way to make it an attractive proposition for players to stay in Ubon Ratchathani.

Our President owned a university, so we gave players scholarships to study and play in the academy. We got a residential facility so we could recruit players from further afield, and we partnered with a local school so players could live, study and train together.

We kept an eye on their grades and highlighted the importance of education. We would talk to them if their grades dropped or they got into trouble at school. One year later, a parent told us she was amazed at the improvement in her child's grades. Like many Asian parents, she previously believed playing so much football would hold him back. Often, you would see Asian parents pull their children away from sport to focus on their studies. They told me it couldn't be done… but we did it!

New Initiatives

The Head Coach, Scott Cooper, asked me to create and implement a philosophy. There were only two teams in the academy leading to the first team when we arrived. We created four new teams to provide a clear pathway to the first team. This resulted in players breaking into the first team from our newly formed B team, who played in the fourth division.

We had to think on our feet as I had unique problems landing on my desk all the time. Road safety was a massive issue in Thailand. Over one particular week, three of our academy players ended up in hospital after motorbike accidents. As a response, we renovated our truck into a bus to give them a safer alternative to get to the pitch.

We also held a road safety workshop and banned players from playing who didn't wear helmets. Thousands of young people die on the roads every year in Thailand. Ideally, we would have banned them from riding motorbikes altogether. But it wasn't possible due to the public transport system in the Thai countryside.

Coach Education was non-existent in our region of Thailand. This presented us with a great opportunity to bring the first national coaching course to Ubon. We also brought Spanish Ekkono coaches from the

Thai FA in to deliver a course. We set up our own coach education classes in universities for local physical education students. We also held weekly workshops for our staff at the club.

Over 100 coaches attended the courses we organised. The vast majority of people in the region didn't speak English. This meant they only had Thai materials and education available to them. We were able to change this, and bring different ideas to supplement what they had learnt before. Courses continued taking place after we left through the relationships we had developed.

We delivered school sessions that gave children their first taste of qualified coaching. We also ran camps for children to attend, and over 300 children were involved in these programmes. Three U17 academy players and seven university interns were involved in coaching these programmes. This gave them valuable coaching experience to open up future career opportunities.

We gave away free Thai League tickets to schoolchildren. The younger academy players were mascots and ball boys for the first team's games; the older academy players were flag bearers. This gave many their first close-up experience of professional football.

First Team

After Scott left, Mixu Paatelainen took over as Head Coach. He was a great man and let me work individually with one of the foreign first team players. I watched a first team game and saw one foreign player getting frustrated. The player was signed by Scott as a number 10 attacking playmaker, but Mixu played him as a striker and wanted him to stay high. He kept dropping deep as he wanted to play number 10.

The player had started three of the first six games with one goal as an attacking midfielder. I told him, if he wants to play, he needs to tell Mixu that he'll play striker and stay high. He did, and Mixu listened as the two foreign strikers weren't performing. He started as a striker in the next game and scored against Buriram United. The President's son and I jumped up to celebrate his goal as our plan had worked.

The player and I co-created a performance programme that went a lot deeper than the chat with Mixu and it seemed to work. The player started the next six games, scoring four goals and providing two assists. This was enough to earn a move to a bigger club and bring in much-needed funds to the club. The success was all down to the player's quality, but he said some very complimentary things about our programme, too. His recommendation led to working with his international teammates and Head Coach.

It was a great experience watching the reigns of three Head Coaches. Scott Cooper led the team to a tenth-place finish in our first season. This included doing the double over Muangthong United, who were a big club. Mixu Paatelainen took over from Scott. I was able to watch a lot of Mixu's pre-season sessions, as it was the academy's off season, and we had some great chats. Sugao Kambe, a Japanese coach, took over after Mixu left towards the end of our time there. They all brought different ideas, which I learnt a lot from.

Sad Ending

The education players were receiving on and off the field had improved dramatically. Our academy results improved, as did grades in the classroom. Players were progressing through the age groups and into the first team. The academy was unrecognisable from the situation we had inherited.

We were also able to make a difference in the community with our school and coach education programmes. The President's son was very complimentary about us to the Head Coaches and his father. The plan was for the President's son to take over from his father one day. He wanted me to become the B team Head Coach before becoming the first team Head Coach when he took over.

Sadly, that dream ended, as the money dried up and they could no longer afford to pay me. They promoted my translator to take over and continue our good work. The club had financial problems and – most sadly – had to be liquidated. A real shame, as it had so much potential. More than 80 people came to my farewell event at the pitch. Several players also surprised me by coming to the airport for my final send-off. It was hard holding back the tears as I hugged the President's son and waved goodbye for the final time.

This experience taught me so much culturally. It developed my managerial skills and taught me how to run an academy and work with senior international players. All of this was perfect preparation for the challenges that lay ahead.

Chapter 8. Foreign Failures: Six Reasons Coaches Fail Abroad

It's not easy moving to a place where you don't understand the culture, language, or local game. It's no surprise that coaches who move abroad often fail. We've all seen it over the years with a high turnover of foreign coaches around the world. Understanding why this happens is crucial, as most coaches don't get a second chance in the professional game.

Coaches have highlighted six reasons for failure abroad:

1. Failing to understand the culture.
2. Unwilling to adapt their coaching approaches to fit the setting.
3. Expecting things to work the same way as their homeland.
4. Poor quality of work and results.
5. Lack of long-term thinking.
6. Accepting jobs that don't have the resources needed to succeed.

Cultural Issues

Michael Yau has seen many coaches come and go in recent years.

China has had a huge influx of foreign coaches in recent years. Not only at the professional level but also grassroots. Some of them haven't been successful. Why? Because they lack cultural understanding.

Sam agrees this is the biggest area coaches get wrong.

It's a failure to understand the culture and adapt from a coaching point of view. You have to be adaptable.

Not understanding the culture and adapting means coaches don't get the best from people. This leads to toxic environments, poor performance, and coaches ultimately losing their jobs. Simon has seen plenty of foreign coaches getting it wrong.

Many coaches are unaware of the context and culture within the club and country. You walk in and bring your European attitude with you, and you're going to fail and fall on your arse. Even if you get a couple of wins and you start barking at the bosses, they're not going to like that.

Scott knows the challenges coaches face when walking into a club in a different country.

When you're a new foreign Head Coach in Vietnam or Thailand, you can be in for a shock. You can learn the culture but is your translator translating exactly what you want? The translator may not be behind you as they wanted another coach to get the job.

You have no idea what the players are saying, what the owner wants, and what he's saying behind closed doors. You've got a week to manage these players, and hope they get your perspective. There are so many unknown commodities when you walk in as a foreign coach. You've got to survive the first two to three months.

You need time to understand the culture and find the best way of working. Unfortunately, coaches don't always get given the time they need.

Failing to Adapt

Sam believes foreign Technical Directors can get it wrong by imposing a style that doesn't work in that country.

Having a Technical Director come in and copy the Spanish model isn't appropriate for a country like Hong Kong. It can set the country's development back years.

If that's what they believe in, then they'll try to coach the players that way. They might try new systems and copy how they've used sports science, analysis, and those sorts of things. If it's not appropriate for the country you work in, and you are taking them down the wrong path, that's where people fail.

Sam saw coaches who didn't adapt their approach to get the best out of those they were working with.

Where people fail is when they try to put their ideas that have been successful in their own country onto other countries. In China, I saw coaches who weren't open-minded enough to change their ways. They forced their preferred methodology onto the players. The players can't do it because they have grown up in a certain way.

You must adjust because if you copy and paste from what you did at home, it's not going to work. If you don't adapt, you'll quickly lose the respect and trust of the people that you're working with.

Cederique knows it takes time to introduce different approaches in a foreign country.

If you haven't worked abroad, it's harder to adapt to the local culture and possess the patience required. Yes, we know it should be like this, but we are in Lithuania and we cannot change everything immediately. We can take some steps towards it, but if we try to copy it immediately – it won't work.

Sam saw many coaches come and go.

Going to China, you have to become flexible in the way you deliver. Some coaches came out and couldn't handle it and moved on quickly – the coaches who adapted stayed there longer.

Home Truths

Michael knows people won't follow your approach based solely on where you come from.

You can't think, I've got some brilliant methods. My way is the best way of working. This is a country where football is less developed, so you must follow my way. If you go over with an attitude like that you're going to fail.

Simon feels a foreign coach's ego can alienate people.

Sometimes, there's a sense of entitlement when coaches go to South East Asia, especially if you're coming from a bigger league in Europe. They think, I'm the superstar here. I know a lot more than everyone in this country – that's why I'm here.

You take that attitude into a boardroom, a meeting with players, or the training ground – they'll pick up on that. That makes it very hard for you to build relationships with players. It's all about building relationships with players and understanding them.

Coaches who can't adapt to the country they're in are setting themselves up for failure, as Steve well knows.

Most foreign coaches who fail in Asia utter the same words "In my country, we do it this way." Well, they are not in England, Germany, or Brazil!

Cederique has seen close-minded coaches who couldn't adapt.

A lot of coaches go to a country and say, "We do it like this in Spain or Italy." They come to China and want to do things the same as at home and it doesn't work. People have different mindsets and ways of thinking.

They may not understand it at the beginning and get frustrated. They say, "This is bad, and this is bad." After three to six months, they are so fed up because they haven't adapted to the local culture, and they leave.

Things are done very differently abroad which can be a huge shock for coaches. Simon knows this can make it a challenging transition.

When it comes to Asia, there are many bumps in the road. If you get thrown off the road at the first, you're not going to be at the club long. You're not going to get your message across. The players aren't going to be interested. Bosses aren't going to want to deal with you. If your mindset is fixed on – here's the target and this is the only path I'm taking – you'll get thrown off and it makes it very difficult for you to sustain work in Asia.

Coaches with a tunnel vision approach and a lack of interest in the local culture are destined for failure.

Poor Performance

Sam believes you'll lose players with poor training sessions.

If you're working with good players, they expect a certain level of training. They expect a certain quality of information from you. If you can't provide that, then the whispers are going to start. Once the whispers start with one player, two players, four players, eight players, then you're struggling.

It's not only the session quality but also the schedule organisation, the ideas you introduce, and the relationships you have with players. Owners ask for players' opinions so Scott feels having poor relationships reduces your job opportunities.

It can work against you if you're a muppet in player management. Going around smashing people. "No, we don't want him. We don't want him." They will hold that against you.

Cederique says poor quality of work makes it hard to sustain work abroad.

The people you know or what club you work at doesn't matter — if you don't do a good job, they will finish your contract and stop working with you. When this happens, it's very difficult to continue working in that country.

Colum has found owners lack patience when it comes to results.

They're not very patient. Everybody wants to win trophies in 20 minutes. It's the same in world football, bar a few clubs that have people at the top with a long-term vision.

Steve knows if you don't win games at first team level, you'll soon be getting the sack.

Coaches have to learn to adapt to the country they're in, and what they feel is the right method to win. Don't forget, it's all about winning. None of this philosophy or project rubbish. If you don't win as a foreigner, you are out as you are expensive!

Long-term is next week in many clubs. The reality is if you're working at the first team level and you don't get good results, you won't be in a job for long. There's not much stability in the professional game with owners being impatient worldwide.

Short-term Thinking

Michael has seen coaches fail in China as they're looking for a quick payday.

Some coaches see it as a short-term project, and the locals have lost patience. They come in intending to make a lot of money and leave. If you're a foreign coach, and you want to leave a mark in China, you're going to have to stay for at least three to five years.

Short-term thinking and adopting a top-down approach is something Sam believes Technical Directors at federations get wrong.

Technical Directors might have played internationally, and they want to work with the U23 and senior teams. If you lose a couple of friendly games at senior level, it's not going to have a hugely dramatic effect. If they focus 100% on the senior team and they have a miracle result and qualify for a tournament – that would have an impact – but I believe grassroots and coach education are the most important.

Sam believes neglecting the foundations of the game can be a Technical Director's downfall.

They neglect coach education and grassroots football, which can have a long-lasting impact on the country. Some Technical Directors prefer to bring in foreign educators to take courses rather than using local staff. But how can that instructor understand the situation of that country? It's difficult. That's why it's much better to have local staff who can deliver coach education to local people.

Quick results may keep staff in a job, but failing to build a long-term strategy can be a Technical Director's undoing. Sustained success requires an intentional strategy with youth programmes and coach education. Without it, you can't succeed and stay in the job long-term.

Wrong Job

Coaches can walk into a position where they have no chance of succeeding. An agent or club can sell you the dream, but when you arrive it doesn't always match reality. The staff, players, budget, and the owner's approach may not allow a coach to meet the expectations set.

You can be a great coach, but Scott knows that isn't always enough.

There's been a lot of very good coaches coming in, and it's not happened for them. They've not had the platform to do it. They may have had an owner picking the signings and the system because they've seen a team they like on TV.

Scott joined a club in Indonesia but felt the internal interference wouldn't allow him to work the way he wanted. They did pre-season in Bangkok, so he wasn't aware of what followed on arrival in Indonesia. He quickly resigned and said if he had visited the club first, he would never have taken the job.

Simon signed for a club in Vietnam that the agent told him had won the league, had national team players, and was ready to compete again. He hadn't been told he was the third coach that season, all but one national team player had been sold, and they were struggling at the bottom of the league.

His hands were tied as a lot was going on behind the scenes that he had no warning of. He didn't last long at the club. This was only Simon's second Head Coach job abroad and he learned from those lessons and went on to achieve success in the region.

Gary Stevens, the former Tottenham and England defender, was due to become Head Coach at Ubon United. On arrival for pre-season, there was a disagreement and they were unable to agree on contract terms. The club had to quickly find a replacement Head Coach with pre-season starting and they appointed Mixu Paatelainen, the former Dundee United and Finland Head Coach.

Scott had left the previous season as he knew it was going to be difficult to compete, due to their budget. Mixu had to manage the squad he had inherited and found himself in a difficult position in his first role in Asia. He was a great person and coach but he was sacked four months into the season.

Halfway through the season, the club released a lot of first team players to reduce the budget and the club got relegated. The club subsequently got relegated from the second division the following season and has since been liquidated. Clubs around the world have had financial struggles in recent years and it's tough for coaches walking into that situation.

Coaches who don't talk to former coaches, players, or football people who know the club and country are setting themselves up for failure. It's not easy getting the full picture before joining a club, but you've got to do as much research as you can. Without it, you can inherit a situation that gives you no chance of succeeding.

Coaching anywhere is challenging, but it can become a lot more complex doing it abroad. Factoring in what *could* go wrong ensures you don't fall into the trap that many coaches do when they first move abroad. Taking these ideas on board can help you build a long and successful career abroad.

Chapter 9. Simon's Journey: Head Coach of Indonesia- "You Must Win!"

In 2015, FIFA banned Indonesia from the 2018 World Cup Qualifiers and the 2019 Asian Cup Qualifiers due to a dispute between the Government and the Indonesian League. They were allowed to compete in the 2018 Suzuki Cup but crashed out at the group stage, an outcome which led to the sacking of Head Coach Bima Sakti.

Simon McMenemy was appointed in December 2018 and tasked with rebuilding the National Team. This was a huge challenge after missing out on two qualifying campaigns and a poor showing at the Suzuki Cup.

When I came into the national team, the plan was to be competitive at the Suzuki Cup at the end of my two-year tenure. I had two years to build towards it. The World Cup qualifiers were going to be used to make us a stronger unit to be able to win the Suzuki Cup.

Group of Death

The plan changed immediately once Indonesia were drawn into a qualifying group with their fiercest rivals.

The World Cup draw was made, and we got Malaysia, Thailand, and Vietnam. All of a sudden, the Suzuki Cup – in two years – was going to be in two months. Whether people were going, "I know it's early," or not, I was going to get judged whether I liked it or not.

As soon as the draw was made, Simon knew he was in big trouble.

Honestly, I thought I was going to get sacked. You have enough experience to understand who you want to come out of the hat, what condition your team is in, and what state Indonesian football is in at the time. That was the worst draw we could have had.

Indonesia v Malaysia

The first World Cup Qualifying game was against their biggest rivals.

For a team that was getting back on its feet and trying to establish itself again to get Malaysia... I mean, that's like World War Three. That's Celtic-Rangers. It's well-known that's going to be a brutal encounter. To have that as our very first game of the World Cup qualifying campaign... and at home as well. The expectation and the pressure on the shoulders of the players was massive. They felt it in the weeks leading up to that first game. You had every member of the PSSI (Football Association of Indonesia) coming in and talking to the players. They were banging their hands on the desk and saying, "This is must win!" There was no reason for it to be a 'must win', especially if you looked at the condition of the players. There was a lot at stake.

Ultimately, the game against Malaysia was overshadowed by events off the field.

As we're walking out onto the pitch, we've got 75,000 in the stadium going mental. The Bung Karno is shaking. On the far side, behind the goal, the fans all hold up a piece of paper. And if you look at it from a distance, it read "F**k you losers" to the Malaysian fans. We've just come back from a ban. Straightaway, the atmosphere in the stadium was tense and aggressive. There were about three or four hundred Malaysians who dared take the trip to Indonesia. They're trying to get at the Indonesian fans from the word go. The Indonesian fans are ripping seats up and throwing them. It's their own stadium. Guys are getting arrested because they're trying to get across the top of the barbed wire into them.

Despite the hostile atmosphere, Indonesia started the game well. They took a 12th-minute lead with a lovely reverse pass which was finished off by Beto Goncalves. Malaysia equalised in the 37th minute when Mohamadou Sumareh ran onto a through ball and slotted it past the keeper. Indonesia immediately reclaimed the lead in the 39th minute, though, when Beto got his second goal with a well-struck curling effort from outside the box. Indonesia went into the half-time break 2-1 up.

Malaysia equalised in the 66th minute, through a headed goal from Syafiq Ahmad, before the referee had to stop the game at 2-2 due to what was happening in the stands.

When they equalised, the fans started trying to get across to the Malaysian fans, and it kicked off. They were getting onto the pitch and there was a pitch invasion. They all got pushed back into the stands, but the fighting continued. They were throwing things across and the Malaysians were throwing stuff back. Now and again, one guy would make it through, and the police went in to get them out. A flare was thrown onto the pitch, which made it all smoky and tense, and the game got stopped. Four or five of our players were going to the fans to try to get them to calm down.

The game was stopped for five or six minutes. Their coach was complaining to me, and I'm like, "What on earth do you expect me to do, pal? Let's be serious for a second. This is Indonesia. You know what to expect coming here." He was saying, "Oh, this is not fair." I was thinking, shut up and get back in your box. There's not a lot I could do about it.

The pitch invasion was a distraction for the Indonesian players, and it cost them. There was a lot of added time due to the stoppages and disaster struck in the 97th minute. The keeper committed himself and failed to intercept a low cross into the box. Malaysian forward, Sumareh, got ahead of his marker to fire into an empty goal at the back post. This was the decisive goal as Malaysia ran out 3-2 winners.

That distraction cost us the game. When that third goal went in, it came from an area we knew it was going to come from. The individuals we knew would score were there, and we switched off. That lack of focus came about four or five minutes after that major stoppage. It was disappointing.

It was a big blow for Indonesia – a loss to their biggest rivals in the first game.

It was an aggressive game right from kick-off. It came from the Indonesian fans, and the players picked up on it. They got nervous in the last 20 minutes, and we gave two goals away. It was a very disappointing way to start our World Cup qualifying campaign. It's this sabre-rattling and sticking two fingers up at Malaysia. Indonesian fans are the best and the worst thing about football in this country. It could have been a better, more positive, and enjoyable experience, but it was ruthless from the word go.

Fail to Prepare...

Simon couldn't prepare the team for the World Cup Qualifiers as he would have liked. He was constantly fighting political battles to get the squad together to prepare.

We were very unprepared for the Malaysia game. It was a really difficult situation because I took the team in January. We had our first training camp around March, then we went to Australia for two or three weeks and did a good training camp there. Away from the media, fans, and pressure, the players were loving it. It was really enjoyable. We beat Perth Glory 2-1, playing good football. We went to Myanmar to play our first official FIFA friendly and beat them 2-0 comfortably. They were significantly above us in the rankings at the time. We started well.

The Indonesian league started late, which also caused big problems for Simon.

The problem was – that year – the league didn't start until late. There was a Presidential election, and they didn't want to start the league before the Presidents Cup, which is a pre-season tournament. You had this political influence going on, especially with the league. Because the league didn't start until late, they had to cram the games in before the end of the year. This had a huge impact on the national team. I couldn't take the players to training camps. The owners of the clubs are very influential, rich guys in Indonesia. They're pestering the PSSI, "They've got too many games. We can't let the players go. We don't want to lose league games because the players are going to the national team."

The political battle meant Simon's requests weren't being met.

You had this constant negotiation. They were asking, "How much time do you need for preparation?" and the acting President of the league was saying, "Can you not just have two or three sessions instead of ten?" I responded, "No, this is the World Cup; we can't do that!" I wanted a month's preparation before the first game. I ended up getting just over two weeks, and I didn't get some of the best players. They were held back by their clubs as the Federation allowed clubs to keep their players, instead of releasing them for the National Team. I only got them three days before the first game.

Even when Simon managed to get players for his two-week camp, the league was still running. Malaysia, by comparison, had two months to prepare for the game.

During the two-week training camp, league games were going on. The league didn't stop throughout the World Cup qualifiers. It's this constant headache. The Malaysian team had two months of preparation for that first game, and they were doing psychology sessions about going into the Bung Karno in front of the Indonesian fans. That's the level of preparation they went into. I got two weeks with half a squad, and people were then surprised when results didn't go our way.

Mission Impossible

It was a terrible time to take over the national team. Simon was told that – and he knew it himself – but you can't turn down such a big job.

It's one of those things that you have to understand. If you don't like it, don't put your name on the contract. You can't turn around and moan about it later. You know what's going to happen in Indonesia. It was tough. You know what needs to be done, but you often don't get the opportunity to do it. You have to put some type of plan together, given the access you've been given to the players. It was really difficult."

Simon did everything he could, but it wasn't enough.

We weren't in a situation to be ready for that sort of judgement, for the importance of the qualifying campaign. It became important because it was Malaysia, Thailand, and Vietnam. I did everything I possibly could – working against the Federation – to prepare us. It was insurmountable, sadly.

Five days later, Indonesia lost 3-0 to Thailand, which heaped further pressure on Simon's shoulders. The following month they lost 5-0 to the United Arab Emirates (UAE), who ended up finishing top of the group. They were managed by Bert van Marwijk, who led the Netherlands to the World Cup Final in 2010. Simon's final game in charge was a 3-1 defeat to Vietnam.

Simon was sadly sacked in November 2019, just 11 months into his two-year contract.

Chapter 10. Managing Across Cultures

Every move to a new environment will cause some level of shock to the system. This could be moving to a new club in your town, another city in your homeland, or a different country altogether. The magnitude of the culture shock will depend on where you choose to work. Moving from London to New York may not provide as much of a culture shock as moving from Manchester to Beijing. Some people will love the excitement of it all, and others won't.

The cultural examples are told from European Coaches' perspectives of working in Asia and Europe. There are Asian and European people who are exceptions to the rule of what we'll discuss. Every individual has a different personality and upbringing, which impacts their behaviour, although you will see similarities in groups of people who were raised in the same place.

It's also important never to stereotype a continent or country; it doesn't account for huge differences between regions and organisations. It's tough comparing places, but the stories are the opinions of the coaches working in Asian and European countries. They may not represent what *you* would find in that country. The coaches' experiences depend on the people and organisations they've worked with. Their insights provide a guide on what to be aware of, and you'll notice trends between countries.

Asia and Europe are the main focus as the coaches have all experienced working across the two continents. There are vast cultural differences between Asia and Europe which makes it challenging to adapt, but a lot of the cultural lessons are transferrable to other regions. The stories aim to share experiences that open your mind to different ways of thinking – a central requirement when working with people from different cultures.

Foreign Cultures

Sam has experienced North America and Asia but found he had to adapt much more when working in Asia. It was very different from what he was used to in England.

You've got to learn, adapt, and adjust what you do to suit the culture that you're working in. Going over to the US is not that different. There are some things, but you don't need to adapt too much. Working in Asia, you have to make significant adjustments. You need to adjust the way that you work, treat people, network, and get the best from people.

You have lots to learn when arriving in a foreign culture. Making a good first impression is key. You must know how to greet and address locals when you first meet them. Ask someone in the country how to greet men, women, boys, and girls and what you should call the owners and members of staff.

I was meeting the mother of a player in Kuwait, and I offered my hand to shake. She was hesitant and awkwardly shook my hand. This was a mistake. I was told, afterwards, that you should never offer your hand to a Kuwaiti woman unless she offers her hand first. At home, it would have been normal to shake a woman's hand in this situation.

I made a lot of mistakes at the beginning, but they made me more culturally aware. They also encouraged me to research how to greet people and be cautious and follow their lead when I'm unsure.

Belgian coach Cederique was well aware of the importance of culture during his time in China.

We went for dinner with Chinese government officials and had to wait before doing certain things. Only when this person sits can we sit. Only when this person starts drinking can we drink. Only when this person starts eating can we start eating. In Belgium, we would think the food is here, let's eat. But by eating, you're already offending the person without even noticing. These cultural norms are very important. You can learn by getting advice from colleagues, friends, and experiencing it yourself.

Cultural Intelligence

There is often a misconception that foreign coaches are being hired to rip everything up and do it their way. But you are *not there* to change thousands of years of culture. You are there to adapt to the culture and tweak things to bring some new ideas which improve performance.

Every country is different. You can't take a programme from one country and plant it in another and expect immediate results. Each country has a different culture, history, constraints, resources, and education system. This has a huge impact on how you work. Get the cultural aspect right by always respecting it, making it a priority to understand the local and sporting culture, and taking time to assess the organisation's culture and resources *before* making changes.

This can make or break you. You might want to rip things up, but you may lose everyone immediately, and you can't do it alone. Take your time to settle in. Look around to see how things are done – first – and then see how your ideas can work in the environment, whilst utilising the strengths of what's already there.

Local Knowledge

Some coaches believe having European licences and experience helps build credibility in Asia. European football may be highly regarded worldwide, but that didn't help Sam in Hong Kong.

You don't get instant credibility, and you definitely don't get it when you work abroad. There is already a barrier you need to pass, as you've got a job a local didn't get. That's something you've got to break down from minute one. Or you're going to have that cloud over you the whole time.

Some people are intrigued by a foreign accent, whereas others don't understand it. Often, you'll be working with local coaches, players, staff, and owners. You need to build a personal bond with them and show them you are genuine before they will buy into your ideas.

Local staff may have had negative experiences with foreigners – coaches who were only there for the money and didn't plan to stay long-term. Alternatively, they may never have worked with a foreigner before and feel nervous and that their job is under threat. You need to get them onside. They can share how the organisation worked in the past: what was successful, what didn't work, and what they feel is the best approach moving forward. This is priceless information!

They can also help introduce any changes you want to make by using their inside knowledge and strong relationships to get others to buy in. It also helps if they like you and feel you're doing a good job. This makes your life easier and encourages them to pass positive messages back to the owner, which strengthens your position. They may have been there for years, have a strong relationship with the owner, and will outstay your tenure, regardless of what you achieve.

Sam knows it's vital to build relationships with local staff off the pitch.

If a coach goes abroad and identifies they'll be working with three or four people regularly, it'd be majorly beneficial to grab a coffee, get some food, or a couple of drinks with them. Getting to know them as people helps them open up. It's a good way of building rapport and trust.

An Asian coach who has spent their whole career in their own country and all of a sudden a coach from France comes in, well, they are going to be tentative. They're not going to be quite sure how things are going to work. Helping them settle their nerves might be as simple as taking a walk or going for a burger.

This isn't something that often happens back home, but Sam recognised its importance when working in Asia.

It wouldn't happen in the UK. When you finish your session in the UK, everyone says goodbye and goes home. When you work abroad, it needs that extra personal touch. It helps you build relationships that are going to help you succeed. The local staff have invaluable knowledge that you can't possibly know. You might be a highly qualified and experienced coach, but you have to get the best out of the local people. If you can't do that, you won't succeed.

Steve Darby would have been in big trouble if his captain hadn't saved him.

Very early on in Malaysia, I was training on the Sultan of Johor's playing fields. A man suddenly rode across training on a horse. I was about to scream "Get off" when my captain dived on me and held me down. He whispered, "I know what you were going to say, but that's the Sultan's son (now the current Sultan). You would not be here if you had said what you were going to say." I learnt "cultural awareness". There are some people you don't say certain things to.

Cultural Comparisons

There are cultural norms you must be aware of when working abroad. Saving face, hierarchies, and religion are some sociocultural influences you'll need to understand to get people on board and succeed.

Cultural influences such as *direct* or *indirect feedback* are on a scale. Countries aren't always fixed at one end or the other. They may lie along different parts of the scale. How another culture appears to you will depend on the cultures you have experienced. All cultures bring pros and cons and you can't say one is better than another. You need to be flexible and – at times – use both ends of the scale to earn respect and get the job done.

Saving Face

Social status is a big deal worldwide but especially in many Asian countries. If you criticise a player in front of the group, they'll lose face in the view of players and staff. This embarrassment impacts their social status, which they believe reflects on their family.

Peter Reid, the former England international, made a wise decision by bringing Steve Darby in as his Assistant Coach. Steve knew the culture which saved Peter during their first game with the Thailand national team.

One of our best players wasn't following our instructions, and it was causing us big problems. As we walked down the tunnel at half-time, I could see Reidy was quite rightly fuming. I grabbed him and said, "If you are going to bollock him, do it one-to-one outside the dressing room. He's a good lad; he'll take it. But not in front of the team as he will "lose face", which is a massive cultural issue in Thailand. He may also suddenly have a hamstring problem, as will some of his mates."

It's important to avoid confrontation where possible, as most people won't respond well to it. Being aware of this helps you get people onside rather than losing them for good. Colum knows confrontation in Cambodia is taken personally and continues long after it has occurred.

If you scream and shout at a player here, boom – forget about it – for the vast majority. That's something the foreign players coming from Europe struggle with. European players shout and scream at each other and it's forgotten about. But here, it's not forgotten. It will linger on for a couple of days.

I've had heated debates with European coaches, which were soon forgotten about. We got on well and could discuss and challenge each other's approaches without taking it personally. It was seen as a way of improving ourselves and the organisation. In Asia, they may take such incidents personally. This shows the importance of recruiting good foreign staff who will get on with the locals. Colum has to take the time to educate foreign players on the culture to help them adapt and fit into the team.

You have to manage foreign players. You're not in Europe or North America anymore. You're in Cambodia, and these boys need to warm to you.

Our U12 coach started instructing players during one of my first U17 Thai Youth League games. I told my translator to tell him not to instruct in a relaxed manner. I didn't want him sending mixed messages. He didn't work with the team or know our game plan. My translator did what I asked, and the coach immediately left. He had lost face in front of the players on the sideline. With any European colleagues I'd worked with, this would not have been an issue. I could have told my translator to pull him aside first but I lacked cultural awareness at that stage. It was another vital lesson.

You don't always need to be direct with feedback one-to-one as many Asian people aren't used to it. If you are dropping a player, you can say you are resting them for an upcoming game, that you will definitely play them in. Indirect feedback is a useful tool for getting messages across without alienating people. Although, if it's serious, then address it directly one-to-one.

Even positive feedback can embarrass some Asian people as they're highly group-oriented. Many Asian cultures focus on maintaining the harmony of the group at all costs. Criticising others openly disrupts the harmony.

Organisational Hierarchy

In many Asian countries, there is a strict hierarchy with the person at the top controlling everything and making all the decisions. Some

European countries believe in giving ownership and making decisions using a group vote. Group decision making is slower but easier to implement. Everyone has a say, so they better understand and are more likely to buy in. One person making decisions is faster, but it takes longer to implement as people below may not fully understand or believe in it.

The Asian hierarchies may mean a European coach has to be more authoritarian, initially, as that's what a lot of Asian people respond to. The coach can then introduce and develop their new approach gradually. It's vital to find the best way to manage and succeed in the culture you're working in. You may have to change your approach as what works at home may not work abroad.

In hierarchical organisations, people don't dare question anyone above them in the organisation. That means players and staff won't always tell you the truth. Read between the lines of what people say. Monitor body language and behaviour to identify any signs of unhappiness. Ask questions about what's going on with the people around them. This is often the only way to find out as they won't always tell you directly.

The President's son would take the Thai coaches out drinking when he wanted to know how they really felt. Social settings are more relaxed and, after some food and drinks, the coaches would open up. This works in Buddhist cultures, but for Muslim players, you can skip the alcohol and take them out for halal food.

An alternative approach is asking a group of people on the same level in the hierarchy to meet. They can come up with feedback on how they're feeling, or come up with new ideas together. They'll be more open to talking to people on the same level and the boss not being there. They can then offer feedback to you on what the group came up with.

Age Hierarchy

The age hierarchy in some Asian countries can make it challenging to manage staff older than you. Getting older staff onside is key for spreading your message, as younger members of staff look up to them. Sam has experienced this throughout his career, but especially in Asia.

I'm 32, which in the coaching world is very young. When I went to Hong Kong, I was 28. When I did my B licence, I was 21. People get that first look at you and think I'm 50 and I've got 100 caps for the national team. Why am I going to listen to you? You're just a kid.

It can be difficult managing older people. The age hierarchy in some Asian countries means no one younger can question them. What they say is often taken as fact, and they don't have to develop themselves to stay ahead of the curve. This can be dangerous within an organisation. It's vital everyone is continually developing to improve the organisation.

We are taught to respect our elders in Europe, but we don't always believe in an idea based purely on someone's seniority. It's important to respect people of all ages and job roles, based on what they bring to the table.

No matter your expertise, the reality is that a few grey hairs command respect in Asia (initially). But it won't last if the quality of work is poor.

Religion

Understanding the different religions of people at an organisation gets people onside. This was essential for Simon's work in Indonesia.

Football aside, everyone needs to get the feeling that you want to understand Indonesian players. Learn about their religion; where they have to be, what they have to eat, and how many times they have to pray. They'll be much more likely to buy into what you're doing. They will start to make an effort back.

Questioning their religion, even if it impacts performance, is a recipe for disaster, as Simon explains.

If you walk in and go, "What are you getting up at five o'clock in the morning for? You're a professional athlete. What are you praying five times a day for? Why are you eating this?" If you start questioning everything, they don't like that. They will take it personally and turn against you.

You're the coach. Expecting them to adapt is not going to work; you're the one that's going to have to change what you do. You have to base your schedule around them.

Steve recommends not forcing your beliefs on other people.

No country will expect you to convert to their religion, but don't try to impose your religious or political beliefs. It is enough of a job getting them to win!

How much religion will impact your day-to-day work differs, depending on the country and who's in your squad. It's vital to find out what religious requirements the players will have throughout the season. For example, knowing when Ramadan is helps you cater to players' needs during that time.

Adaptability

Sometimes, you have to deal with situations you have no control over. Including family coming before football in Asia, as Steve discovered.

I got a call one morning from my international striker, telling me he couldn't come to training. I asked why? Thinking injury, illness, transport? But no, he said he had to take his Mum shopping as his dad was sick. No matter what I said – be it a fine or a dropping – he had no choice as his Mum always went shopping on that day, at that time, and there was nothing he could do.

Number symbolism is sacred in certain cultures. If the numbers align, it doesn't matter if it clashes with your game – there will only be one winner, as Steve found out.

My centre back, also an international, gave me an invite to his wedding. I looked at the date and it was a match day. I said, "I know your fiancée and she would understand you were playing." He replied it was nothing to do with him or his fiancée. The two families had got together and the "numbers" maintained they had to get married that day. And they did.

Things like this happen very rarely, so it's not a massive issue. But if you try to fight these situations, you will never win. Accept them and negotiate – when appropriate – to get the best outcome you can.

You will find other situations that test you on a more regular basis. These moments have helped Michael become more adaptable in China.

Sometimes there are changes and last-minute things that might be different. Training might be delayed by a sudden meeting. Or you have to attend an event that's been decided last minute. You have to be very adaptable here, both on and off the pitch. You always have to be ready to accept the unexpected and not create a fuss. It's important not to let the things that you can't control affect your mentality and mood.

We were holding open trials, and over 1,000 players registered from all over Thailand. I spent two days training the admin staff to handle player registrations and run the event. It was going to be a very challenging process. On trial day, the President decided he needed the admin staff to sell tickets. He sent us two other staff members who had no idea what our system was, and who turned up late on the day.

Simon feels working at different levels has helped him deal with such unexpected situations.

Working at youth levels, and doing the school sessions in the UK, has helped me so much. You're at a pro club in the UK; you've got the tools you need to do the job. But when you come to a top-level club in Indonesia, and you've only got five balls pumped up or the pitch is crap, or you don't have a set of goalposts – because you've worked in schools in the UK and worked with kids, you learn to problem-solve. Little Johnny is sick today; we've only got three guys. Right, this is the game we're going to play.

There are Asian clubs that are run much more professionally than European clubs and there are many that aren't. It's important to be prepared for all eventualities.

Match Fixing

It can be hard to grasp the perspectives of those from foreign countries when you don't know what they're going through. Players may be responsible for providing for their family; some may even be providing for their entire village!

This is tough when you haven't been paid for three months, and when someone calls you saying they will give you a year's salary; it can be hard to refuse. Steve is completely against match fixing, but he now understands the position players are in.

I used to think if you fixed a match, you were a cheat. It was a black and white issue. This coming from a background where I thought it was non-existent. The reality is that there are shades of grey. What do you do if you or your family are threatened? Or you haven't been paid for months and have three kids?

Steve was told his team were going to win as he walked towards the tunnel, with the score 0-0 at half-time.

Match fixing isn't easy to spot. Especially if you are winning. I was coming off the pitch at half-time and the foreigner on the other team said we would win 2-0. Sure enough we scored in the 84th and 89th minutes. No time for us to get a third, and they weren't going to score as they had bet on a two-goal spread. When you are winning, you think it's down to your coaching, not the bookies.

Simon has experienced similar incidents.

After losing 3-0 away, the owner of the opposition — with a big smile on his face — told me he influenced the referee. He told me I was never going to win the game. I've had the referee call the owner of the club I'm working at. The owner called me saying, "Coach, the referee has told me that three points tomorrow is going to cost four thousand dollars. What do you think?" I said, "If you pay him, then you need to pay up my contract. I need to know I can influence the game."

Simon says it's hard to prove and eliminate from the game.

It's very difficult to stamp out. It's a brave man who walks into the offices of club owners and starts taking their phones and laptops away, because that has consequences. They're all connected. Police shy away from doing anything about it.

The referees are also under huge pressure, which Simon sympathises with.

The referees are only human, and they're not particularly well paid. They're under all this pressure with 30, 40, 50, 60 thousand fans all wanting to kill them. Which Indonesian is going to give a penalty against Persija in the last minute that leads to them losing? He's not going to do it. He's thinking about his family. You can't blame these guys.

Managing Up

The amount of political interference you experience depends on your role. Sam experienced a lot of interference when working in a National Association.

If you go in as a manager, Technical Director, or any position of power, you are going to have to deal with political influence. You can't just do what you want. You need to find a balance between everything, whilst developing football. If you try to find a balance and make everyone happy, you can't do anything.

Cederique was only involved in the training as an Assistant Coach in China League Two. This worked well for him.

I was only involved with the training process. I didn't notice too much about the hierarchy and the people above me.

All coaching roles in football involve some form of managing up. The higher you go, the more challenging this becomes. How long you remain at an organisation often depends on your relationship with the owner. Scott Cooper says you need to ensure you're working for an owner you can get on with.

You won't get anywhere unless you're working for the right owner. You've got to visit and go into the boardroom. See how it functions and get a read of people early. Speak to coaches, journalists, or agents linked to any players or coaches that know the club.

Anybody taking a job in Asia should ensure it's an owner that you can create a really good relationship with. You can forget the stadium, the fans, the history, the location, and the players to some degree. Players are going to be important, but none of that makes any difference unless you can build an understanding and work with the owner. If you don't have that, you're in trouble. It's just a question of when that trouble comes, not if.

In some Asian clubs, the owners will lead team talks before games and sit on the bench during games. Some will attend every training session. Scott highlights how clubs are run differently in Asia.

Asian football is unique. You work with an owner and often the owner's family. The GM may be a relative of the owner. Football clubs in Europe are run by a GM that's experienced in the football industry. Sometimes you get clubs in Asia with an owner who wants to sign the players. His son, nephew, or best friend is going to be involved in running the club. While the business components are there, the football aspects aren't always.

Colum experienced different sporting structures in Cambodia and China.

My club in Cambodia had a Technical Director, CEO, and owner. It was quite frustrating because in China I was running it all. Not that I wanted to do everything myself but I'd have liked more of my own staff.

Finding out how much control you'll have is critical for Steve.

Role descriptions must be established early. The most important being who picks the team! Know what your role is, what you can comment on, and learn the policy of the club. In reality, your role is to get the team to win! Try to gear everything and everybody towards this aim.

You may have a team manager who handles all the logistics and sits on the bench during games. You could be in direct contact with a director or the President's Assistant. Whoever the person is, you need to build strong personal relationships to get things done.

Cederique was fortunate to have a manager who understood him.

I was always in contact with my Chinese manager at Dayu FC. He lived in Belgium for eight years, so he was already westernised.

This makes life a lot easier. People who have lived in different countries can help you learn about the differences between cultures. They're also more likely to understand different ways of thinking.

First week at a new club

When Simon is appointed Head Coach, he feels it's vital to get a snapshot of the hierarchy at the organisation.

Who are the major players that are going to be making decisions over you? What do they want? What are they looking for? Do they want to win the league? Do they want to play well?

With Bhayangkara, we were a police-run team. There's a very different hierarchy within the ownership of the club. Rather than one rich guy, it's multilevel and the ultimate boss is the head of the police. He cares whether we win or lose. It's not, "They did well today," it's "Did you win tonight?" "No, we lost." OK, pressure on your shoulders. "You must win next week."

That's not about football or players. It's the culture of the club.

Sam found this to be an important process when working at a National Association.

Put yourself in a position where you understand what the owners are about. What they do, what they like, what they don't like, and try to adjust yourself to fit in with that. You have to try to understand what person x's motivation is, what their pressure points are, and where it comes from. It can help you to anticipate what's to come.

Understanding the political landscape helps put you in a position to succeed. You have to develop the understanding over time – through speaking to people and your experiences working there. It's not easy. The owner will have a series of relationships that are very important to them. In some cases, they may link with national governing bodies or even the government. In that regard, you're a small potato.

Simon identifies the people at the club who will help him.

Who are the guys that are going to help you? Who are the guys that are going to put you under pressure? Also, identify the guys you don't need to bother with because there are always hangers-on at clubs. Work that out in your head, and get a feel for the context in which your work is taking place.

Simon feels building relationships buys you time at the beginning.

Creating relationships with the important people you've identified helps with those early bumps. The first loss, when we've got four or five players injured or the training ground's crap… it makes those discussions easier.

The football will come. Getting a snapshot and meeting the key people is the initial priority for Simon.

Most guys walking in with any sort of qualification know football. Once they get on a pitch, that's the easy part. It's the bit leading up to that. It's when you're sitting in rooms and waiting for people to turn up, and you're taking phone calls. You're getting introduced to the boss. That's the bit that can make or break you.

Scott believes constant communication is essential.

I would meet the owner every couple of days. If you're in constant communication – and it's healthy – you've got that backing. You don't get the craziness behind your back that can happen. There's no confusion or uncertainty about what the coach is saying and what he's doing.

Educating Up

You have to educate the owner in the correct manner to get what you want; they won't always come from a football background or be students of the game. This has proved to be a challenge for Colum.

The process of trying to get the club to understand that football works fast can be difficult. You can sign a player or lose a player in a matter of hours. You message the owner asking, "Where are you?" and they respond, "I'll get back to you in a few days." It's frustrating when 20 other clubs are trying to sign the same player!

Simon knows you have to be clever in how you approach it.

As a Head Coach in South East Asia, you educate up as much as you educate down. That means going into boardrooms and educating people. How you do that will have a massive effect on how long you stay at a club. You have to tell a boss when they're wrong because you want to get to where you're going. How you do it is crucial.

Some foreign coaches come in and go, "This is all shit. This is terrible. What's going on? This is not a proper training ground. These aren't proper players. The balls aren't pumped up. We've got no cones left. Why is the bus there?" You could go on. Unless you pick your battles, the boss is going to go, "This guy is an arsehole. I don't want to deal with him anymore. Let's get rid of him and get another one in." It's a conveyor belt. Unless you're aware of that, you're not going to be at the club long.

One coach introduced expected goals (xG) to his owner to help them analyse games on more than just the result. He believed this bought him time when things weren't going well, as they were creating good chances but couldn't find the back of the net.

Staff education programmes are also essential. Managing and recruiting staff in a location far from home is a challenge since people have different beliefs based on their upbringing and the country's education system. In many regions, coach education courses aren't available. In turn, locals may not have many good resources available in their language. Educating staff and the owners is essential for getting buy in, implementing your approach, and navigating the battles that lie ahead.

Picking Your Battles

Guiding the owner to what you want has been the most effective approach for Scott.

It's picking your battles and knowing how to navigate those battles. I might disagree on something, but while you're up for having a battle, you don't fight. You steer them in a way that you want and you know they'll understand at some point. When they get there, you get there too. You both tell each other how great the idea is and then you've got what you wanted.

Scott will relent on some of the owner's requests but he will never compromise if it negatively impacts the team.

You give up the things that aren't going to damage you. I wouldn't release something that would damage the team. I would release something that didn't have that much impact and, actually, I could go this way instead. So, it's not a problem for me.

It's how you try to keep it because you can't demand it.

Steve Darby knows the challenges all too well after receiving a phone call from the President. He told Steve to play 1-4-4-3, which was sure to work with 12 players on the field!

Be like bamboo. Bend when you have to but keep your principles. It's better to die on your feet than live on your knees. Have certain non-negotiables, e.g., who picks the team. Be prepared to die by your methods rather than somebody else's. No matter what, you will be sacked first, so you may as well be sacked for your mistakes, not the President's.

Sam says you have to pick your battles as it's not hard for owners to replace coaches.

You always have to remember — you're expendable. That can make life very difficult for coaches. A coach may be asked to substitute a player, put a player in the squad, or run training a certain way. You have to pick your battles. What are you going to push back on? Because if you do it with everything, you're going to lose your job.

Some owners or agents will force players on you that you need to keep on the payroll, as Steve found in India.

I signed for a club in India after the squad had been selected by the committee. It was a massive squad and at least five of the players should not have been there. Nice lads who tried hard but were not good enough. I was told if they weren't under contract, they would have no money to feed their families. And they were also related to people on the committee.

People inside clubs and agents may put pressure on Head Coaches to start certain players. They may be getting a percentage for every appearance they make. A high-profile player only agreed to join a club, if they signed his two friends. His friends joined and agreed to pay him for every appearance they made. The coach was unaware and didn't play them. As a result, the player wasn't getting his money, so he told the owner the coach wasn't up to the job. The team was doing well but the owner still sacked the coach. The player then persuaded the owner to hire a coach he knew he could manipulate. It can be a ruthless business.

A third division owner once told a Head Coach not to win games as he couldn't afford the costs associated with promotion. Despite this, it didn't stop the owner from asking questions when the team started losing games! It can be very challenging for Head Coaches to deal with. Simon makes it clear he won't tolerate such interference.

I've made a point everywhere I've been that I don't want to get involved in the political side. Don't ask me to favour this or favour that. Have respect for me and let me do my job. If you don't like it, I'll go. It's no problem.

You won't always agree on things, but try to manage the differences as best you can. This can be the hardest part for coaches who have to stay true to their principles. Sometimes, it's not possible, and you have to walk away.

You can have the best methodology and be the best coach in the world, but if you don't adapt to the culture – and build a strong relationship with the owner – you won't survive. This won't be taught on most courses, but it determines your success as Sam well knows.

What I've learned is, whether you work in England or any country, the culture that you create, and the culture that surrounds it, influences absolutely everything. If you don't understand it, you simply won't get the best out of the situation you're working in.

Chapter 11. Michael's Journey: From Grassroots to the Chinese Super League

Michael Yau has always been football mad and originally wanted to become a professional player. He didn't make the grade and got into coaching to give young people the coaching he was never fortunate enough to receive.

I wanted to understand more about the game and gain more knowledge. I wanted the kids, who had a dream like me, to have access to quality coaching. To give them the opportunity to learn and improve.

Michael volunteered at grassroots and was fortunate to progress into a full-time role with a private company. Despite this, Michael didn't see a pathway into the professional game in England. This led him to take an opportunity in China.

It was difficult for me to progress because of my playing experience. In 2014, I had a chance to go to China. I went there the year before, to visit family and friends, and I came across a company that was owned by British nationals.

I was fortunate to see them at work, speak to them, and I gave them my contact details. They were a company that was developing local football and they had a good philosophy. They wanted to give Chinese kids a different football experience.

Beijing, China

Chinese football was on the rise as President Xi Jinping laid out a plan to host and win the World Cup by 2050. The plan involved having tens of thousands of schools playing football across China.

This was a good opportunity as Chinese football was booming. In 2014, Xi Jinping wanted China to progress in football, and there was a lot of emphasis on the game. I was quite fortunate I came at a time when the spotlight was on football.

Football was on the rise, but Michael also wanted to live in the country his family was from.

I wanted to live and work in the country that my parents were brought up in. When I was younger, we went to China every summer. My girlfriend was also Chinese, which gave me the confidence to go for it. If it wasn't for her, I wouldn't have come. She was able to help me navigate problems and make it a smoother transition. It's very different from being brought up in the UK.

It turned out to be a great move for Michael. The work and lifestyle in China were a great fit for him.

When I started working here, I really enjoyed China and the environment. I did miss my friends and family at home, but I wanted to try something I hadn't experienced before.

The grassroots role in Beijing was a great experience for Michael.

I'm so fortunate they gave me a stepping stone. I met some amazing coaches. I felt it progressed my coaching and developed my methods and way of working. It was a massive springboard for me.

Shenzhen, China

After two years working in grassroots, Michael moved into professional football in 2016. He joined Shenzhen FC, who was playing in China League One at the time. Four-time Champions League winner Clarence Seedorf was their Head Coach, before former England manager Sven-Goran Eriksson took over at the end of 2016.

Michael's friend from University was working for the Chinese FA and recommended him to the club. Michael feels being in China already was a big help in getting the role and adjusting to life at his new club.

Without the grassroots experience, I would have struggled. You can argue you're working at grassroots level with kids who aren't that interested in football. If you can get those that don't like football to enjoy it, then you're not going to have problems with professional players. It helped me understand how Chinese children learn, how they think, and how they interact. A lot is connected to how they were brought up.

I saw how they developed through adolescence. At the professional level, I understand their behaviour patterns more. Professional players are sometimes like big kids. By having that experience at grassroots, you know how kids work and why they behave like that. Then you can apply those principles to your session design and delivery.

It was great timing for Michael as China's professional leagues required clubs to have youth teams. This meant clubs had to find youth coaches.

The club was under new ownership and they wanted to build a youth system. Having youth teams was a requirement for the first team to enter the professional league. There was a massive surge of needing coaches.

Michael was hired as a U17 analyst and Assistant coach but he was also involved in the sessions on and off the field.

I would take part in the planning of sessions, parts of the delivery, and the evaluation of the sessions; as well as working with individual players and doing group sessions. It wasn't only recording games or training sessions and then analysing that. It was delivering what I'd identified through analysis presentations and putting it onto the training pitch. It was a very valuable experience as it allowed me to better understand the game.

It was a challenging working environment for Michael, initially. It was the first time he had worked with a Chinese Head Coach.

The whole experience was in Mandarin. The coaching staff couldn't speak English, so it was a massive culture shock. It was hard at the start as I'm not a Mandarin speaker. Speaking Cantonese helped, but Cantonese and Mandarin are very different. It's like Welsh and English.

I was having to learn a new language and having to deal with more complicated and challenging work. The first couple of years were really hard.

The Chinese Head Coach was very different from the other coaches Michael had worked with.

He was more hands-on, wanted to have control of everything, and was very specific in what he wanted from you. If you saw anything that needed to be improved, he was willing to listen. He was open to ideas but he would make the final decision.

Michael felt the Head Coach didn't like him to begin with, and it took time to gain his trust.

At the start, I don't think he liked me. Initially, it was like – you listen to what I want you to do, and you do it. That's because he didn't know me. Professional football is a very close-knit family. It's hard fitting in if you're someone from the outside and haven't played professional football; especially if you haven't got a name in the country that you're working in. I was no one, and I got invited to this family. I had to prove myself and earn his trust over time.

Michael was able to impress the Head Coach and Chinese staff by being proactive and passionate.

I won them over with my attitude and taking the initiative. Those who have been brought up in the West take initiative. We are different from Chinese coaches. If we see problems, we'll try to solve them. We don't wait for something to happen. We identify it and have a solution for A, B, and C.

He said I was very proactive and he'd not experienced that before. It's not common among the local coaches. They're happy to be told what to do, and they'll do it. He found that to be a positive asset. I was also very passionate about football and wanted to help him and the players. They embraced me in the end; it was like a family.

Earning Promotion

In 2018, Former Real Madrid Head Coach, Juan Ramon Lopez Caro, led the first team to the Chinese Super League for the first time in seven years. The competition was fierce after becoming the world's highest spending league in the winter of 2017 with around $420 million (USD) being splashed on players such as Carlos Tevez, who reportedly became one of the highest paid players in the world on $820,000 (USD) a week. In 2019, Michael earned a promotion of his own after impressing the staff and hierarchy.

I worked with the U17, U18, and U19 teams for three seasons. The following season there was an opportunity to go to the reserve team. We had a new Portuguese Head Coach and he needed more staff. The club was determined to develop their staff and didn't want to bring anyone else in. There was an opportunity for an analyst. I can speak English and Chinese, which was a good asset for the Portuguese Head Coach.

A lot of the U19 players were also moving to the reserve team. It was a big step up for both Michael and the players as they were now facing seasoned professionals in the reserve league.

We were playing in the reserve league, which was a great learning curve. We were no longer facing players in the same age group. The reserve team took place the day after the first team. We were facing first team players who were returning from injury or regaining fitness. This was a good opportunity for the players to compete against top professionals.

Michael also learnt skills that would help him further down the line.

It was also a good opportunity for us because the quality of our work had to improve. The analysis was more in-depth than before. Before it was individual analysis but it became team and opposition analysis. We played home and away, so there was a lot of travelling. It was the first time I'd had that professional experience. I was also given some new roles, including the athletic development of individuals and selected groups.

In 2019, the first team finished second bottom (15th) in their first season back in the topflight. Juan Ramon Lopez Caro had been sacked mid-season after a long run without a win. He was replaced by former Italy Head Coach Roberto Donadoni, who was unable to lift the team up the table. The club was saved from relegation due to a rival club – Tianjin Tianhai – filing for bankruptcy.

In 2020, the Covid-19 pandemic caused a lot of changes in Chinese football. Some clubs scrapped their reserve teams and the reserve league stopped. This meant Michael no longer had a team to work with. Donadoni was also dismissed and the club appointed Jordi Cruyff.

Due to the pandemic, there were a lot of changes at the club. The club decided to stop the reserve team. They felt there were no players in the reserves that could make the progression to the first team.

I didn't have a team to work with towards the end of the year, so the club decided to send me to the U15 team temporarily. I was working as an Assistant Coach but focused on physical preparation.

The pandemic had cast Michael's future in doubt. Two months later, however, it helped him earn a further promotion to the first team. Jordi

Cruyff and his staff went home during the off-season. When it was time for pre-season, they couldn't re-enter China due to Covid-19 restrictions.

The first team was short-staffed and they asked me to go with them for pre-season. I was there to support the physical work that the foreign coaches had set the Chinese staff to do over pre-season.

The players and staff liked Michael's work and he was able to develop good relationships with them.

During pre-season, the players and Chinese coaches got to see my work. They were impressed with my attitude, organisation, passion, commitment, and willingness to help.

The club sent Michael to work individually with the foreign players who were arriving back in China. The goal was to prepare them physically for returning to first team training.

The club sent me back to the base to work with the foreign players. I was getting them ready to return to team training. They hadn't trained for quite a long time. They were coming out of quarantine and weren't in the best physical condition. I worked with them and learnt a lot from the experience. They enjoyed working with me, and I really enjoyed working with them.

It was a great experience working with players like Juan Fernando Quintero who was the first Columbian to score in two World Cups, Dyego Sousa who won the UEFA Nations League with Portugal, and Morteza Pouraliganji who played at the 2018 World Cup with Iran. Michael impressed with his work, so Jordi Cruyff decided to keep him with the first team.

When the foreign staff finally got back, they felt that I had done a good job while they were away. As a result, the physical coach (ex-Valencia, Brighton, and Maccabi Tel Aviv) had requested to the club that I stay and work in the first-time set-up permanently.

Cultural Bridge

Michael used his Chinese heritage to his advantage. It was a key asset in his progression to the first team.

That's where I get my biggest advantage. I'm Chinese with a Western education. This allows me to be accepted here because they see me as Chinese, and I'm happy for them to see me like that. They expect the way I look at things to be different from them, which is normal because I was brought up in England.

Understanding both English and Chinese languages and culture is a huge asset.

At a professional level, I can bridge between Chinese and Western thinking. With the foreign coaches, I can comprehend their thoughts and accurately transmit the information and work to the players and domestic staff without breaking any cultural norms. I can bridge what they need from the foreign coaches and vice versa. This helps develop better relationships and operations on a daily basis.

Michael is in a position to continue the legacy of each coach and offer some continuity.

The issue we have with foreigners that come to China is they leave with everything. When a new Head Coach comes we start from scratch. It shouldn't be like that. Every foreign coach who comes in is a massive asset, and the things they do well should be kept at the club. My understanding of that allows us to continue the legacy by continuing to implement it in our system. This allows the club to develop something that's going to be sustainable. That can help the club grow and improve.

Michael has also been able to act as a translator at times for the foreign staff.

When I'm working with the foreign staff, they may need to speak to the players individually. I can understand exactly what the foreign coaches want, and translate it into Chinese. Translators don't always understand football enough to get the information across. The translation is only one aspect, alongside my Western experience, education, and football understanding. It's a massive asset for the club.

Michael loves the game and is passionate about his career.

I have always dreamt of working in the professional game. I'm very fortunate that I've always been full-time in football. I don't see it as my job as I always tried to pursue happiness. I've liked football from a young age, always been inspired by those around me and by a nation that loves football.

Jordi Cruyff led Shenzhen to a respectable 13th position in the league table in the 2020 season. Cruyff left to join FC Barcelona midway through the 2021 season and the club appointed Jose Carlos Granero as his replacement. 2021 proved to be a good season, beating Guangzhou Evergrande for the first time and finishing 6th in the league.

In 2022, new Head Coach, Lee Jang-Soo, kept Michael on his coaching staff for his 8th year in Chinese football. What a football education it's been, working under Seedorf, Donadoni and Cruyff!

Michael's language skills and cultural understanding have helped him stand out and survive many staff changes at a time when Chinese football was booming. He used his assets to his advantage to forge a good career for himself in the game he loves.

Chapter 12. Cross-Cultural Coaching Approaches

Coaches often assess the personality of individuals and the group's behaviour. These two approaches are very important when working with people from different countries, but you also need to assess behaviour through the appropriate cultural lens.

You arrive at a new Chinese team and are coaching a group of local players. You stop the session, ask a question, and wait a few seconds, but no one speaks up. You might assume the players are more introverted as they don't want to answer, but this would be confusing personality with culture. Sam knows this is a major factor in such a scenario.

In China, it's very much a teacher-led, autocratic style of delivery. In schools, kids don't need to think too much beyond listening and writing down. That impacts your football coaching environment.

Having experienced this from a young age, players will initially struggle when asked questions. They aren't used to answering questions verbally, and they also don't want to lose face by getting the answer wrong in front of the group.

We need to assess things from individual, group, cultural, and generational perspectives. Each generation has been raised differently and has different norms which affect their behaviour and the leadership style they respond best to. Assessing these angles gives you – the coach – a more vivid picture of what's causing certain behaviours.

It's also important not to stereotype anyone based on where they come from, as previously discussed. The insights shared are European coaches' perspectives of what they found coaching in different European and Asian countries. The chapter on Managing Across Cultures focused on national culture and managing up. This chapter focuses on how culture impacts your coaching environment.

Different Approaches

People raised in Asia and Europe often have different cultural beliefs. A Thai coach went to England to do the FA youth modules and returned excited to implement ideas from the English approach. He wanted to give the players ownership and more freedom but was immediately shot down by the older coaches around him. They told him it doesn't work in Thailand, so he reverted to type and started delivering in line with the coaches around him.

Some Asian coaches focus more on the quantity of training rather than the quality. Steve once switched training from twice a day to once a day and the President went berserk, but thankfully the team kept winning!

This isn't to highlight that one coaching approach is better than another. This shows how hard it can be to implement new ideas when people have always believed in a certain approach, especially when other cultural factors are bubbling under the surface.

Encouraging autonomy can be difficult as many Asian players are used to following their coach or teacher's instructions. They may also not be used to group work. Sam had to adapt in China as his approach didn't work at the beginning.

China taught me that what I learned on my FA youth modules doesn't work in every country. In England, we were encouraged to ask a lot of questions to players, to speak to them individually, and take more of a democratic coaching style. It works in England because of the culture we have. Kids can think creatively, make decisions, discuss things together and solve problems.

Asking Chinese kids to write down ideas on a whiteboard and discuss them together is difficult. Particularly for students in the local schools. They haven't grown up in that environment, and they need a lot more time to get used to it.

Sam had to adopt a mixed approach due to working in both international and local schools.

You can't copy and paste the method you've learned from your own country. You've got to adapt to where you are. When I went to China, I had to adjust to more of a mixed approach. There were times I would be working with international school kids – so that required a different approach than when I was working at a local school.

In international schools, you could give challenges, ask questions, and give them ownership. If you're in the local school, you need to do that less and take more of a command approach. That's what the players were used to, and they responded to it. If you go around trying to ask lots of questions, you'll get nothing. The kids aren't going to get anything out of the session. You've got to try and find that balance.

Developing Behaviours

In a foreign country, there are aspects of the culture that can't be changed. You must adapt to the socio-cultural factors, including religious practices, hierarchical structures, and saving face – which are deeply ingrained. The national culture is there to be respected but within your environment, there are aspects you can adjust. You can develop the desired behaviours you believe will lead to improved performance.

In Asia, this may involve moving from a more autocratic approach to a democratic coaching style. It won't happen overnight, but this process can work. It requires a more direct approach (initially). The idea of great coaching for many in Asia is someone who is dominant and has all the answers. If you ask a lot of questions – at the outset – you may be met with silence, which wastes a lot of training time. The players won't get anything from it. They may also not buy in and will wonder why you're being indecisive and don't know the answers.

Initially, Cederique found it hard to adapt his coaching in China. But he benefitted from being surrounded by colleagues who provided guidance.

In the beginning, it was difficult. We had weekly coach education sessions. You were also working with other foreign coaches so you could see how they did it, and they shared ideas of how you could approach things. Having an experienced translator also helped to adapt my behaviour, and I became a more patient person... in all aspects.

It's important to introduce your approach, its benefits, and positively reinforce when it's done well. Players need to feel safe enough to open themselves up to answer questions in front of the group and to take on added responsibility without fear of making mistakes. Cederique had to find ways to introduce this approach in China.

I started by asking questions. I let the players know that they need to think, speak up, and answer. I was full-time with the players in China. This helps you create a different bond than when you have the players only two times a week. Before training, we showed a presentation of what we were going to do in the session, especially at the beginning. We showed tactical ideas, asked questions, and encouraged as much interaction as possible.

It took a long time before it happened; they always felt like, I don't want to make a mistake, so it's better not to answer. For us, it's not a mistake. OK, you didn't give the answer we wanted to hear, but maybe it was a good answer and we can discuss it.

Culture Shift in Hong Kong

Sam was part of a multi-national coaching team at the Hong Kong FA. Here's how they shifted the culture of their Youth National Teams.

In Hong Kong, a lot of the school work is extremely autocratic, following what the teacher says. They don't have as many opportunities to work collaboratively with others. We'd schedule a two-hour training slot but we'd only train for 90 minutes. For the first 20 minutes, the players had ownership over how they wanted to set up and start the session. When the players arrived, they brought all the equipment out and set up their warm-up depending on what the session was. Players got to the point where they could set up the pitch for us as well.

Players were able to interact and it didn't eat into Sam's session time.

We let them work together to find solutions. If we said, "Use the cones to set up a circle", then they had to work together to make sure that it was set up properly. It encouraged them to discuss things with each other and solve problems. They were working with one another in a way that they wouldn't have an opportunity to do elsewhere... due to the culture.

By the end of our time there, they would arrange everything by themselves but it takes time to get to that point. This meant that when we started the hour and a half session properly, we could get straight into it because it was already set up. We didn't lose any session time. Then you have ten minutes at the end to pack it all away.

It helped them assess the players' character and to develop life skills.

It was a good way of identifying which players had different characteristics. Who would be willing to arrive early to help set up? Who would lead the others? Who will follow and do nothing? When they're asked to do something, can they do it or not? Who will step up in a difficult moment? It can give you an indication of what players might be like on the pitch.

It was also helping them develop skills that are going to help them later on in life. Once they go into the workplace, they're going to need to be able to work with people. They might need to manage people, listen, and organise projects.

The coaches wanted players who could step up and take responsibility.

We were conscious that parents in Hong Kong do everything for their kids. If coaches do everything for them too, kids will go through their youth thinking they don't have to do anything for themselves. We wanted to develop that sense of – if we work together – we can achieve our goals. Ultimately, that is what you have to do on the pitch.

The players would often have an 'auntie' to look after them. That might be things like dropping them off at the pitch or carrying their stuff. We made a rule that once they arrived, they were responsible for carrying their equipment. Ultimately, once they step onto the pitch for the national team, potentially at 13 years old in the under 15s, there's nobody to do it for them. They have to do it themselves. They can't keep looking to the coach for every answer all the time.

They needed a team approach to help Hong Kong succeed.

We wanted to develop young players for the future of Hong Kong who can take responsibility. Players who take ownership of what they do on the pitch and also work together. Not selfish players who think, I'm the best player in centre midfield and everything must go through me. We needed to take a team approach because Hong Kong is not a strong country. Hong Kong does not qualify for the World Cup and barely qualifies for AFC competitions. They haven't done for many years. They need a collaborative approach if they are to qualify for future tournaments. It won't work if we have 11 individuals on the pitch.

This approach took time but enabled Sam to adjust his coaching style.

Once you start, it takes a lot of time to change the behaviour. But once the behaviour changes, you can take a more democratic coaching approach. You've trained their minds to open up and accept this way of doing things. That means you can start asking them to do group work and ask questions in front of the group. All the carrying of the equipment and setting up sessions for a couple of months has led us to this point. You have to stick with it. It's not going to work on the first day. It's going to take a lot of time.

The habits needed to be ingrained from a young age, which everyone loved.

That's why we need to have training sessions with the youngest age groups, such as the under 11s — to give them more training time, but also to teach them the right habits. They're not getting that at home, and they don't get it from their club or school. That's why we have to step up. People say parent management in Hong Kong is difficult, but it's very easy if you talk to them. We'd arrange a meeting at the start of the season, saying, "We're going to try this" and the parents loved it because that's exactly what they want their kids to be taught. The players enjoyed it too!

Football Culture

You have to capture the culture within your training and management.

Sam is absolutely correct here. Coaches need to get a feel for the *football culture* as there can even be big differences between areas within the same country. Countries in the same region can also have huge differences as Simon found working in the Philippines and Indonesia.

In the Philippines, you get three men and a dog watching the games. There wasn't pressure on the players to go out and perform. You guys are national team players; there's no one watching out there and the games are very rarely on TV.

In Indonesia, you play at one o'clock on a Wednesday afternoon. There are 60,000, salivating at the mouth over how important this game is. You don't need to motivate anybody! We're arriving at the games in armoured personnel carriers because the bus will get trashed.

The passion and life-or-death attitude to winning and losing is so different in Indonesia. In the Philippines, that passion and motivation have to come from you as a coach. Whereas, in Indonesia, it's already there, so you're trying to contain it and work against it. It's two ends of the scale.

The passion for the game plays a massive role in managing the group but also in developing talent at youth level. Working in a country where football is the number one sport makes it easier to recruit, fund, and develop committed players. It can be an uphill battle in countries where football is competing against more popular sports.

Mentality

Players' mentality can be different when working abroad. This needs to be factored in when interacting with individuals and planning sessions. Michael's seen this in the top leagues in China.

The player's behaviour is different. In China, they don't like to be pushed too hard. Whereas in the European setting, the players love to be pushed hard.

What is expected of professionals and their behaviour – on and off the pitch – may differ between Asia and Europe. This is due to culture, their football education, and the role models they have around them.

Despite this, you will find plenty of top professionals too. Our Thai players were disciplined, respectful, and hung on to our every word. There were fewer egos involved as they are all about the team as it is ingrained within the culture. Many players were driven to succeed and provide for their families. You will find pros and cons in all cultures and environments.

Sam has also experienced big differences in mentality when working with the Hong Kong Youth National Teams.

My experience in England is that players of a certain level have a drive. They have inner confidence because they know what's expected. Whereas the players in Asia tend to be more tentative; a bit less confident in their ability. This makes it more difficult for them to step up.

When we went to a tournament, players would be extremely nervous. Some were even scared of participating at international level. They were also tentative moving up through the age groups, from under 15 to under 18 and 23. Once they got to senior level, it wasn't so apparent.

Being aware of the differences was crucial as Sam had to adjust his approach to get the best from them.

That required more of a soft touch from me as a coach. To encourage them and let them know they are in an environment that will be difficult for them. But there's no pressure for them to perform. They're here to get experience, and they'll be all the better for it. Whereas it's a little bit different with the lads in England. Sometimes, you have to do the opposite and calm them down a bit. Overconfidence versus under-confidence is the general difference between England and Hong Kong.

At Simon's club in the Philippines, he had British players with Filipino heritage. They were very different from the Filipino and Indonesian players. The British players were more confrontational and ego-driven, which was a challenge for Simon.

The problem is when egos start to kick in. If we don't get a win, everybody's got an opinion. Filipinos won't say a word. But the Brits are chirping up, and that becomes too much and affects the dressing room. It could help when it was respectful but there was a point when it was getting quite difficult and I had to put my foot down. It's something you don't often get in South East Asia.

Training Sessions

Cederique doesn't feel your training exercises need to change much when coaching in different countries.

My sessions in the professional academies in Belgium and China didn't change too much. Football is football everywhere in the world, and your exercises can fit. But you need to adapt to the level and qualities of your players and the style of play.

Sam's sessions were similar, but how he coached them was different.

I kept the practices similar to what I would do back in the UK but I adapted the coaching style.

The players in Indonesia didn't have the same football education, which meant Simon had to adapt his approach.

In England, you can take shortcuts because players have a good understanding of the game. Especially guys who've been through academies. They know this stuff by the time they get to 18 or 20 years old. The Indonesian guys haven't got that bank of knowledge. They haven't had the basics. A lot of the time, you find yourself going right back to square one before you can go to level eight of your coaching.

The technical content – where I want to get to – is the same. A lot of the sessions are the same. Tactically, it might vary depending on where we are. But how I coach it, understanding the environment I'm in, is the main difference.

Scott Cooper also highlighted how football education impacts your coaching.

The football education that a lot of Thai players had wasn't to the standards of the UK. You're dialling it back a bit. There were sessions I would do with the Leicester U15s that I wasn't doing with Buriram's first team. It took a while for them to grasp some of that.

Buriram had good players but it takes time to understand different sessions, principles, and ways of working.

The professional game in many Asian countries is very young compared with top European football nations. As a consequence, Asian players may not have had access to high-level academy programmes. Clubs haven't always focused on youth development or been required to have an academy. This is gradually changing as many professional Asian leagues now require clubs to have an academy and a Head of Youth. There are now some excellent academies in Asia but, like anywhere in the world, some football education and youth systems are still lacking.

Individual Feedback

We've discussed the importance of saving face in Asian cultures – it plays a huge role in how individuals respond to feedback.

Scott feels managing individuals is the most important part of his job.

Football comes down to your man-management skills and your tactical awareness.

Simon had to adapt his approach when working with players in Indonesia. The more direct feedback approach (which he is used to in England) doesn't work there.

If someone bollocks me on the pitch in England, fair enough. It's not because he thinks I'm an arsehole, it's because I've not done something right. I respond to that. You do the same thing in Indonesia, and they take it personally, especially in front of other people. They think, I like you, coach. Why don't you like me? Why did you shout at me? It's a very different thing.

There is a time when you have to coach, and put things right. You point out too many things that are wrong in front of the wrong people, and they'll take that very personally. That will upset the relationship with that player.

It's important to separate the person from the action when providing feedback. Simon says it's also beneficial giving individual feedback away from the group.

Take them to one side and say, "I know what you're trying to do but have a couple of goes at this." They buy into you doing it away from everybody else and explaining why. They like you for showing them respect, and they'll show you respect back.

If you go in there and bollock them for a bad performance, it's not going to work. How you approach that specifically, you have to use their culture to do that, not your own. You've got to take that on board. Otherwise, you're going to struggle.

Scott worked with Theerathon Bunmathan early in his career and often met for coffee to discuss the defensive side of his game. Theerathon went on to become one of Thailand's top players and one of the first to play in Japan.

At that stage, Theerathon didn't want to defend. He only wanted to attack. He was a left wing-back and I always thought to myself, what would I do against Buriram? I'd put it behind him and attack that space. We told him that – subtly – and he committed to the defensive side of his game.

When giving feedback, Scott used videos and tapped into the players' personal goals. Not many Thai players were playing abroad at that stage. The goal for the top players was to move to the biggest Asian leagues, like Japan.

We'd talk to Theerathon about his defensive transition. "Have a look at this video." I would always start with positives first. "You're doing this well, you're doing that well, and I'm loving this. You're the best left back in the league. You should be aiming for a move to Japan."

"There are a couple of areas that would help you move to that next level. You want to look at them?" He'd say, "Yeah, I want to look." We would go through the positives, and then build them up to asking for the negatives. You want them to ask for feedback. Explain why they need to do it, and what it will do for them.

The way you communicate the feedback is essential for Scott.

I wouldn't say, "You don't do this, you don't do that." It's better to say, "Imagine if you did this instead of that." It always works a treat. If you get a player who wants to get to that next level, then nine times out of 10, it's going to work.

Theerathon moved to Japan to play for Yokohama F. Marinos under coach Ange Postecoglou. He became the first Thai to win the J League, scoring in the title-deciding game in front of 63,000 fans. Scott's individual chats were vital for getting him and the other leaders onside.

If Theerathon or Suchao Nuchum weren't having me, I would have been finished at Buriram. You're dead because they'll speak out. But once they put their stamp of approval on me, everybody followed. If you get the leaders onside, it's a lot easier. I would spend a lot of time individually talking to them about the game and what I thought they did well. I'd also take an interest in their family and where they grew up. It shows you care about them.

Getting players onside is crucial for Scott.

I could do a session with a group of 20 players that don't like me. They'll do the session. But with a group of players that respect you, and with who you've got a good relationship, you'll get more because they're willing to open their ears to listen. They'll add the extra bits of movement, communication, and work better with other players. You'll get that bit more from them each time.

Group Feedback

Group feedback is different. It can be given in a team setting as long as you don't target individuals excessively. Simon also gives individual messages indirectly in the team setting. Asian players are usually better at reading between the lines and receiving messages, due to not typically communicating as directly as many Europeans would.

You do things indirectly. If someone's doing something, you say it to the group — rather than targeting individuals — and hopefully the message goes through. If it doesn't, you take them to the side.

Scott says there are times when you need to provide individual feedback in front of the group. He would be a lot harder on the senior and foreign players, who he knew would respond well to it.

Generally, I'll bring a player in and speak to them on my own but you can correct players in front of the group. With Victor Cardozo, it will be different than Siroch Chattong. If I had a go at Siroch, he would be shaking for the rest of the day. Victor needed that, but Siroch needed something else. There are no rules that you shouldn't do that, or shouldn't do this. You need to figure out what's the best way to get that player working harder, playing better, and developing.

Some coaches fear highlighting Asian players' mistakes in front of the group. They don't want to face the backlash that can come. Scott says you can do it if you approach it the right way.

Some coaches fear what happens next. You smash a good player and he thinks, F**k off. Under his breath, he's muttering and he goes back thinking he's a d*ck. If you're comfortable with your relationship with that player, you can be direct. I could stop Theerathon and say, "Hey, you are better than that. Your delivery is better than that." Or "Hey, any chance of you running back on that transition" and he'll laugh. That type of feedback.

Scott would only hammer a player if he thought they were disrespecting people at the club.

There aren't many players that you want to bring in and rip to shreds. Unless they've done something off the pitch and disgraced themselves. I would also hammer a player if he's openly trying to leave the club, he's not working in training sessions, or he's being disrespectful to the owner. You're not using him anymore and he's not with the group. That's when you can do whatever you want. But that's not happened very often to me.

Knowing when to interject is the key for Scott.

It's the right moment of interjection. That's what defines a really good coach. It's also picking what you think will make that player tick. That's not only Asian players… it's all players. That may be more important than any tactical aspect. You're not going to get what you want unless the players want to do it for themselves and you.

Simon agrees with the importance of knowing when to do it.

You can't shout all the time. Eventually, they get numb to it. He's off again. They don't listen. But there has to be a time when you do raise the roof and take the paint off the walls to get a reaction. At half-time, you've got eight minutes to say something that will change the game. There is no time to put your arm around eleven players and say everything's going to be all right. If most of the time on the training ground, you're one-to-one, you're explaining things to them in detail, then all of a sudden, at half-time, you're going mental. Straight away, Jesus, coach isn't happy; we've got to step up here. You get a reaction and that's what you're after.

If Simon gives critical feedback to someone in front of the group, he will pull them aside and explain things afterwards. This ensures everything is understood and reduces any negative feelings.

Sometimes, you need to bollock someone, and they need to be big enough to handle it and react to it. And then, after the game, you can say, "Do you understand why I did that?" and you can point things out using videos. Every so often, you need that reaction. There's a time and a place for everything.

Language Barrier

Skilfully delivering these individual and group messages while facing a language barrier is a great challenge.

In an ideal world, you'd do intense language lessons before getting a job in a foreign country. Unfortunately, you don't always have much time to prepare. You can be approached one week, and be landing in the country with no idea of the language or culture the following week!

Becoming fluent can take a long time. Each region has a different accent and may use different words, which can make it difficult to learn the language without being immersed in the environment. You will improve over time, which helps to develop connections with locals. Try to learn five keywords or phrases every day. Bounce them off your translator and practise them around town. Sam feels learning the language is a message that you *want to stay* and *make a difference* in their country.

One of the ways you show commitment to the job, and the reason you've been hired, is by embracing the culture. Learning the language is a massive part of that. It doesn't mean becoming fluent. It means making an effort to understand what's going on. When you start to feel more confident, try to use some of the language with players and in sessions. It helps to develop relationships and shows locals that you're there to make a difference and not there for the money. It's a key part if you want to have long-term success in that country.

Colum made a big effort with the language in Cambodia, which he feels paid off.

The big thing for me was coming in and speaking the language. I'd only been in the country for two weeks, but I did intense classes. That got me onside early. They were a bit shocked. "How is he speaking our language already?"

Cederique learnt key football terminologies to use on the field.

Communication is always very important. In China, I learned the language by speaking it and being on the field. It's not perfect and never will be. Making an effort to speak Chinese creates a stronger connection with the players. You can communicate directly rather than through a translator.

In a club with a wide range of nationalities, it's important to try and get everyone speaking the local language. It's not always possible when you're signing foreign players, but it's important to ensure locals and foreigners are united. Cliques can develop when groups speak different languages. This may spread mistrust and confusion when people don't know what others are saying around them.

Translators

During my first week in Thailand, we played Buriram United. I was standing in the stadium's technical area, and I soon realised there was no point in me standing there. I couldn't communicate with anyone! My translator went into the technical area, and I sat in the dugout and fed messages through him.

Finding a good translator makes a huge difference. My best translator spent three years in England doing a degree in sports coaching. He spoke good English and understood the differences between English and Thai culture. He had a background working in football which meant he understood *football language* and the value of different coaching approaches. He was also switched on, so I could trust him to deal with the logistics and paperwork, which was all in Thai.

Working with a translator encourages you to become more concise and gives you time to think of your next message when the translation is being given. It also encourages you to prepare in more detail by telling the translator what you'll be doing in sessions and games. The translator has a great command of the language and culture which is invaluable. They can help you to speak the language, learn about the region, and with logistics and life off the pitch.

There are also downsides to working with a translator, including the translation may not always be accurate or convey the same tone or body language. It also takes much longer to get messages across. It can be hard finding a good translator and it may discourage coaches from learning the language.

One of my translators was unreliable and didn't turn up for one of my first Thai Youth League games. I was in the dressing room with 16 players, a goalkeeper coach, and a physio. None of them could speak English and my Thai was limited. Thankfully, we had trained with a translator all week. I put the cones down in our formation and moved them around to reinforce key points. The leaders in the group would reinforce my messages in Thai. During a break in play, I'd show a nearby player a drawing on my notepad, and use trigger words and basic Thai. He'd shout over to the player I wanted to get the message to.

Cederique had to intervene when the translator couldn't understand his Croatian colleague.

The club got two student translators who didn't know anything about football. We were training and the Croatian coaches had very thick accents. It was difficult for the

126

translators to understand. The coach was explaining the exercise and the translator couldn't translate. He was constantly saying, "What did you say?", "What?" while he was translating. And it was a bullshit translation. I could speak some Chinese, so I stepped in and started shouting in Chinese. All the players looked at me and started clapping before doing the exercise.

Steve Darby had similar problems with translators in Vietnam.

I realised the value of high-quality translators in Vietnam. When I went in 2001, virtually nobody spoke English. Even with a degree in translation… as some of them had. One of my first translators kept saying "yes" to me. I eventually asked her: "Are you a Giraffe?" She said, "Yes, of course."

I then got a brilliant one who was self-taught. She was angry when I was angry, and translated jokes. But even she had her moments. I shouted for players to, "Get it to the far stick." Next minute the players were pinging balls to the corner flag. I asked, "What are they doing?" She said, "You said, hit it to the furthest stick!" It taught me not to use slang.

One of my translators spoke perfect English but didn't speak football language. They also didn't have the personality to connect or command respect from the players. At this stage, the players and I had worked together for months; they knew what was expected, and how we worked. I communicated using body language, physical demonstrations, video footage, cones, tactics boards, our trigger words, and basic Thai. After a while, it feels like you don't need a translator to run sessions. But they're still vital for giving the detail and sorting out logistical issues.

Working with a Translator

Sam feels the biggest change in how you coach abroad is your communication.

The main way of adapting the session is from a communication standpoint. You need to go through somebody to get your message to the player.

Scott found it wasn't always easy getting his point across in a foreign language.

You've got to tone down your language, so it's easy for them to understand and get your point across. That takes a lot of emotional intelligence to tailor the message and see if it's being received.

Scott recommends building a relationship with the translator.

Make sure the translator is your friend so that they've got empathy for what you're saying. They'll try their best to make sure it comes across. You need to use basic English or come in with local interjection words when you can.

It's not only what you say; Scott uses body language to communicate.

Ensure your communication is effective and touches them in the right places. It's got to come through translation and body language. You can get players with your eyes and a smile. They can see that you're there for them, and you're happy to see them. It might be a laugh or a joke. You might tease the colour of their sneakers. Light-hearted things like that show your human qualities. They have to see different aspects of you as a person.

Cederique has experience working with a lot of translators in China.

Be patient because – for a translator – it's difficult, especially in the beginning. Sometimes you get translators who are straight out of school. They don't have experience in football yet. You're explaining something and they misunderstand and explain it wrong to the players. The players will do something completely different. You're thinking in your mind, how can they not understand this? It may have been a mistake by the translator or I didn't explain it well enough.

Cederique meets the translator before training to explain exactly what they'll be doing in training.

I quickly go over the plan and explain the exercises. It helps a lot. For the translators that have worked with me, it's only one minute. For new translators, it takes 10-15 minutes. I explain what I expect from them and what we will do in the exercises. It works because they already know what to do.

Colum feels planning makes the difference with translators.

Your session design has to be spot on to make the session flow. That's something we improved a lot and reflected on with the translators. Showing my translator the sessions beforehand was beneficial. I had to prepare meticulously and know the colours and language I would use. I also cut out the translator when possible.

Sam realised the need to be concise with messages when working with a translator.

You have to say things using fewer words that have the same impact. It needs to be short and sharp. The translator needs to understand what you're saying; otherwise, the players have no chance of understanding. Use a lot more demonstration when you're trying to show what you want from the players, particularly with younger players. If it's easy to explain, you can show using a demonstration only.

We developed a list of key trigger words linked to our game model. The translator explained the terms to the players in Thai. That meant I could say one word or phrase and the players knew exactly what I meant. It also showed whether the translation was accurate as I could see their reaction to the trigger words.

Trigger words are crucial, even when you speak the same language. It creates a common language, condenses information, and makes messages easier to receive and retain. The result will be the whole team speaking the same football language. This improves communication regardless of what language you all speak!

Chapter 13. Scott's Journey: A Football Rollercoaster

Muangthong United

After leaving Buriram United, Scott Cooper was attracting interest from Japanese clubs after Buriram's stellar Champions League performances.

The Champions League results and being ranked the seventh-best team in Asia spurred some interest from J2 teams (second division). You couldn't have envisioned our results – for years, Thai teams were getting beaten in the group stages and then, suddenly, we were pushing on to the quarter-finals.

One of Buriram United's fiercest rivals also approached Scott.

We let one of the Buriram players go mid-season, and Muangthong United picked him up. He called me saying, "The Muangthong people are asking all about you: can I give them your number?" I said, "Sure." The owner called and I said, "I appreciate it, but I'm going to Tokyo Verdy." At that stage, it was almost done and there was another J2 club interested. For some reason, the communication fizzled out and it died off.

I was in Bangkok, and we started enjoying life there. I then discovered Muangthong was very close to where we lived. I met the Muangthong owner in a restaurant to have a chat. Out of respect, I put a call in to the GM of Buriram United to ask how they felt about me signing for Muangthong. I didn't want to be disrespectful. He said, "Do what you have to do. It's fine. Nobody's going to be against it." We decided to take the job, signing a three-year deal.

Things didn't turn out how Scott had hoped, and he resigned early in the season.

I went into the job, but it wasn't for me. I left Darren Read in charge and the team was playing well. We were top of the league, and Darren carried on with those performances and they kept winning. It wasn't anything to do with the players.

It was a different type of ownership from what I had been used to before. I didn't feel I could be myself. It was about the way I wanted to work and I didn't feel it was going to be possible, so I decided to leave. I didn't go out and say anything untoward, and neither did they.

Indonesia

After Muangthong, Scott was at Suphanburi FC when he got approached by an Indonesian agent.

I was at Suphanburi, helping them oversee things, but I wanted to coach and they'd already got a coach there. I wasn't going to stab him in the back, so I kept quiet and did my job. Then an agent contacted me from Indonesia, saying, "Do you fancy the Indonesian league?" I wasn't sure but I looked at it and wow, that's a passionate league with a massive fanbase.

I said, "Okay, I can meet you." He said, "We'll do our pre-season right where you live in Bangkok. We'll stay in a hotel near where you live with the whole squad there for three weeks. You can do the pre-season, then you can decide." I said, "Okay, let's do that." They came over and we trained at an International School.

Pre-season performances were good, which convinced Scott to sign for Mitra Kukar.

We played Ratchaburi, Army, Air Force, and won all of our pre-season games. I said, "Okay, let's do it!"

Scott was in for a shock once he landed in the East Kalimantan rainforest.

I flew over to Mitra Kukar, and it was an eye-opener. It's hard to get there but it's a nice little town with a good stadium. The team was already assembled, so I had to deal with what they'd got.

We started, and the signs were on the wall. It looked like some major interference was coming from inside the club. I didn't like that. It felt like it was interference without any reason because the bosses hadn't been to training sessions or seen what was going on.

Scott was getting stopped by fans which wasn't what he was used to in Thailand.

Indonesia is a massive football country but what you've got was worse than Thailand, where you're getting stopped left, right, and centre by fans.

During pre-season, there was a legal battle going on, which allowed Scott to escape.

We went away to a pre-season camp and there were legal issues between the league and a breakaway league. Politics got involved and FIFA shut down the league. The club wanted to keep training and wait for the league to start. I was told on good authority that the league was never going to go ahead, and it didn't. I said, "Let's cut the contract. You don't need to pay me and the team can train with the domestic staff." They didn't want to, but I pushed for it.

It was a lesson learned for Scott about doing your research before joining a club.

Do your homework on the league, the country, and the ownership group. I should have known better. If I had visited and seen what I saw, I would never have taken that job. Even though they came to do pre-season in Bangkok, the money was fine and the team wasn't bad.

I was fortunate that the league didn't go ahead. It allowed me to manoeuvre myself out of a situation where I wasn't going to be at my best. When I came back to Thailand, the league folded. I dodged a bullet there because I didn't think it was going to be right.

Football is huge in Indonesia, but you don't take a job based on how many fans they've got.

The agent did a good job of selling the club and the league. There's no question Indonesian football is passionate. But you don't take a job based on how many fans are in the stadium and their passion for it. You've got to do it based on how well you can do the job.

Ubon UMT United

After Indonesia, Scott received a call asking whether he wanted to meet the owner of a third division Thai club.

I was passing through Thailand on vacation before going back to our home in Florida. I was still in touch with Muangthong and they asked if I wanted to meet the Ubon owner. They were a T3 team and you can imagine me saying I'm not going to T3. But I knew he'd got some finance behind him and he had ambition. I thought, Okay, I'll go and meet him.

Scott hit it off with the owner right away.

He had a big smile on his face and I liked him instantly. He showed me around Ubon and introduced me to the players. He said, "I need someone to come in and help me control it all." I said, "What's your goal?" He responded, "I want to put my town in the Thai Premier League (T1)."

I told him, "You're in eighth position in T3. It's not going to be easy as it's mid-season. What's the budget?" He showed me the budget, which he didn't increase during that season. I said, "That's not a bad budget for what you've got here."

Scott saw the club's potential but he needed to make it through to the mid-season transfer window.

I gave him my verdict on the players that were there, and what I felt he hadn't seen. He told me to come and watch a couple of games. I watched the games and thought we could do something. But I needed to get the team through to the end of the first leg (mid-season break).

Scott's biggest request was for direct communication with the owner, and to let him do his job.

For me, it was understanding him and asking him questions. What happens with a lot of Thai clubs is that there are a lot of people around owners or GMs. These people have their say, and there's interference and complications. I made it clear that if it was me and him working together and making decisions, it could work well.

The owner agreed and stuck to his word.

He made it against the rules for players to contact him or the admin about any football matters unless it came through me first. So, contractually, nothing could come, and he liked it that way. He said, "I'm not as busy anymore", and we hit it off right from the start.

Scott took a big risk going to the third division, which could have backfired.

It could have been career suicide going to T3. What would have happened if we'd lost six of the first eight games? I could have been done. Then where do you go from there? It was a decision I made based on the owner, the budget, and what I thought we could do.

Arriving a quarter of the way through the season was a huge challenge.

At that stage, they were 15 points behind the leaders, Khon Kaen United. I couldn't spend money to bring players in and had to deal with the players they had. That was the hardest part because I went into a team that wasn't mine and they were overaged and lacked motivation. They were only playing in T3 to get a paycheck.

I told the owner, "Some players… we're not going to be able to use. After the first leg, we're going to need to change things. We need to bring some younger players in, some loan players, and some new foreign players." He said, "I will leave everything up to you".

The owner gave Scott the freedom and backing he needed.

The power the owner gave me allowed us to work with the players and get rid of those who didn't want to work hard. Then we topped it up with players like Victor Cardozo, that came on minimal funds. Victor was booed for the first two or three games by some fans, and the owner could have easily said, "I don't want him", but he didn't. Victor went on to win the Thai league with Bangkok Glass years later.

He put the budget in place and never questioned any signing I made, or anything I did tactically. When I thought we could upgrade the hotels on away games, or instead of going for one day, we'd go for two days; everything was okay as long as it fell into the budget. The key is knowing the budget, but you're only as good as the owner allows you to be. I'd been blessed with an owner at Buriram that's passionate about football and was willing to spend, and an owner at Ubon that said, "This is your club."

Scott overcame an early scare before going on a long winning streak.

We lost the first game and I thought, "Oh my word, I'm going to be a T3 coach forever." And then we won 12 on the bounce, including nine straight away games. At any level, that's not easy. The results saw us climb the table to reach the promotion play-off final.

We played Sakon in the final and that's probably the best game I've ever been part of. We won the first leg 7-0, and they were a really good team. We won the away leg on Boxing Day 2-0 to win 9-0 on aggregate and earn promotion. I'm pretty sure that's never going to be matched again!

Ubon had a tough opponent in their first T2 fixture.

That T2 season we had Thai Port, PTT Rayong, Songkhla, and there were some other big clubs in the league. Our first game of the season was away at PTT Rayong. I remember the waiter at breakfast on the morning of the game. He said, "You're playing PTT Rayong today, who is a big rich club. How do you think you'll do?" I smiled and said, "It's not possible to win today", but we won 2-0.

The Ubon fans travelled well and filled that side of the stadium. It was amazing because we didn't know how we would do that season. We only brought in a few players. We kept almost the same squad from T3 to T2. We went with the group that won all those games and got us promoted.

The owner was repaid for his trust in Scott as they got promoted to the top division.

I was given the time and trust, and when we went to T2, we were the favourites to be relegated. I only promised him one thing, and that was we won't get relegated. That's not happening. But we got promoted again. That PTT Rayong game showed us straight away that we were more than equipped. That one and the promotion-winning game against Chiang Mai stand out. They were pushing for promotion themselves with four games left, and we beat them at home.

Scott was full of praise for the owner's approach.

It was one and a half seasons from T3 to T1, and that was down to the owner of the team. He needs to take a lot of credit for that because he stepped back and said, "I'm going to enjoy the football. You make all the football decisions." He never had an opinion when we drew a game or this or that. We'd speak after every game, and there was never any pressure.

Scott and the team had a great first season in the Thai Topflight.

We won the first game of the Thai Premier League, beating Sisaket 2-0. We always started well. We played Army, who were second or third at that stage, and Chiang Rai in the cup, and we beat them both at home. It wasn't end to end; we put it on them, and we beat them well. They were really good performances.

Despite having had a great season, Scott decided to leave as the club's budget couldn't match his ambitions.

The owner never intruded, and he kept it that way right up until the end. I left Ubon because I felt I couldn't do anything more with the budget we had. I wanted to try and win the Thai Premier League with Ubon. We drew eleven games in that Premier League season, and we finished 10th. We were the better team for a lot of those draws. There was a good eight to ten points that would have put us third or fourth.

The club sold some key players, which made life difficult for Scott.

The budget was fine when we were in T2 or T3, but in T1 it was difficult. If we had not sold Siroch and increased the budget, we could have challenged Buriram, Muangthong, Chonburi, and Bangkok United at the top of the table. We were a 25 percent budget increase and not selling two players away from it. But we went the other way and sold five players. The sponsors didn't come in, and we kept the same budget.

Scott was relying on the recruitment and development of young players to progress the club through the leagues.

I couldn't keep unearthing foreign and Thai players. We'd got the right Thai players in T2, and we'd prepared them for T1. I couldn't find hidden gems that were ready to be thrown straight into T1 games. The nucleus of what we had at the club wasn't working. We could have done a deal with a T2 club and got the right coach in there to keep bringing those players through. It was something that I planned to do alongside raising the budget a little.

Scott felt the club couldn't progress which is what happened as the club went on a downward spiral.

We won the last three games 2-1, and they were all struggles and I felt the writing was on the wall. If we didn't get it right, we were always going to be a mid-table team. I wanted to do more.

The thing about Ubon is we had total control. The owner was amazing; he did everything he said he would. Towards the end, I felt we had to bring in a major sponsor or we couldn't take that next step. I didn't want to stay and devalue what I'd done by dropping down the league. Sadly, it fell to pieces shortly after I left, and they're liquidated now.

Police Tero

After leaving Ubon, Scott was contacted by one of the owners at Police Tero.

Brian Marcar contacted me after I left Ubon, and the Japanese clubs were calling again. I'd always had a good relationship with Brian, having dealt with him at Ubon when we were buying and selling players. It was a new club. Police and BEC had combined their two ownership groups and backed it quite well.

We met for dinner, and he said, "We've got some exciting young players" and that he'd let me sign seven or eight players if I came. He said, "Don't go to Japan. You know Thai football," and he did a good job of selling it to me. He let me bring all of my staff in.

The team didn't get off to the best of starts.

The team was misfiring at the start of the season. We had some good moments and some average ones. We won away in Chainat and lost a couple of games 2-1. There was a bit of frustration kicking in.

Scott's Mum – who was back in England – suddenly became ill after an away game.

We drew 0-0 in Chiang Rai which wasn't a bad performance; I thought we could have won that. After the game my mum became ill. She had pneumonia but we didn't think it was too serious.

Suddenly things changed and they said, "We're going to have to put her into an induced coma because her vital organs are shutting down." A couple of days later, they said, "Listen, we think you should fly here; we don't think she's going to make it."

This was a huge shock to Scott, who thought his mum seemed to be pulling through.

This was my mother, who was laughing and joking the week before. I told the club, "I need to fly", and they said, "Hey Scott, fine, I hope she's okay." I flew and I'm glad I got there. She was in a coma for two or three days, and then her vitals were picking up, and she was doing well. I was thinking, thank God, I'm glad I'll be here when she wakes up… she'll be happy.

Things, sadly, took a turn for the worst.

I got home that night, and the phone rings at 3:00 a.m., and they said, "You better get over here. Everything's crashing." "What!" We get to the hospital. The Doctor rolled mum's eyelids back, and her eyes were blank. They said, "She's not going to make it through this. We could keep her in this coma, but she's not going to make it."

We decided that we had to take the hard decision to turn the machine off. I had to sit there and go through that. It wasn't easy for my dad and my sister… it was just me who sat there to do it, and I held her hand as she slipped away.

Scott told the club he had to stay and arrange the funeral.

I contacted the club and said, "My mum has passed away, and I'll be staying for the funeral arrangements." They did an autopsy, and then we had to wait for a funeral and we couldn't get a funeral date for three weeks. That's seven or eight games I'd miss.

During that time, my dad was in a state because my mum fell ill and died suddenly. My dad previously had a stroke, and he couldn't speak properly and didn't know what he was doing. My sister's a ballet teacher in Austria with her own school. It was only me, and I wasn't going to leave my dad. I said to the club, "I've got to stay here for three weeks until the funeral, and I'll miss the seven or eight games."

The club relieved Scott of his duties.

A week to ten days later, I got an email from the club saying, "I'm sorry, but we're going to have to let you go." I didn't mind at that stage as my priority was my dad being right. I understood it. The club got some criticism from the fans, but it wasn't written in a bad way. It wasn't anything nasty. They had to carry on and were in a bit of limbo.

They let my staff go too. Darren Read went to become the Udon Thani coach. They carried on with Rangsan, who did a good job for a while. Then Coach Ban, who won the league with Muangthong, took over; he got fired after eight games. Rangsan came back in, and they got relegated.

We'd won two, lost two, and drawn one. But for me, it wasn't important and the club did the honourable thing. The financial agreement and everything were all followed properly. It was a shame it ended that way.

Scott wouldn't have been in the right frame of mind to continue anyway.

Even if the funeral had been the week after, I'd still have stayed to make sure my dad was okay. It was never going to be right, and I wasn't right in the head. Even if I'd come back, it wouldn't have been me.

Scott was very close to his mum.

My mum was the most inspirational person in my life… I talked to her every day. She was a big Irish personality. Then, for her to be gone is just heartbreaking. I fell out with religion, and with everything and everyone at that stage. I was in no state to do anything.

I spent a bit of time with dad, and in Serbia with my friends there. It wasn't an easy time. I was in no state to be coaching. They made the right decision for the club – you can't blame them for that.

Philippines

Later that year, Scott joined the Philippine Football Federation.

I resurfaced thanks to my agent. A couple of Filipino players also wanted to introduce me to the Federation when Coach Dooley left. Javier Patino – who'd had me at Buriram – was a Filipino international. He'd talked to Daniel Palami at the federation, who liked what we'd done at Buriram. He also liked the work at Ubon as he wanted a coach that could build something, because they needed to bring players in. That's how I got the job there.

Scott held various roles at the federation. His first was Assistant Coach to former England captain, Terry Butcher. Scott encountered some problems due to needing to revalidate his coaching licence.

It was off and on because I had to get the licencing sorted out. I didn't do the CPD, so I couldn't revalidate my licence. I came in as Assistant Coach to Terry Butcher. Terry didn't stay – for his own reasons – and then I became the caretaker coach.

Scott got thrown into the hot seat for two friendlies in the Middle East. He no longer needed a translator as he did in Thailand, which helped him get off to a good start.

I had a baptism of fire with Oman and Bahrain away. Two very different games; we drew both 1-1 and did well. I felt my man-management skills were at their best as the players all spoke English. I was able to go in and we started well.

Sven-Goran Eriksson, who was at Leicester City when Scott was an Academy Coach there, then became the Philippines Head Coach. Things didn't go well in the Asian Cup, so Scott took over, signing a long-term deal.

Sven came in, and we got to the semi-finals of the Suzuki Cup but we lost every game in the Asian Cup, which was disappointing. Then the President and the Azkals Chairman, Dan Palami, said, "We only wanted you to be here." They gave me a three-year deal, and then we extended it to six years.

Scott had to make changes as the Philippines (Azkals) had an aging squad.

As a national team coach, you've got to get off to a winning start straight away; otherwise, you're in trouble. The Azkals squad was an aging squad of good players and good lads. I was able to start looking at younger players and changing some things. We had new players coming through who were looking good, and we were writing a domestic plan.

Under Scott's reign, the Philippines recorded their most ever points in a World Cup Qualifying campaign, although the campaign ended in a Covid-19 bubble in Dubai. It was a big challenge for Scott with injuries and players who couldn't travel due to the Covid-19 pandemic. Finishing third behind China and Syria put them through to a third-round qualifying spot for the Asian Cup qualifiers, but Scott wasn't satisfied.

We got the points record, but to me, it didn't feel like a success because we came third in the group. We needed to be top two to qualify for the next round. Beating Guam 4-1 was the biggest away win the country has had in a World Cup qualifying game. The goalless draw with China saw us become the first South East Asian team in 60 years to take points off China in a World Cup qualifying campaign. But can you look at a draw as your best result? We beat the Maldives away, but we didn't do anything I could say I'm pleased about.

Scott pitted his wits against World Cup-winning coach Marcello Lippi, who was in charge of China.

He was great to me. It was fantastic because my dad is Italian and I spoke the most broken Italian to him. He was surprised, but what a humble guy – he was under immense pressure.

The Philippines hadn't fared well against China in previous years.

Three years before, the Philippines lost 8-0 in China. Then we lost 3-0 with Sven in the Asian Cup. I had already played against Lippi's team with a young Azkals side, in a full stadium in China. We couldn't call up many players, and we lost 2-0.

137

We played well in the last 20 minutes after having a player sent off after 60 minutes. After the game, Lippi came over to me and said it's a team for the future.

Lippi was very complimentary about Scott and his team before and after their goalless draw in the Philippines.

A World Cup-winning coach was saying, "They're well-coached, this is going to be a hard game, and this guy knows what he's doing." After the game, he was disappointed because we held them to a draw, and that cost them, with Syria winning the group. But he was so humble and complimentary afterwards, telling the press, "Our national teams do well against the weaker opponents. But when we play stronger opponents or teams that are well-coached like the Philippines, we struggle." Hearing that – when it felt like we were nowhere near where we should be – gave us confidence.

Scott changed the system late on, and they could have won the game against China.

It was a tactical stand-off. We were 5-4-1, they were 4-3-3, and we were holding them and countering. With less than 10 minutes left, Mr. Lippi took off their two centre backs and put on two full-backs for mobility – to keep the ball moving. I responded and put on a big striker in Angel Guirado. So, they went small and we went even bigger.

We went more direct to Angel and it started causing massive problems. Balls were dropping around him and they couldn't deal with him. They were holding him and he was flicking things on. It was mayhem and we had three or four chances to win the game at the end. Neil Etheridge made a point-blank save for us in the dying moments, which was a monster save. We had a shot blocked that was going in, and the Chinese player just got his boot to block it. For the last five to ten minutes, I was thinking, we're going to win this.

A big chance came at the end with a free kick. The Philippines had a big height advantage and a set-piece specialist in Mark Hartmann.

We had a free kick on the corner of the box. It was too wide to try and score and the height difference in the box was massively in our favour. I was thinking, this is it, because I know Mark can put it on a penny. Schrock came over, and I waved him away because he's more of a snapping rebound player.

Mark tried to whip it into the top corner and the keeper read it. The whistle went a few minutes after. I was pleased with the result and I was proud, but I said to Mark, "What did you shoot for?" He said, "Shrocky told me to." God, it killed me because I thought we were going to win the game at that moment.

Scott put a worldwide scouting system in place to find the next generation of Filipino talent.

We put a scouting system in South America, North America, Asia, and Europe, and it was working. Filipinos are such well-travelled people, and it's a large population. There are a lot of full- and half-Filipinos all over Canada, the US, South America, and throughout Europe.

We identified hundreds of players and had many conversations with players about A. Did they want to play for the Philippines? B. What do they know about the country, the team, and how do they feel about representing it? C. Where do they see themselves long-term? We also had to ask if they've got the passport. If they hadn't, did they need to apply for it because their mum or dad has the passport? Then we had to go through birth certificates.

It was a massive game of communication and gauging what's the best team you can put out, based on the players' quality and their desire to play for the national team. It was a unique process we went through. I don't think any other country has gone through it on the scale that we did.

Scott faced questions from the Chinese media about naturalising players. The Philippines had only naturalised striker Bienvenido Maranon in 2021, although he had played in the Philippines for over six years. All other players who were called up had Filipino parents.

We took a bit of stick with people saying, "Oh, you're naturalising players." No, we weren't. These players had Filipino blood in their veins. China naturalised three Brazilian players who played in their league. That's naturalising. We were giving passports to players that were biologically Filipino under FIFA laws. If your grandparents or your parents were Filipinos, you qualified.

There wasn't anyone with even a grandparent. All our players had a Filipino parent (other than Maranon), and some of them even spoke Tagalog. What made them less Filipino than somebody that's grown up in Manila? It's debatable. We had a very good pool of players to choose from.

Some of the players were at top European clubs. Having players raised in top European academies and pushing towards first teams at big clubs was great for the country. Unfortunately, the 2021 Suzuki Cup took place outside a FIFA window, which meant the majority of the players at European clubs weren't released by their clubs.

Scott had to rely heavily on locally-based Filipino players and those playing across South East Asia. The Philippines won two and lost two but finished third, which wasn't enough to qualify for the semi-finals.

The full potential of Philippines football can only be realised during FIFA breaks when the players could be called up. At the same time, we weren't closing the door on the domestic players. But we needed the league to do well, and we needed a new regional restructuring of domestic football – so that it became a north, south, east, west, with the regional teams playing each other. We were also developing a national training centre.

The Philippines team had grown up around the world, and Scott was the perfect man to lead such a diverse dressing room.

My mum's from Cork and dad's from Rome. Neil Etheridge comes from England; we had German lads and players from Japan. I was ready for that because I've experienced different cultures and spent time reading different characters. Once you've been coaching in different places, and you have signed different foreigners, you get used to the differences. My Assistant Coach and physio and Goalkeeping Coach were Serbian. It was a good mix, but I don't find that challenging anymore. I didn't have to overthink how I man-managed.

The Philippines had a great team spirit, and all felt immense pride playing for their country.

Our dressing room was fantastic with the Azkals. I understood that they came from different cultures. When we were in camp, the atmosphere was not like one culture – it was a mix of everything in there. People brought different characteristics to the table.

One thing the players all shared was a strong desire to play for the Philippines. I always promised players that no one would ever come into the national team unless they felt something and wanted to fight for the flag and the country. It felt like a football club. Different players and characters, but all fighting for one purpose. Everybody was fiercely proud to be Filipino and wanted to achieve something.

Stephan Shrock was one of the Philippines top players, having played in the Bundesliga. He had fallen out with the previous coach, but Scott brought him back into the fold.

I made Schrock captain. He was out in the wilderness under the former coach who had left him out of the team. There was a big fallout, and media outbursts against each other. I didn't have that with Shrock. He came in for me, and he was fantastic. I had a captain that called me every couple of days to check how I was doing. A captain who worked his socks off and was selfless in what he did around the squad. We talked together about the team, the structure, and the plan going forward.

This is a guy who came and played in the SEA (South East Asian) games as an overage player. Imagine asking the captain of the national team, "Do you want to play in a regional under-22 tournament, as one of the overage players?" He said, "I'll do that for you. No problem." It comes down to your management of players. He's the best captain I've ever had. But then somebody else would say he was this or that.

Scott has had some amazing experiences as a Head Coach and Technical Director, but the best is yet to come.

The AFC Champions League quarter-final against Bunyodkor was amazing to go through and win – fantastic. The game in Esteghlal – what an atmosphere with 96,000 fully charged fans. The Ubon promotion evenings were fantastic. I've got more to come and I'm looking forward to them and trying not to look back.

After resigning from his Philippines role, Scott took over one of the top teams in Thailand, Port FC. It's yet another exciting chapter in Scott's fascinating career path. The vast experiences he's had leave no doubts that further success lies ahead!

Chapter 14. Coaching Abroad: The Reality

Many coaches move away from home to develop their careers. Some do it due to the lack of full-time jobs at home, and others fall into it as an amazing opportunity appears. Some follow a loved one to their new job, while others want to experience living in a new place or to travel the world. One thing all coaches abroad have in common is the huge impact it has on not only their careers but their lives.

Professional Opportunities

Moving abroad provided the coaches with the opportunity to break into professional football. Simon went from a part-time Assistant to National Team Head Coach, which transformed his career. Moving to China also provided Michael with the opportunity to work in professional football.

You might need to leave your country to get more opportunities. In the UK, it was very difficult for me to work at a professional level because I didn't play professionally. I always wanted to have an opportunity to work in professional football. There's less competition for jobs in developing football countries which creates more opportunities.

Michael has lived his dream working under Roberto Donadoni, Clarence Seedorf, Sven-Goran Eriksson, and Jordi Cruyff, plus their backroom staff.

Those that I've worked with are top people in their professions. These are things I can't get from a book or qualification. They've had experience at big clubs. It works for the players and the culture that I'm working in. If I didn't work with them, it might take me five to 10 years to get that experience.

Michael has learnt a lot from watching them work every day.

They've shown me the importance of managing players and how they think. Some players don't want to train – how do you deal with that? How do you communicate with those in the hierarchy at the club? Being with them, I've been able to develop from the coaching itself, but also gained transferable skills such as organisation and communication.

Getting yourself into a good working environment is priceless for your development. Sam Bensley had the opportunity to work at national and AFC level with the Hong Kong FA. He was fortunate to work alongside a team of experienced UEFA and AFC Pro licence coaches.

You've got the Heads of Grassroots, Coach Education, Women's Football, Elite Development, and the Technical Director. Somebody has an idea because they're from

Japan. Someone's got a different idea because they're from Spain. Mixing all those ideas means you never stop learning in that environment. It's best to work in an environment with good people who you can bounce ideas off and learn from.

Sam learnt a lot from working at different clubs and a Football Association abroad.

Working at the Hong Kong FA, we were always thinking on a country-wide basis. You take in all sorts of other factors: politics, what the government is saying, local culture, football culture, and the level of local coaches. Every single variable is having an impact on what you're doing.

In a Chinese football club, we've got our philosophy; we don't need to worry about what other clubs are doing. But when you're in the FA, you've got to worry about what all the clubs are doing. You've got to give the overall direction. It helped me understand how things work on a national level, AFC level, and how it filters down to the players on the pitch.

Having the opportunity to develop football on a national scale was a great experience that Sam wouldn't have got at home. Working at that level taught Sam much more than he could learn on any coaching course.

The informal part is far more valuable because it's real. If we decide the future of a grassroots project – under a five-year plan – it needs to be the best for the country, players, funders, and sponsors. And it has to be an informed, correct, well-thought-out decision, which you can never get on a course.

Foreign Coaches

Michael believes it's important to reach out to coaches in your region.

You're working in China, and you know other foreign coaches are in a similar position. You can talk and share experiences. They might have some good practices that are working for them, and you can share information. You get to learn more about the culture and what works or doesn't work.

Colum had 16 coaches – from England, Northern Ireland, Spain, and Belgium – to bounce ideas off whilst in China. Working with coaches from different countries was fascinating; it presented many new ideas and lightbulb moments. The coaches were all highly motivated and eager to share ideas and improve.

Colum's grassroots club held weekly in-service sessions with different coaches leading each week. He learned about things that are not always covered on coach education courses.

I learned a lot about session design in China. It's not something that's covered in-depth on coaching licences. FAs have to cram a lot of content in to tick the boxes.

The coaches in China would also meet in the office daily to discuss session plans for the day. The club created a great learning environment for coaches to develop. Colum also found working under a good leader made a real difference.

I want to be told when I could have done something differently. The Director of Football in China was really good. He never let me get away with anything. He always made me keep my standards high, on and off the pitch.

Sam worked with Colum in China and found the foreign coaches were great at supporting one another.

In Beijing, we had a good mix of coaches from Europe. We were all going through the same difficulties of living and working in China; we could bounce things off each other and support one another.

Foreign coaches don't normally stay in one country long-term. The coaches in Beijing have moved around the world, which has subsequently opened doors in over 20 countries. Cederique has benefitted from working with coaches from around the world.

I've been lucky to work with coaches from different countries. It gives you different angles and a much bigger view of working in football. It's been beneficial working with Spanish, Irish, English, Croatian, and Lithuanian guys. Every culture and view of coaching is slightly different. You can always learn – it's been fantastic.

Greater Responsibility

Going into a club with a small budget, or a club in a less-developed football nation, can put you in a higher position within the organisation. There are many highly-qualified coaches in developed footballing nations, but in some countries, coach education isn't as accessible. This means staff might not be as highly-qualified, and the owner may want a figurehead to run the project. This can help you stand out and get higher-level jobs with more responsibility.

Clubs with smaller budgets may also not have as many staff members. This means you can fulfil multiple roles and be a key decision-maker within the club. You'll learn new skills and experience different aspects involved in running an organisation. You can learn from working at well-run clubs. But being in a club where the structure is not so strong is a great opportunity for you to build one. Cederique found this working at clubs abroad.

In some clubs, there's a fantastic structure. It's good for developing as a coach because everybody has the same idea. Your colleagues' work is at a good level, and you can learn from them. In some clubs, the structure is not so visible. But you can develop by building the structure. You may have a couple of colleagues that aren't so good. Your task is to help them develop into the structure you're trying to create. It's people management and an education role from your side.

Coaching in less-developed nations provides a great opportunity for change. The game and academies being less developed offers real opportunities for growth. This can come through coach education, creating youth leagues, and better youth programmes.

I became an Academy Director at a topflight club in Thailand at the age of 25. This would never have happened back in Europe. It was a different type of learning experience. Previously, I had been Head Coach of teams; in Thailand, I was running the academy. Having full control of a professional academy brought a lot more responsibility. I had to recruit, develop, and manage the staff and players. I was working with full-time players, which was an amazing experience.

In Beijing, I was learning from the coaches around me. In Thailand, though, I wasn't surrounded by high-level coaches in our academy. I learned from watching the Pro Licence coaches in the first team, but we often trained at the same time, which meant I couldn't always watch. Learning from the challenges the job presented me with was the best experience.

You're under more pressure as a foreigner. They've flown you in and will expect a lot from you. You have to show *why* you'd do a better job than others in the region. Many people will look at you as an outsider and may want you to fail. Doing a good job and impressing the first team staff and hierarchy can lead to promotion within the club. It can also lead to opportunities at other clubs or federations in the future.

Michael believes you can work your way up to succeed the foreign staff once they leave.

If you're working at a professional club abroad and they have foreign coaches, they're not going to be there forever. One day they might leave or be going on a course and then an opportunity comes… if you deliver, you'll get a chance.

New Experiences

Sam has found coaching abroad to be a positive experience for his development.

Going abroad and working with people from different countries, cultures, and levels has a massive impact. You can adapt your coaching style, sessions, and learn how to coach in different contexts. You can visit different countries, meet new people, learn a new language and see different types of football. All this is majorly positive and something I wouldn't have got if I'd stayed at Norwich as a coach.

Coaching abroad has opened Michael's mind.

It's an opportunity to become more open-minded. Going to a different country and seeing different cultures and ways of doing things – it opens your mind. You become more willing to accept different norms than what you were raised to believe in.

Michael found it has helped him focus completely on his career.

Working abroad has been enjoyable but tough as my family and friends aren't here. I don't have any distractions. I can focus on developing and progressing in my job.

It's been brilliant for Michael's development.

You become adaptable because you have to adjust to different situations all the time. It improves your communication skills; not just your verbal but nonverbal as well. When you can't speak the language, your non-verbal communication has to be excellent. Otherwise, they won't know what you're talking about without a translator. You also learn to become extremely organised to deliver effective sessions.

Colum was coaching multiple sessions per day in China which was great for his development. His session plans had to be on point due to the language and heat.

You get so much time on the grass; that's the best learning you can have. You make mistakes, and you reflect on them. Your session design has to be meticulous, and with the heat – you want to be on and off as quick as possible.

Managing the intensity during training and games is vital in hot countries.

Personal Growth

Simon feels the experiences abroad help you grow as a person.

You find out about the type of person you are. When you leave your comfort zone and your support network, you meet a group of people that you've never met before. You don't speak their language; you don't understand their culture or religion. How do you get them playing football the way you want while maintaining some kind of morality and positive effect on people? It's a massive challenge.

You're representing your family and friends. Simon has a tattoo on his hand that reminds him he's not alone when he's on the touchline.

The support you get from those people – and representing that support in the best way – is a pressure. I would never, ever take it for granted. It comes at a price. That tattoo on my hand. When I'm wearing a suit, on the sideline, that's the only tattoo I see. It's to remind me how many people are standing behind me. It can be incredibly lonely standing there when you're getting battered by the fans. Even if you lose games, you're always representing someone. I try to do it to the best of my ability.

Coaching abroad has helped Simon put things into perspective.

You're putting yourself into challenging situations. Being able to come out of it – good or bad – builds strength and confidence. Firstly, in yourself as a person and your ability. In situations where you think this is life or death, where you think it's really serious, it's not. It's just a game.

Succeeding in different countries has given Simon the confidence that he can go anywhere in the world.

It gives you this confidence when someone calls me, "Do you want to go to the Peruvian Premier League." "Yeah, alright. What's it like? Let me do a bit of research." It gives you this confidence that I know what I'm about. I know the situations that I do and do not want. Would I go anywhere in the world? Yeah, I probably would – as long as it's right for me and my family. But I now know what's right for us and what's not.

Challenges

Coaching abroad presents many challenges, including finding the right job. Sam says it all comes down to your research.

Have an understanding of where you'd like to go. What are the potential vacancies in that area? What are the salaries? What's the lifestyle like? How much is accommodation? All those things.

Visiting different countries helps you identify places you'd like to work. Sam flew to Hong Kong on holiday before moving there.

Some people may go somewhere on holiday to get a feel for it. That was the case for me in Hong Kong, having already visited a couple of times before I applied for a job there. I did it because I made the mistake of not doing it before going to China.

It can be risky not doing your research, as Sam outlines.

I knew that China was a growing market but I didn't know much about the cultural points of view. The way I did it was so wrong. I applied for a job with the idea of going somewhere that doesn't speak English and doing some coaching and seeing how it goes. That's not the way I would advise anyone to do it.

Sam recommends having face to face meetings – before taking any job – if you can.

When I went to New York, they recruited in the UK. You already met them face to face, I had a strong feeling that it was a very professional organisation and that I'd be well looked after. Whereas when I was going out to China it was all done online. That was the most blind I'd been. It was taking a leap of faith.

Sam knows you need to be brave to step on that plane.

You need something in your head that tells you it might be a good idea in the first place. Some people say, "I'm not going to do it; that's not comfortable for me. I'm quite happy in my hometown and I'll try to find something closer to home." You need bravery to get on the plane, not knowing what's going to greet you at the other end.

It's hard researching jobs and working environments in countries you have no connection with. Colum knows it has backfired for coaches.

I've heard of people going abroad, and salaries haven't been paid. Get a feel for the people that you're going to be working for. Speak to an agent or someone you know in the country. Go on LinkedIn and reach out to people working there.

Sam echoes Colum's advice.

Sometimes people go out to clubs and it's not what they expected. Speak to people who are already working at that club. Look at the club's website, social media, and get a flavour for it before committing. It all comes down to research and knowing what you're doing before you commit. So you don't arrive and end up not getting paid or experiencing visa issues – all those horror stories. Some people sell their house or car to make that commitment and then get stitched up.

Find out the contract length, salary, bonuses, working hours, job requirements, day(s) off, holidays, sick leave, notice period, and grounds for dismissal. Will they cover your visa, accommodation, insurance, and flights? Will you have a translator if there's a language barrier? What facilities do they use and how much travel is involved, and is it included? Ask the organisation, people who have worked there, people in the country, and visit yourself to gain the best possible insight.

Work-Life Balance

Michael has found you don't always have a good work-life balance in professional football abroad.

You're living in Shenzhen with 18 million people. Life is very quick. You don't get much downtime when you're working in China. There's no work-life balance. That's one of the things I find hard and haven't adapted to yet. You don't have your own time when you work in professional football. Your time is given to the job and whenever the coach or club needs you, you have to be there. You can't plan things because servicing the team and players is your main responsibility. It takes priority over everything else.

Colum finds it difficult to switch off away from work.

The job demands your time. I have nights when I try to leave my phone in the house for a couple of hours, but it rarely happens. I had to get two phones, but it doesn't work as you take them both everywhere and you end up answering the work one.

Sam was working hard in Hong Kong.

The lifestyle I had in Hong Kong was just working. We used to do six days a week; your day off was for sleep.

Colum didn't have a holiday with his partner for years due to his workload, Covid, and work schedule clashes.

We didn't have a holiday together for about six years.

This is the reality of working in full-time football but – of course – it can be the *best job in the world* in the right environment!

Fewer Foreigners

It's only natural that the majority of coaches in a country will be local. Countries want their citizens to get jobs, which can make it harder to get a visa for grassroots positions. It also costs a lot more flying a foreigner in, with their salary and additional benefits. Most professional leagues will be made up mostly of local coaches. Organisations either don't want foreign coaches or don't have the budget to hire them. This reduces the window of opportunity, unless you are well-connected to the recruiters.

Owners who do have the budget, and want a foreigner, will be looking for a specific type of coach. Some owners may want a Spanish or German coach. Coaches from countries that are doing well on the world stage are hot property amongst owners.

They may also discard certain nationalities. They may have had a negative experience with a coach from that country before, or the coach's country may not have a strong football pedigree, or they don't play a certain style of football. We can't control this, but if an owner likes football in your country, then make the most of the opportunity.

Foreign Football Ignorance

Simon has found people in the UK don't understand the experiences he has had abroad. This makes it difficult to get good jobs in Europe.

There's a credibility factor. The guys who make decisions back in the UK and Europe don't know Asian football. They don't understand what it takes to be Head Coach of the Philippines. They don't have a grasp of what that even means.

When they're comparing you against a guy from the UK… he maybe hasn't got a CV like yours, but he's from the UK. It's experience they can break down and understand. There's a real difficulty in trying to get back to the UK, I find.

I sent my CV to a guy who was head of Manchester City's Academy at the time. I asked him what I should apply for in the UK. Should I be applying for Conference jobs, Assistant Manager, youth jobs, or academy jobs? He sent me a long email back saying, "Si, to answer your question, I just don't know."

Simon has enquired about roles, but the level and packages available can't compare to what he gets in countries such as Indonesia.

I had a discussion with a manager at one of the biggest clubs in the Conference. I spoke to him a couple of times on LinkedIn. He was looking for a first team coach, so I messaged him saying, "Can I send you my CV, and you have a look at it?"

He said, "I can consider you." I asked, "What's the salary package roughly?" He said, "It's about twenty-five grand a year." I thought, I might be able to do it.

But I'm thinking about my life and how my standard of living would change going back to the UK, earning twenty-five grand a year. Not getting a house, not getting a car, and all the things that come with contracts in this part of the world. Also being in the Conference, and not even English Football League level.

Simon has been a national team Head Coach, won titles, and earned five figure monthly salaries (USD). Despite this, he wasn't even considered for a lower league job in Scotland on £450 a month.

I had a chat with the owner of Clyde, Division three in Scotland. I sent my CV, and he called me back and went, "Wow, you've been a national team coach. You worked in so many different countries. You've handled budgets of over a million dollars. You've signed Premier League players. I have no idea how that fits into what Clyde wants to do."

I tried to break down the experience for him, and he said, "I've got no idea how you would fit in here." I asked, "What's the salary package you offer?" He said, "It's about £450 per month." £450 per month? To not be considered for £450 a month is a kick in the teeth!

Coaching abroad allows you to experience things that aren't possible in the UK. Simon is well aware of this.

I'm at the point where the more I get knocked back from the UK, specifically England, I think to myself, why would I want to go back? I can't do what I do here in the UK.

Simon has a reputation in Indonesia which helps him get good jobs.

I've been a national team coach and I'm well-known here. I'm not that guy back home – I can't be that guy – so why would I want to go back? There's always a pull, and you'd always love the opportunity. But the reality is there's a whole world of football out there. It's just spoken with a different accent in every country in the world. You love the game, why would you not want to go and see it in lots of different countries?

Coaching abroad has given Simon some unbelievable experiences.

With the Philippines, we had 90,000 in the stadium, 15,000 in the car park, and 450 million watching on TV. They are numbers that you can't get to in the UK; there aren't enough people. There are things I've done in this part of the world that Premier League managers haven't done. It doesn't correspond a lot of the time. Owners want a safe option as opposed to something they don't know about. That credibility will always be an issue. To get from here to there – I need a stepping stone.

I need something in the middle that is a bit more understandable and credible for them. It's been a nightmare.

Returning Home

Sam found the same thing when trying to secure a job when he returned to the UK.

In job interviews, I explained how my experiences abroad would be valuable to that organisation. I understood from their perspective; they've got a lot of applications to look at. One that says China and Hong Kong might get discarded straight away. They think I don't know anything about China and Hong Kong, or they might not value the experience. They'd rather have a safe bet; somebody they already know. He hasn't got the experience, but we know his face.

Michael doesn't think he can get a job at a professional club back in the UK, even though he works at the highest level in China.

It isn't going to be easy. I've been looking at the requirements and qualifications the clubs want. I don't meet the criteria. A lot of them were asking for experience working in the UK academy environment. UK academies were a very closed environment. If you've not worked in them, then you don't get the experience, and they want you to have that experience. If you can't get in, how are you going to get that experience? I don't know.

Colum went straight back from China into a job with the Irish Football Association. He got it through people he knew, and who he had kept strong relationships with. Scott Cooper has also been offered jobs.

I've been offered jobs in the UK and Europe a few times. You're not going to go from Asia to a top league… unless you're high profile like Rafa Benitez was in the Chinese Super League. If you're in the Thai or Vietnamese league, you might get a job in Poland, Estonia, Austria, Denmark, Finland, or somewhere like that. Then it's up to you to make your mark before making that next step to the bigger leagues.

Scott believes Graham Potter is a great example. He went into the Swedish fourth division and got a team promoted to the topflight. From there, he earned a move to Swansea and then Brighton in the Premier League. He impressed there which earned a huge move to Chelsea.

Look at Graham Potter in Sweden. He took a team from nothing and built them up. He did a great job and backed it up in the Premier League.

People in Belgium don't value Cederique's experiences abroad.

Working abroad hindered my career in Belgium – but only in Belgium. Obtaining my A license in Belgium while being abroad was very difficult. Getting onto the Pro licence when you're working abroad would be nearly impossible.

In Belgium, some clubs look past it because they know my qualities. People that I have never worked with would say, "I don't know you. You only worked in China."

Even though you worked there at one of the highest levels. There's so much money involved. Academies work more professionally in some ways than in Belgium. But some clubs will always say, "It's just China."

This didn't stop Cederique as he successfully returned to his homeland. He impressed with his work at United World's Al-Hilal so they moved him to their Belgian club, Beerschot.

There's a different story when you enter into negotiations with people who don't know you. Coaching abroad should be seen as a positive – building up more experiences – but those experiences aren't always given the value they should back home. It's best to stay in Europe if you want to work in a top European league. There aren't many examples of coaches excelling outside Europe and moving to top European leagues. This may differ at academy level.

Roles at top professional clubs are in high demand. You'd need to know someone or have done a very good job in Europe. Without having connections, it's very difficult getting into a senior role in a top European league. This is why it's important to decide where you want to be long-term, and plan how to get there. Factor in both your career and the lifestyle you want to live.

Build your network and profile in the country you want to be in, long-term. Develop a name for yourself and work your way through one of the five pathways discussed in Chapter 4. You need to make yourself visible, keep improving, and connect with the right people. Disappearing to another country can leave you out of sight and out of mind.

There are opportunities to coach at higher levels in less-developed football nations. The roles can be great for your development and lead to better opportunities in that region. But it won't always lead to opportunities in the more developed footballing nations.

Final Verdict

Simon would highly recommend coaching abroad.

It will make you a better person. Away from football, it will make you more forgiving, more understanding, and more grounded. It will make you a different person from the one that's landlocked in a UK bubble. Look at what you get to do in this part of the world. Look at the food you get to eat, the people you meet, and the experiences you have.

In the UK, there'll always be a pull. You'd always love to go back to work at a big club back home, in front of your family and friends. But look at the quality of life you have in other parts of the world. It's still football. You're doing things that people in the UK can't even comprehend; the experiences you're having. I'm a big advocate of getting out of your bubble and going and doing it!

Scott would recommend coaching abroad if you've got a desire to succeed. It won't come easy, so you need the drive to push through those moments. Cederique also recommends coaching abroad.

It opens your view of the world and football. It needs to be something for you; not everybody can adapt. But if you are an aspiring coach and you want to do something different, going abroad is fantastic. I know people who left after one week or one month. It's not for everybody, but I recommend it 100%.

Sam also recommends going for it.

I would encourage anybody who wanted to do it – just go for it! You don't have to go abroad for ten years. You can go abroad for a summer internship or you can do a six-month contract. You don't have to commit yourself. If things don't work out, you don't like it, or it's not what you expected, you can go home. You're going to love it and gain a lot from it. It can help you in everything you do in life and football.

Colum agrees, especially if you have nothing tying you down.

It's a big advantage for a young coach that's single. If you've no attachments, I don't know what you're waiting for. The worst thing that can happen is you go back home and say you didn't like it.

Further down the line, you can make a long-term decision which Sam has been through.

If you stay longer, you might think: do I want to stay here for the next 10 years or the rest of my life? That question comes naturally as you get older. That is when you have to make that decision about the positives and negatives.

Coaching abroad isn't without its challenges but it has offered amazing opportunities and experiences. Cederique played against Bernd Schuster in China, Simon faced Bert Van Marwijk with Indonesia, and Scott pitted his wits against Marcello Lippi with the Philippines. Michael's team faced the likes of Fabio Cannavaro, Rafael Benitez, Giovanni Van Bronckhorst, Oscar, Hulk, and Paulinho. They've faced top pros in amazing atmospheres, with up to 100,000 passionate fans.

It's not only helped the coaches' development, but it has also created a different lifestyle. Three of the Head Coaches working in bigger Asian leagues earned monthly five-figure salaries (USD), with a car and house included. One coach reportedly got a six figure pay-off (USD) when he got sacked in Asia. It should also be pointed out, however, that the vast majority of coaches are on much lower salaries and will never reach that level. Other coaches have got by on $800-2,000 (USD) per month.

No matter what salary coaches earn abroad, though, they will leave rich in life experiences. There should be parity between the amazing life experiences you encounter and your bank balance; your quality of life will suffer if one is out of balance with the other. If you choose to go abroad, it'll be a roller-coaster, but it'll be a life-changing experience!

Chapter 15. Sam's Journey: There's More to Life than Football

Sam has always loved football but didn't think he could make a career in the game. He surpassed all expectations, starting in the UK, and has since experienced working at the same club as Thierry Henry in America, cultural adventures in China, and political battles in Hong Kong. It's been quite the journey for the Englishman.

Norwich

Sam started volunteering with the grassroots team he played for. He then joined Norwich City Community Sports Foundation, where he led school sessions, holiday camps, and grassroots teams. Sam enjoyed his coaching, but didn't have a clear idea of what path to take initially. He applied for university at 18 and got accepted, but he chose not to go.

I was a young boy from Norfolk; we're quite isolated out on the East Coast, and we don't go out much. I was apprehensive, didn't feel confident, and wasn't mature enough to go at that time.

Sam started working outside the sporting world but soon realised he didn't enjoy it. After a year of work, he decided to leave home to do a sports coaching degree, as he had greater aspirations.

I thought… I've got to go to university because I can make something better for myself.

He took a big step and set off on the six-hour car journey from Norwich to University in Preston.

Preston

At university, Sam started working for Blackburn Rovers, Morecambe, and Preston North End in coaching and analyst roles. He worked for six clubs in total during his time at university, which made him realise coaching was a real career.

Those experiences at professional clubs made me think I can make a career out of coaching. I've loved playing football since I could walk, so I thought that if I can make a career out of it, then I want to try.

Leaving his hometown also opened Sam's mind.

That inspired me to be more open-minded. It opened my eyes to a different part of the country and different people and ways of doing things. It led to me thinking, I'll try something different and apply for a job in America.

New York

Sam's first foray abroad was to the United States, where he worked for the New York Red Bulls. He saw the role on a job site and decided to apply as Major League Soccer was on the rise. There was a lot of excitement around the club after making a huge marquee signing.

Thierry Henry had just gone there, which was a draw alongside the fact that it was New York, one of the major cities in the world.

Sam believed his experience working in professional academies appealed to the club.

When I applied for the job at New York Red Bulls, I had a lot of experience working in different pro academies part-time. It also helped that they'd seen me deliver a practical session.

The club hosted a training day in England, which gave Sam a feel for the club and allowed them to see him in action.

When I went down to do the training day, we had to do a series of practical sessions and group work. We were observed and watched in different situations. Throughout the two days, I had a good feeling about the club.

Sam was there for seven months as a youth coach at partner clubs and delivered coach education and summer camps. Going to New York gave Sam a feel for life abroad, which lit a spark.

Norwich

Sam returned to England to work for Norwich City. He coached the U15 girls' centre of excellence, the women's team, and the advanced boys' squads. He also worked as an Assistant Manager with a semi-professional men's team who played in step 4 of non-league. The club had an academy that offered a BTEC course, full-time training, and the chance to play in the national college league. Sam enjoyed his spell there, but decided to leave after the club's manager got sacked at the end of the season.

The new manager was very old school, and I was a young coach. I wanted to play football a certain way, so there was no match there.

Sam decided to go for a second spell abroad, but this time he wanted to try somewhere different.

I thought I'm going to go abroad. America is not too much of a strain for English people, so that's when I looked at China. I wanted to move to a country that didn't have English as its first language. My initial thought when I went there was, to see how it goes and if it doesn't suit me, I can always come back. No harm done.

Sam would have stayed in England if it hadn't been for the sacking of the manager. It's a big deal uprooting your life and moving to a new place.

It's always come with being open-minded and a bit brave inside. Screw it. I'm going to do it and see what happens.

Beijing

Sam's first steps in Asia were in Beijing after finding an Assistant Director of Coaching role on a job site. He worked for a grassroots club with a range of age groups. Sam ran coach education and a youth league, which would be vital for his career progression.

Sam was living with Michael Yau, which was a big help for him.

Michael arrived in China on the same day as me. He speaks Chinese which helped massively with the language barrier, getting about, and understanding how things worked. Michael is Chinese and knows different foods and places to go, which helped me settle in.

Sam's focus changed once he got to China.

When I was in China, I wanted to do the best I could because I was so far from home. I was away from my family and mates. I didn't want to waste the opportunity by going out partying and not concentrating on my work. I wanted to enjoy the travelling part of being in Beijing, but also to work hard and push myself. It's my career at the end of the day.

Sam believes he got the job in China due to his degree and qualifications.

I had the right qualifications – which are important in China with the visa requirement – and the experience I had was also attractive to them.

Having a range of experiences helped Sam stand out.

I had experience across a broad spectrum. I'd worked in men's and women's football and grassroots football with different age groups. I also had a UEFA B licence and a degree in sports coaching. They thought I would be able to integrate quite well into what they were doing.

Sam had also already worked abroad in the US, which helped. After two years in China, Sam decided he wanted to move to Hong Kong, so he started planning his move.

I opened up an Excel file and put all the criteria in. We've got these potential clubs to choose from... this is the contact person. As I was making that document, I went onto the Hong Kong FA website. They had a vacancy for a Grassroots Football Manager which closed that day at midnight.

I had training and got back at half-past 8. I arrived at the office and I had three and a half hours to complete the application, right before it closed. One of the managers came down and chatted with me for an hour and a half. All I was thinking the whole time was, I've got to get this application in here, and it's eating into my time. I was extremely fortunate I found it that day and not the day after.

That was the first time I'd made a map of what was in the area and what to apply for. The other jobs came through online sites, where I had a membership and they sent me all the jobs.

The role not being shared widely by large online platforms helped.

The role was only advertised on the Hong Kong FA website, which narrowed the field and did me a favour.

Sam was fortunate as more recent Hong Kong FA jobs have been posted on job sites, which makes it more competitive. It worked well for Sam who was moving to Hong Kong for personal reasons.

The move to Hong Kong was influenced by the fact that my girlfriend was there. I also liked Hong Kong when I visited. I applied, and they offered me an interview. I decided to fly down to do the interview face to face because I really wanted the job.

He knew flying to meet them face to face would create a stronger impression and connection. Sam learnt that from his previous experience at the New York Red Bulls recruitment day. Every step Sam took on his coaching journey saw more doors open along the way.

Step by step, each part of the process opened up a little more. When I got offered the opportunity to work at a National Association in Hong Kong, of course I was going to take it. National Associations are one of the highest levels you can work at.

Hong Kong

In China, Sam delivered coach education with Premier Skills, which was the British Council's international partnership with the Premier League. He believes that this – coupled with running a youth league in China – helped him get the Hong Kong FA (HKFA) job.

I had the experience of the Premier Skills programme and I'd also been running the BIJFL (Beijing International Junior Football League). HKFA was looking for somebody to come in and run their grassroots programmes. The Technical Director wanted to create a competition for eight to 12-year-olds. The fact I'd had experience managing those two projects helped. Along with having different English professional clubs on my CV, that made them feel I was a suitable candidate.

Having spent time in China helped Sam adapt to working in Hong Kong.

I already had two and a half years of working within the Chinese culture. Hong Kong and China are different, but there are a lot of similarities. That helped me a lot; I didn't put my foot in the mud again with the same mistakes I made in China.

It also helped Sam adapt off the pitch and know how to approach things.

When I went to Hong Kong, my partner was there already. I was older and was thinking more about where to live, places to rent, and what I needed to do about tax. All those important things, which my partner was able to help me with.

When I went to China, by comparison, it was more about where do I go to eat, how do I speak to people, and how do I get about. Because I'd already had that experience in China, going to Hong Kong was a lot easier. As was the fact most people spoke English.

Earning Promotion

When Sam went to Hong Kong, he wanted to work his way up through the organisation.

My target was to get promoted and do well within the organisation, because that was going to help me later on.

Sam started as a Grassroots Football Manager, which gave him the platform to make an impression.

My main responsibility was to look after all the grassroots programmes. We had one huge programme that covered 4,000 players across the entire region from ages four up to 18.

Alongside this, Sam developed a project which he believes was crucial for earning promotion within the Hong Kong FA.

I developed the Golden Age project, with my colleagues, which focused on eight to 12-year-old players. This was a strategic objective the Hong Kong FA had identified. They wanted to give young players more playing opportunities and high-level coaching.

They felt under-15 and 18 players were lacking in certain areas, and that was affecting the country's ability to compete in international competitions. The Golden Age project was developed to help players become better in the younger age groups. The aim was – once they reached under-15 to 18 level – they had a more solid grounding and would be able to compete better.

Sam created a youth league for a range of teams across Hong Kong.

Before, in Hong Kong, everything was siloed off. The clubs were in one silo, the districts in another silo, and the private soccer schools in another. They rarely competed against each other unless it was a one-day competition. These competitions were all about who could qualify out of the group and win the competition. It wasn't particularly helpful for player development. We brought them together at our new training centre and ran a massive league for the under-10 to 12 age group. This was one of the projects that helped me get promoted.

The large number of players participating in the league caught the eye of Sam's bosses.

We had 1,500 players and almost 100 teams who all came on Saturday mornings. If you went down to the pitch, there was a wow factor with how many people were there. Senior Hong Kong FA officials came down and saw it. It was a lightbulb moment for them as they saw it as a good way of using the facility and providing opportunities to play.

Sam feels developing relationships and contributing well on other projects also helped him earn a promotion.

In the beginning, my direct line manager was English, which made it easier to build a relationship. This helped when an opportunity came up because I had a good relationship with the person who was hiring. Second to that are pieces of work like the Golden Age competition, which showed that I can do what I say I'm going to do.

I worked with my colleagues to develop the Hong Kong National Football Curriculum. Through this work, feedback was going back to my boss that I was making a good contribution. We were working with people from across grassroots, women's, futsal, and elite football at the HKFA. The conversations people were having about me also helped in that regard. It's number one doing a good job, and number two building those internal relationships.

Elite Development Coach

Sam was promoted from Grassroots Football Manager to Elite Development Coach.

That required working with the under-18, under-17, and also a bit with the under-15 national teams. In Hong Kong, we also had under-13, 12, and 11 age groups. They weren't national teams but training squads which gave us more contact time.

They were only training twice a week with their clubs. Whereas Japan and Korea, who were at a much higher level in the region, were training four or five times a week. We needed to bridge that gap, so we put extra sessions on for those age groups.

The job role entailed a lot more than the title would suggest.

There was a lot of work off the pitch, which included finishing off the curriculum. That process took about 18 months to two years to develop. It took a great deal of time and effort.

I also wrote a five-year football development plan. The plan went to the Hong Kong Jockey Club, which was our major funder for grassroots football. The five-year plan detailed everything the FA was going to do to seek funding from the Jockey Club. That included the grassroots programme with 4,000 players, referees, futsal, women's football development, and coach education.

Rather than focusing only on high-level refereeing, the Jockey Club was more interested in young grassroots referees. With coach education, we weren't interested in having 50 Pro licence coaches. We were more interested in the quality of the D and C licence coaches who were working with young players. Percentage-wise, the role was 75% off the pitch and 25% on the pitch.

Political Unrest

Sam decided to leave Hong Kong after three-and-a-half years to end a memorable six-year spell in Asia. Various factors contributed to Sam's decision to leave the Hong Kong FA and return home – one of which was the political unrest with violent protests being held across the country.

The political situation had a big impact on my job. A lot of events were cancelled. We'd been preparing a select team from the 18 districts for a showcase tournament. We were due to face teams like Manchester United in one of the stadiums. That got cancelled one week before we were due to play. It was a big project we'd been working towards and doing all the preparation with the team for a year. It was a huge blow.

It was becoming difficult to travel in Hong Kong due to the political rallies.

The national team training started getting cancelled because the government advised people not to travel. Different things were going on in the streets, and we didn't want to put the players or their families at risk. That meant we weren't training, and it snowballed into something that became difficult. When you work in football, the game is the result of all the work that's happened before, and we didn't have that.

The constant battles within the FA were also making things increasingly difficult for Sam.

I was handling extreme political pressure and interference in almost everything. No matter what you were trying to do on the pitch, or putting long-term plans together, you faced constant interference, which wears you down.

What's the Cost?

The work versus the off-the-field challenges made Sam question whether it was all worth it.

When creating a long-term football development plan, the most important thing is having everyone on the same page. When you don't have that, you're losing 1% here, 2% there, and another 1% over there. You end up questioning if it's worth doing it because we've already scrubbed off so many different aspects of it.

That was extremely difficult to try and overcome. You multiply that with missing my mum getting remarried, my sister finishing college, and all those sorts of things, and I began to think, what is the benefit versus the cost?

The political situation within the Football Association also played a part.

My contract was coming to an end. I'd been promised a new five-year contract by the CEO at the time, but there was an inside political situation happening. Staff members at senior level had changed and the politics of Hong Kong football was evolving.

The people who were coming in as a result of this change didn't want foreign staff within the FA. It meant there was a domino effect with one person going and then another and another after that. It became the perfect storm.

Sam thought it was time for a lifestyle change back home.

After years of being abroad, you miss out on so much with your friends and family. If everything had gone smoothly, we would have stayed in Hong Kong for another year or two. Moving home suited the situation for me and my girlfriend. We were conscious that we wanted to get back to England and have a lifestyle change. Working in football, you're Monday to Sunday and evenings and weekends. I wanted to take a step away from that and get my life back.

Norwich, England

Sam had some amazing experiences during his six years abroad. He delivered Premier Skills programmes for the Premier League and British Council. He worked with National Youth Teams, the Asian Football Confederation, and the Hong Kong FA was even voted AFC Member Association of the Year. Sam managed national programmes with over 500 coaches, 4,000+ players, 200 teams, and a budget of $1.8 million USD.

You'd think this would set him up for a good full-time job back in England, but sadly this wasn't the case. Sam applied for over 100 jobs, had seven interviews, and was unsuccessful in getting a full-time job for a year.

That was surprising. I thought the experience of working in a National Association and working with AFC would have left me in a very good position. My CV looked quite strong.

Sam knows recruiters may not understand the value of his experiences in China and Hong Kong. He goes into great detail to help them understand how his skills abroad would transfer.

When I make an application, I try to add rich detail. I highlight the various things I've learned working abroad. Dealing with partners or board members is usually on the criteria. I write in detail about how we've dealt with that in Hong Kong, linking into the AFC to try to bring it to life. But that then requires a person to read it in detail to get that understanding.

Covid-19 made it hugely difficult with a large number of people losing their jobs.

We decided to move back to England before the Covid-19 pandemic started. That was something unforeseen that was thrown into the mix. It had a big impact as people lost their jobs, or got put on furlough. Numerous England FA staff didn't have their contracts renewed. It was awful timing because it put us all in that job pool together. The market in football and sports development is extremely competitive with hundreds of people applying for every job. If it weren't for Covid, I don't think it would have taken a year to get a job.

Getting knocked back from multiple jobs took its toll on Sam. He had to remain mentally strong to keep going.

Patience and perseverance were the major factors. I had a spreadsheet of all the jobs that were available at that time. I had a drop-down menu, whether I'd be interested in it, when the deadline was, what needed to be done, and kept tabs on it. It required a lot of determination. There was lots of, "We're not doing this job anymore because of Covid." They copy and pasted the same emails to everybody. It was very frustrating receiving that email multiple times.

I had seven or eight interviews. To prepare for the interview, then give your best and hear back that you haven't got the job was dispiriting. It happened again and again and again. You've got to have some mental fortitude to get up in the morning and sit in front of the laptop. OK, let's start looking for the next job to apply for.

His age was also still being held against him.

I went for a job and got down to the final two, and the excuse they gave was that I didn't have enough experience. I can't make myself be born earlier. Even to still hear that at 32 left me scratching my head. At what point do you not hear that excuse anymore: is it 40, 45, 60?

Sam thought about changing industries but decided it wasn't for him.

I had an interview for something completely different and they offered me the job, but I turned it down. If it came to it, then I would have had to do something because I needed the money. I didn't want to do something where I wouldn't be motivated in the role. It'd be very difficult for me to get the best out of myself.

I had to be patient and keep waiting. It's not like I couldn't get an interview and I was doing something wrong or didn't have the experience. It was once you got the interview; you need that interview panel to take the leap and hire you. Getting interviews was giving me confidence but getting knocked back was tough. I was getting up again on Monday morning, dusting myself down, and going again. What else are you going to do? You can't sit there, sulk, and moan about it.

Lifestyle Change

Sam didn't want to work evenings and weekends but would have for the right job.

Going for a job in football, you have to work evenings and weekends. I would have done it because I'd enjoy the job. But it would have been a blow not to be able to keep to the schedule I wanted.

After all the setbacks, Sam was able to overcome it all and secure a full-time job as Locality Manager at Active Norfolk, where he works closely with local government to advocate for the benefits of physical activity and influences local policy.

I only work weekdays and have my evenings and weekends free, which is exactly what I wanted. My girlfriend and I can now spend time together in the evenings, which we never had a chance to do when I was coaching.

It also means that if I want to coach, I can – as an option – rather than being obligated because it's my job. At the moment, I do a couple of nights a week, which is for enjoyment and to work with some good kids. There's no pressure. I still have my toe in the water, but I can now tailor it to the needs of my lifestyle, which was the major thing.

Working in football can take its toll, and priorities change as you get older. Sam took a long-term view and knew he needed a change.

When I turned 30, that was something I became a lot more conscious of. Some nights I was getting home at 11.30 pm. After training, we reflected on the sessions and spoke as a group of coaches. I'd get home at 11.30 pm and get up in the morning to do it again and again. I wanted something different in the future.

Sam realised some things are more important than football. What an important lesson for everyone working in the football industry!

Chapter 16. Top Tips for Living Abroad

Choosing the right place to live impacts your career, quality of life, and happiness – which should be high on any list of priorities! You can have the best job, but your life won't be complete without a good support network and lifestyle.

Travel

Football can take you anywhere in the world. During my first six years living abroad, I was fortunate to visit 22 countries. Being based in a different region opened up a new world of travel destinations. In Singapore, I was a short boat trip away from stunning Indonesian islands. From Ubon Ratchathani, I was able to do a road trip to Angkor Wat, the largest religious monument in the world.

Colum's experiences abroad have surpassed his expectations.

We've had amazing life experiences like hiking the Great Wall of China on Christmas Eve; I never thought that would happen.

Sam benefitted from visiting amazing places from Hong Kong.

You can fly and visit many different places like Thailand, Cambodia, and Vietnam. It opened up the opportunity to visit different countries, cultures, and get a chance to recharge and refresh.

Travelling within regions like South East Asia is more time- and cost-effective, too. People spend thousands flying from other continents to South East Asia on their holidays. Living there gives you the luxury of cheaper flights around the region, and it doesn't need to eat much into the little holiday time that coaches get. You can even set off for an adventure on your day off!

Culture

There's nothing more exciting than stepping off a plane into a new country. Sam recommends getting out and exploring.

Go out and experience the different sights of the city you're living in and learn more about its history. It gives you a better understanding of the culture and the reason people think as they do.

Michael agrees and offers three tips for living abroad.

Understand the city, the culture, and the language of the country. It allows you to understand the city that you're living in and how to better communicate with the locals.

Living abroad changes how you see the world. Only once you live amongst the people can you see how things are in that country. Cederique has experienced this first-hand.

In Belgium, we have a very narrow view of countries abroad. Belgian people say a lot of China is bad and everything in other countries is bad. When you experience it yourself, it's so much better than people told me. There are some things you dislike, but it opens your view as a person.

Colum's mind has been opened, having had very different experiences in China and Cambodia.

Being away opens your mind. Many things are different from home in both football and everyday life. Beijing was the most hectic place to live. It's much more tranquil here in Cambodia, and the people are more laid back and friendly. In China, people had to get places, and you had to get out of their way.

Working in an organisation with locals can help you off the pitch. Your colleagues can teach you new phrases and show you the best places to eat. They can also show you how to greet people and make you aware of cultural norms. Steve feels this is essential in a foreign country.

Try to learn what is offensive. Drinking alcohol, swearing, going topless, and showing your feet are all habits that may be acceptable in one country – but offensive or even illegal in another. Remember, you are a guest in the country and it doesn't matter what they do or accept in your country.

Culture has a big impact on the feel of a place. If the locals are kind and helpful, it's easier to ask for help. It can be harder to ask if they're less friendly or they don't speak your language. I once asked a Japanese lady for directions in Tokyo and she was amazing. She was walking to work but stopped and walked for five minutes – in the other direction – to show me where I needed to go. Such kindness massively impacts your actions and makes you feel a lot more comfortable in a country.

Food

'Not spicy' is always the first phrase I learn in Asian countries, even though the locals often have a different definition. When they tell me food isn't spicy, it always sets my mouth on fire.

The parents of an academy player once asked my translator if I liked frogs. I said, "Yes." Next thing I know, they'd plated up a frog for me to eat. I was saying I liked *the animal*, but I had to accept their kind offer. They told me it wasn't spicy, but it was the spiciest frog I'd ever had!

Eating foods that your body reacts badly to affects you on and off the pitch. You won't be able to do much if you're running to the bathroom every five minutes. Michael agrees that food is a big challenge for coaches.

The food is very different, which takes some getting used to.

It can be tough getting to know the local food as menus may be in a foreign language and you don't recognise the pictures. Try to find out online or ask locals to help identify what you like. Sometimes, it can be really basic foods like chicken and rice, but knowing how to say it in the local language helps. Trying local food opens up more delicious options, and it's often cheaper. Colum loves the seafood in the local Phnom Penh markets in Cambodia.

Food is a big one for me. We've got all the fresh seafood coming from the coast every day.

Your favourite foods may not always be available, though. In certain countries, some food and drink are illegal due to religious beliefs. In other countries, it's not always easy to buy certain products. If you find food from back home, it may be more expensive as it's either imported or seen as expat food.

A professional player moved to a club in a small city and lost a lot of weight as he couldn't find the nutritious foods he liked. This affected his performance and how he felt about the country. Over time, he found foods he liked and was able to settle in and spend years playing there.

The weather also has a big impact when adapting to a new country. Michael said the heat in Shenzhen can make life difficult.

The weather is extremely hot here in Shenzhen. It's very humid, which can be a struggle at times.

The weather has a massive impact on your life and what you can and cannot do in a country – which needs to be considered.

City Life

When you live in a large cosmopolitan city, you'll usually find most of the shops, restaurants, and home comforts you need. It's also easier to meet people and have a social life around your busy coaching schedule. There should be plenty to keep you entertained away from work.

Things are normally more expensive in big cities, which are full of wealthy locals and expats. As a consequence, salaries may be higher too with more investment in the city. The cost of living in big cities differs – even ones that are close together – so it's important to do your research. Sam found Hong Kong to be an expensive place to live.

The cost of living in Hong Kong is astronomically high. Coaching is not always the most well paid, particularly if you're working in a soccer school. If you need to pay for accommodation in Hong Kong, it's a significant percentage of your salary. You have to ask yourself whether that is a deal-breaker for you.

Accommodation may require sharing a small apartment with someone else. This isn't the case in all big cities, as some are cheaper, but it's something to be aware of. Colum feels the lifestyle and cost of living are much better in Phnom Penh than back home in Northern Ireland.

The way of living is better. I had a swimming pool in the condo and an 18th-floor gym overlooking the city. Everything is cheap. I went home and had to watch my money, but that's not the way here. You don't think too much about what you eat or where you go on holiday. It's a better way of life.

In big Asian cities, you often find markets with cheap products that range from clothing to tasty local food. It's quite an experience walking around local markets, haggling over prices and taking in the atmosphere.

The traffic is often bad in big cities so public transport may be the best option. Air pollution may also go up and down due to traffic, factories, and the time of year. Colum has seen people who didn't like city life abroad.

Some people will land in the country and after 24 hours think – "This isn't for me. People whizzing past me on motorbikes – I don't fancy it."

Quiet Life

Living in smaller cities or towns with few foreigners is a real cultural experience. It's also a great opportunity to learn the language as you'll need it every day. Michael feels the language is a big challenge for foreign coaches in China.

They struggle with the language which isn't easy.

It can be lonely living by yourself without many expats or locals who speak English. You may also struggle to find shopping outlets or the foods you like to eat. People may ask for pictures and you can become a celebrity around town. Sam would be wary of going to such a place.

Some coaches get posted, by themselves, at a school in a town or city as the only expat. That's difficult because you don't have any mates to bounce things off. That's going to take a special type of person to be able to deal with that from a mental point of view.

If you have a child who needs schooling, your family may have to stay in a bigger city, so you may end up alone.

When you live in a smaller city or town, the cost of living – accommodation, food, and activities – will generally be lower. Salaries may be lower too, as there's less money in the region (unless you're at a wealthy club), but your money will go further.

Foreigners

In some countries, you'll stand out; in others, you'll blend in. Countries only grant permission for foreigners from certain industries to work there. This is usually for people with skill sets that are lacking in the country. This means foreigners generally get paid a good salary to move to a new country, and they may receive additional perks such as accommodation, transport, and medical insurance. Sadly, this isn't always the case for coaches, unless you're working at a good level.

Colum and the coaches were able to save money in China due to the salary and cost of living.

The young lads who went over to China in their early twenties were putting a good few quid away. Speaking to some of my colleagues, you're almost losing money if you're working in an academy in London. They're travelling here, there, and everywhere in London. They're leaving at 6 in the morning and getting back at 10 at night.

Foreigners can get treated differently. They may have to pay a higher price than locals at certain tourist attractions, get approached by scammers, and don't always get the same benefits the locals get. Countries look after their citizens first, which is the same everywhere.

My colleague got in a taxi and gave the driver a map of where he was going, as he didn't speak the local language. They were driving for a while but the driver couldn't find the destination. My colleague refused to pay as the driver hadn't taken him to where he wanted.

Things got a bit heated as my colleague tried to open the car boot to get his footballs out. The taxi driver hit his phone out of his hand and cracked the screen. The police came and the taxi driver told them my colleague had hit him and the local witnesses backed the driver. He had to pay the taxi driver a large fare to get away with it.

People may treat foreigners differently, but I've met so many kind-hearted people who would do anything to help you. After crashing my motorbike in Phuket, I lay at the side of the road and a Thai lady came to clean my wounds and called an ambulance. In my experience, the good people have always outweighed the bad, but you need to be wary.

Off the Pitch

It can be hard switching off from football, especially without family or friends around. Initially, coaches without family may end up spending a lot of time alone, away from work. This gives you more time to reflect, develop yourself, and do your own thing. But it may not suit people who need constant social interaction. Michael says being single abroad can be challenging.

Being single can get lonely. Your work keeps you occupied, and you've got friends as well. But when I'm off, other people are working; and when other people are off, I'm working. If you're a young coach it's fine, but it's more difficult if you're getting older and your close friends are married. They've got their families to look after so sometimes you're restricted with options, socially.

Simon warns not to let the loneliness lead you astray, especially when you've got a partner at home.

Stay out of the bars. The best advice someone gave me about moving to Asia was to get my wife out quickly because it gives you a focus. You don't get drawn off in another direction because some pretty girl talks to you – it's going to happen.

You're young and high profile in football – people know who you are. You can get yourself in a massive amount of trouble and that affects your home life. Your family is relying on you to do this job and to provide. If you're using that job and the profile to 'go and have a bit of fun', it's a nightmare waiting to happen.

Simon learnt this the hard way in his first role abroad.

A nightclub owner said, "Come to my club." We had just played the Suzuki Cup semi-final and were going home in the morning. It wasn't a big drinking night and we were out of there by 11 pm. There was a girl in that club who targeted me because I was high profile in Indonesia. I didn't click onto it because I wasn't of the mindset that I'm someone people know. It was my first job. I was still just a kid from Sussex.

I had a photo with her like I did everybody else but – stupidly – I leaned into her and put my arm around her. When that photo was taken, she uploaded it to social media that night and she had over 500,000 followers. The caption read, "It's Coach McMenemy, he's come to see me. I'm going to Manila to start something."

Simon noticed something wasn't right the next morning at the airport.

I noticed that everybody was looking at me – not Phil Younghusband, Neil Etheridge, the good-looking guys – I was thinking this is really weird. I got to the gate and Sarah called me from the UK, "Have a good night last night, did you?" I said, "What do you mean? We were out with the players. Did you see the pictures?" She said, "Yeah, I saw the pictures. Who is the girl?" I replied, "What girl? What are you talking about?" She responded angrily, "That girl – you need to check the internet", and slammed the phone down. I typed my name into Google and almost every news source in Jakarta said: "Simon McMenemy in nightclub meet up with Indonesian celebrity model." The picture was everywhere.

Simon learned a difficult lesson and approaches things differently now.

It's my fault; I put myself in a bad situation. Now when I have a picture, especially with a female, my hand goes behind my back. It was a valuable lesson. Don't put yourself in situations where you can make your life difficult and ruin your marriage.

It can be hard finding time to socialise as you're preparing for games or travelling at the weekend, while most people are out enjoying themselves. You also won't always get the same holidays if games are ongoing. Colum found it hard to spend time with his partner as the coach and teacher schedules didn't align.

In China, I was with my fiancée but I was working a lot. She was working during the day and I was coaching in the evenings. It was hard to spend time together.

It's important to plan your days off which is easy to forget. This gets you into the cycle of only working and not doing much else.

Find things you enjoy, away from work. Some roles abroad are very isolated, but in others you'll be surrounded by expats. Colum said there are lots of social groups you can get involved with, in big cities.

I went to Gaelic football twice in Cambodia. It's important to get away from the same people. There are big expat communities in all the big capital cities in Asia. It's great for getting out and meeting new people.

Try to find expat groups or other events where you can meet people. I met a great group of people at a Gaelic club in Kuwait and ended up playing tournaments in Oman and Bahrain. These events were amazing with thousands of expats from across the Middle East coming together to enjoy the weekend.

Make Friends

Michael thinks it's important to have friends away from football.

I'm football mad. My life is just football, football, and more football – which is not good. It's important to have good friends away from football when you're living abroad.

Cederique also recommends making friends.

If you're only focusing on your job, it's good for one or two months, but you will get homesick after. It's very important to build a group of friends that you can hang out with to switch off from work and explore the city. It makes it easier to adapt, and they can give you tips on living abroad.

A work-life balance is important for Sam when coaching abroad.

Try to get a work-life balance because that can often get overlooked. You go abroad and you're very keen. You want to do as much coaching as possible, and then you end up working six-day weeks. You need to get out and socialise. Make mates, whether that's through playing football, your colleagues, or going down to the pub; whatever it is that you like doing.

Make sure that you can separate yourself from work, so that when you're at work, you're fresh and you're on it, and when you're away from work, you're enjoying yourself. Make the most of the situation because you've committed to being away from your friends, family, and home. You've got to try to enjoy it and make the best of it. Otherwise, it's a waste of time.

Football won't be there for you when you're sick, nor keep you company or support you. You need hobbies and a social support network when you're feeling down. Football can give you a great life, but don't let it be the only thing in your life!

Missing Out

Hugging loved ones while saying goodbye is the hardest part of leaving home. It gets harder each time, as life progresses. It makes you question what you're doing, but it inspires you to make the most of the experience and motivates you to make your family proud.

Colum didn't see his family for years due to Covid-19.

Being away from my family is tough. I didn't see my two nieces for two years. I missed the rest of my family too.

The further you move from your family, the harder it is to see them time-wise and financially. The time difference also makes it difficult to talk, depending on where you are, and it's been hard for Colum to watch big European games.

It's not easy having to stay awake until 3 am to watch the Champions League!

Scott misses his family at home, but modern technology helps him stay connected.

You've moved away from your family, friends, and home. You're not part of the weekly sessions at the pub anymore but thankfully – with modern technology – you can stay in touch.

I can't imagine what it must have been like, years ago, when you had to write letters home. Nowadays it's much better, and you can easily video call your family and friends. It's still tough and, despite advances in technology, it hasn't stopped Sam from missing key moments in his family's life.

Missing weddings, funerals, birthdays, big family moments, and people growing up. You don't notice it when you go back for Christmas. Since I've moved back permanently, you realise more of the details you've missed. When you come home for two weeks, you don't realise the impact that has had when you've been abroad. That is the difficulty of being away from friends and family and missing key milestones in people's lives.

Moving away from home teaches you vital life skills like cooking, money management, and signing contracts. It also makes you appreciate your family and home more. You soak up every moment you spend with them on the rare occasions you're home. It makes you realise what's most important in life.

Challenges

Settling down abroad is tough due to issues surrounding residency, and you can't always pick where you work. Some coaches have partners who work online, which makes it easier to accept jobs abroad, plus online projects are also useful for bringing in money when you find yourself out of work.

Living abroad suits single coaches who don't mind moving around and having exciting experiences in different countries. It can be more challenging to make it work with a family. Colum knows how expensive education can be if you've got a child at school.

A lot of coaches want to move abroad with two kids and a partner. Schooling is expensive in these countries. The partner needs a job and the salaries, aren't going to cover that expense – unless it's a high-profile coaching position.

If you have a partner who is a qualified teacher, they could get a job at an international school. Some international schools offer reduced school fees for the children of their employees. Other coaches base their families in one location so their children can get a good education while they work elsewhere.

Sam has seen different ways to make it work with couples moving abroad together.

I've met people where the wife was a teacher and the husband followed her to Hong Kong. He was a former player and was looking for work as a coach. We had one coach in the HKFA from Spain whose wife came with him. There are lots of different situations. In any situation, having your partner there is a massive help.

Simon advises first team Head Coaches to settle in before bringing their family out.

Don't bring your family straight away – stick it out for the first month or two – to get your feet under the table. No owner wants to be dealing with your wife's requests. They've signed you, not your wife, you have to ease that into the deal. You want to set off on the right foot and show them you're committed. I'll be away from my family and focus on the job. Just stick me in an apartment and don't worry about my family. Let me get on the training pitch and start working.

For a player, it's easier to negotiate because the Head Coach is saying, "That's the only guy I want." When you're a coach, it doesn't often happen like that. There are many more coaches out there that don't have jobs than guys who have jobs. There's a conveyor belt. There are always coaches who will take your place quickly.

Simon knows showing your commitment and the quality of your work strengthens your position when making requests.

Then, slowly, as you start to gain the trust of the players, good feedback goes back to the bosses, and the boss starts saying nice things to you. Maybe they get you a nice car or allow you to go away on a training camp somewhere. Once you start to feel that trust, then you can say, "Boss, my wife's coming next week. Can I move to the house now? Would you mind paying for the ticket that you agreed to?" If you try to push too much too early, especially as a coach, you start becoming a bit of a problem. It can then cause problems in your family life.

Cederique said your partner needs to keep themselves busy when they don't have a child or job.

One of the challenges is work. If your partner is sitting in the room all day, they will get homesick and not like it there. She needs a group of friends and activities to do, so she's not only watching Netflix and getting bored.

Getting a visa for your partner can be tough, as Cederique discovered.

My partner's visa was an issue because, for Belgians in China, the visa is quite strict. She could only get a visa for one month. Every month she was flying to Hong Kong to get a new visa. Financially, we didn't earn a lot of money from her salary because all the money went to the visa, but her job wasn't about the money. It was about her being busy, having friends, and feeling good there.

Support Network

Having a partner with him has been key for Cederique.

It's very good having your partner there. If you have a long day and you're always thinking about football, football, football, and you're getting a little bit frustrated, it's nice to come home and say, "Let's go to the city." Going to eat something nice, taking a walk, or going to the cinema. It's nice spending time with somebody you love. I feel her support.

Having a partner from Hong Kong made all the difference for Sam when he moved there. His partner's family also lived close by, which made the transition easier.

Having family there is a big help. You've got people that you can speak to and bounce ideas off at family dinners.

Scott says you need a life off the pitch, and family plays a huge part.

Life isn't a dress rehearsal; you only get one chance. Family has got to be important. We try to live a good family life behind closed doors. We enjoy the holidays, birthdays,

Christmases, and movie nights with pizza. We don't have phones at the table in the evenings.

A player might not have performed at training, and I'm not happy with him. I don't bring the complaints into the house and drop them on everyone else... Not that anybody's interested in my house. You've got to find that balance. You can't be happy by only winning football games and not having anything at home. But also, having everything at home and not having anything outside of it – does that satisfy you too?

Simon's family help to release him from the pressures of the job.

Once you get to places where there are obstacles, and there are things you're going to have to deal with, there is nothing better than coming home to your family after work. I have a young son. He doesn't care whether I win or lose. He doesn't care that I'm under pressure from my boss. He just wants me to play with him for the next hour.

After playing with him, I'm ready for the next day. It gives you a sense of perspective. It helps me stay grounded, regain focus, and puts emotions to one side; not get too caught up in the fact the referee cost us, or the game was bought. It's the best medicine in the world.

You need coping mechanisms, and for Simon, family plays a vital role.

Doing it on your own under pressure – it's really hard. It takes its toll. You have to find your way of coping with it, there will always be pressure in the game. Winning's easy – you go home, sleep like a baby, and you get money in the morning. But you're going to lose games which is catastrophic and it's all on your shoulders. You have to plan for that and how you will recover, personally. Family plays a massive part in my recovery.

Simon also plays golf to take his mind off football.

It's healthy to have an escape. I can't think about football when I'm playing golf, otherwise I'll be in the trees all the time. It helps me calm down and focus; try to get to the green now. I've got to do this swing and I can't think about football at the same time.

Life Decisions

Simon would struggle without his family.

I can't stress how important it is. I couldn't do what I do without the support of my wife. She's my biggest fan and my biggest support. You need that. When you're on the other side of the world and it's not going well. If you don't have a support network, you don't have a fallback. You're in an apartment in a strange country, staring at the ceiling. You're wondering why you didn't win, and you're worried about getting sacked in the morning.

Family helps Simon put things into perspective.

If I get sacked, so what? We can go home to a country I love, surrounded by family. Once you go through a few sackings, you realise it's not that bad. The anticipation over the sacking is much worse than the actual fallout of it happening. It gives you a bit of impetus to go in a different direction. When one door closes, another door opens. Sometimes, when you're on your own, things seem a lot more life or death. But family is life or death... football and jobs aren't.

Simon has turned down national team jobs due to his family.

The first one I turned down was the Pakistan national team. They sent me the contract and it was good money. More money than I'd earned before. I thought about my wife in Pakistan. At the time, it was just me and her, and she's blonde. I couldn't imagine the life that she would have. I'd be away with the national team for a week or three weeks in other countries. I wasn't prepared to put her through it.

Simon also turned down the chance to sign for a South African club.

There was a potential move to the South African Premier League. It was a good club and league. If I had done well, I could have maybe got into the Middle East or Europe. But it was when the agent said, "Don't forget, your house needs a panic room." I asked, "What does my house need a panic room for?" I'm not going to a league or country where my family needs a panic room.

As a Head Coach, you're away every other weekend with the team for three to five days at a time. People know you're away and your house needs a panic room. They said, "Oh, carjackings don't happen that often." The fact that they don't happen often means they happen. In the end, we discussed it and we were trying for a baby. A lot was going on, and I wasn't prepared to take that risk.

Life Changing

People can have different experiences of the same country, and places evolve over time. You can ask people who have lived in a country, and read all the information online, but the ultimate research is going to experience it yourself, before deciding whether to move there.

There are pros and cons to anywhere you live. Feeling the atmosphere and seeing day-to-day life is critical for determining if it would suit you to live there. It's also important to remember you will be working there, so factor in day-to-day life as a coach and not as a tourist. You're there to work, and you don't get much free time as a coach, which limits the activities you can do. Travelling and living abroad teaches you some of the best lessons you can get. You learn about different cultures, meet new people, and see new ways of doing things. It can be a release from the social pressures and expectations at home. The experiences and life lessons have opened my mind and shaped me into the person I am today. It's not for everyone, but if you don't try, you'll never know. It could be the best decision you ever make!

Chapter 17. Colum's Journey: Head Coach Springboard in Cambodia

Northern Ireland

It seems UEFA Pro Coach, Colum Curtis, was always destined to become a football manager. His brother got him into the game at a young age and he loved it!

I've always been mad into Football Manager. It started with Premier Manager in 1997 when I was eight years old. I spent many hours of my life over the next 15 years playing those games.

Colum's coaching career transferred into the real world when his brother asked him to help out at the club he played for.

My brother was coaching at one of the grassroots clubs that me and my Dad played for. I went down to help him one session, caught the bug, and I haven't stopped since. If my brother didn't get me into it, then life could have been very different. I also helped out the school team a year below me and travelled to games, which I really enjoyed.

Colum had to overcome the devastation of losing his father at a young age. He was living in Newcastle but moved home to be with his family. This helped him get more time on the grass due to his contacts at home.

I went to Newcastle University for a year to study sports coaching. When my Dad passed away, I came back home. The contact time I got at grassroots over the three years at home was priceless.

Colum's family has always been hugely supportive throughout his coaching journey.

My family encouraged me. They always said, "Go for it, be fearless, and say yes to the job." Having good people and energisers around you helps; people that will always push you and help you during the tough times.

Colum was coaching part-time alongside a full-time job to make ends meet. The job helped Colum grow and learn from a brilliant supervisor.

I was a training consultant with Save The Children. It involved delivering a training project in schools. I was only 22 and it was very daunting. The first school I delivered in had my old nursery teacher in attendance. She was 30 years older than me and I had to give her advice. There were people with over 20 years of experience and PhDs. I remember thinking, what am I doing here? After doing it… your confidence grows.

My supervisor's leadership skills and ability to engage a room full of people from different socioeconomic backgrounds, cultures, and opinions were nothing short of amazing. She would observe me and give advice that would go on to have a major impact on how I approach the management of staff and players to this day.

Colum would often sit at work dreaming of coaching abroad.

Every day, I thought I need to get these coaching badges and experience. I would spend lunchtime at work on the computer looking at coaching jobs around the world. I finished work at 4.30pm and ran up the road in my shirt and tie to get the session set up for 5pm. I was doing that three or four times a week and then taking the kids at the weekend.

USA

Colum's first adventure abroad was a summer in the US.

I reached out to the only coach I knew abroad, who was in America. He got me out coaching for two summers. I had started coaching in schools before, which was great. I loved America and met one of my best friends there.

Colum always knew he wanted to coach abroad.

When I first started seeing my partner, Sinead, she was studying languages. She wanted to go abroad and had lived in France and Spain. I always said if I can get a job coaching football and it's on the moon, I'll be going. I didn't think it would be China. It was a bit from leftfield, but I saw it on a job site and chucked my CV in.

Colum got offered the position when he was in the US. He flew home for three days to get his visa and set off for a new adventure in China.

Beijing, China

Colum was Assistant Director of Coaching at a grassroots club with 16 full-time European coaches. Colum learnt a lot from the experience.

It taught me to be disciplined. I wanted to be the first one in the office in the morning. I got my work done so if the coaches or bosses needed anything I was there to help them. We had a good group of coaches who wanted to improve.

The sessions in China were also testing, at times, as you had to coach a range of ages, abilities, and motivations.

I was always being tested with sessions. I never coached the little ones but after one of the lads got sacked, we almost lost our contract with a school. The boss said, "Colum, you go in and coach it for a couple of weeks." I was getting advice from the lads and I went in and faced a load of toddlers. Coaching the youngest age groups is the toughest coaching you can do, but I enjoyed it.

Working in schools teaches you to be adaptable and how to engage with young people, which helps at all levels of the game.

There are 25 kids and you've only got a small hall. Five of them like football and the rest don't. You have to try and engage them. It's a good challenge and I always tried to go back to the office with a smile on my face.

Colum feels his stint in China was great for his development. It was challenging, but it was great managing coaches and getting more time on the grass. It also proved he could adapt to life working in Asia.

I went to a hospital in my second year in China with chest pains. They were saying you need to chill out and stop working so much. The hours were long and I didn't have time to do anything else, but I wouldn't change it. Those sacrifices early on help you further down the line.

Irish Football Association (IFA)

After three years in China, Colum and his partner decided to move back to Northern Ireland for a year.

My partner started teaching kindergarten and loved it, so she wanted to go home and train to be a teacher. She was a bit isolated in Beijing which was tough with my work schedule. I was also beginning to find work less challenging, so we decided to go home.

During his time in China, Colum came home to do his UEFA A licence which put him on the IFA's radar.

I went to China and got a load of experience. When I came back to do my A licence, my assessment feedback was good. This made a good impression on the coach education department who recommended me to the IFA Elite Performance staff.

Colum was in regular contact with the IFA coaches during his time in China and put on a session to showcase his work.

I went for two weeks with Jim Magilton and Declan Devine and put on a few sessions. They were happy and offered me the job. I wouldn't have been at that level if I had stayed at home and not learnt from the Director and coaches in Beijing.

Colum learnt a lot from the IFA's UEFA Pro licence coaches, including Jim Magilton. Jim had played in the Premier League and managed the likes of Ipswich Town and Queens Park Rangers.

Jim implemented a fantastic programme which the country didn't have previously. The players were training together three times a week, had training camps in Spain and the Middle East, and were playing against Premier League clubs, Real Madrid, and other nations. He wanted the best coaches, analysts, strength and conditioning, physiotherapy, and did everything to give the players the best chance of succeeding.

Working alongside Jim changed Colum's views on youth development.

I was taking the U16s for a possession practice in a very tight area and I was delighted with how it was going. Then Jim walked onto the pitch and you could see some of the players crumble. After the practice, I said to Jim, "That was going great until you arrived." In my mind, I was questioning whether he was too demanding of them. He replied, "That's not good, because I want them to be playing in front of a full Windsor Park and be in English senior dressing rooms within the next two years."

I instantly thought he was right. These lads needed to be ready to cope with the pressures that senior football brings. That was the moment it became clear I would have to be a bit more demanding. I had thought, they were only kids, but that was an eye-opener of what it takes to make it at the top level. Fast forward two years and a few of those lads had already made their senior debuts for Northern Ireland; Isaac Price made his Premier League debut for Everton against Arsenal, and Conor Bradley made his Champions League debut for Liverpool in a win against AC Milan at the San Siro.

Phnom Penh, Cambodia

Colum's wife got offered a job at an international school in Phnom Penh, and Colum researched the Cambodian league right away.

Sinead got offered a job in Cambodia to teach. I did some research on the Cambodian League, despite how much I loved working in Northern Ireland with the rain, snow, and six layers on. I saw the level of the coaches and thought there would be a chance to get into professional football there. If not, I had to go and support Sinead as it was a great opportunity for her, and she made the sacrifice to move to Beijing with me.

Colum was meeting people as soon as his feet hit the ground in Cambodia. This groundwork led to a job at topflight club, Svay Rieng.

I did a scouting report for Conor Nestor, a Head Coach from Limerick. I delivered a session and he got me in as an Assistant for the final four months of the season. I loved getting to know the players and testing myself with national team players and foreign players who had played at decent levels. It was a successful season for the club. We won the league, losing only once all season, and lost in the Cup Final on penalties.

Colum took a risk leaving the champions, but he only had to wait a few days before being snapped up by the topflight team who finished third.

We couldn't agree on a new contract, but I was happy with my work and was doing some coach education on the side. Two days later, I got offered a role at Visakha.

First Season

Signing as Head Coach at Visakha FC was a special moment for Colum.

It was a dream come true. A moment I had thought about for as long as I can remember.

On arrival, Colum immediately needed to raise the standards.

I observed the first session and the standard of training needed to improve from the session design to the player's application. Players were taking their jeans off at the side of the pitch and running in when the session had already started. We were training on a 5-a-side pitch because the stadium pitch was under maintenance. I said I wouldn't be leading any sessions until we had a 11v11 grass pitch. It was sorted within a day.

Colum's first signing was a friend from back home.

I called Stephen Corner, who is a physiotherapist and strength and conditioning coach with 10 years of senior football experience in England, India, and Thailand. I needed Stephen badly as there was nothing in place for strength and conditioning and the medical care for the players was non-existent. We introduced nutrition plans and educated the players on the importance of taking care of their bodies away from the club and why we trained as we did. The players were used to 2.5 hour training sessions at medium to low intensity. Everything we did was new to them, from video analysis to gym work before training. We changed a lot in the first month.

Despite the improvements, Colum felt they couldn't win the league title.

In my first board meeting, I made it clear that we didn't have the squad to compete for the league. I had come from the current champions and knew they were ahead of us in almost every department. They also had Privat Mbarga who was the best player in the league by a distance. Two years later, Privat moved to Bali United and played a key role in them winning the Indonesian league.

They needed new players but Colum felt they had a chance in the cup.

The squad I inherited needed an overhaul. We had 32 players who were all expecting to play. Players who weren't in my plans were released or sent to the academy if the club refused to release them. It wasn't only about playing ability, there were disciplinary issues in the squad too.

For the cup, I thought we had a chance as foreign players were ineligible which reduced our opponents' strength. In the league, you were allowed four foreigners on the pitch, but I mostly played with three, as some of the local players were slightly ahead of them.

Colum was summoned after a defeat in only his second game in charge.

We played two games, winning one and losing the second game 1-0, after conceding from a corner. I was called for a meeting the following day to explain our loss. I was shocked but I went in and showed them the video analysis of the opposition attacking corners that players were shown individually and collectively. Defensive set pieces were something that needed to be improved, as over 40% of goals conceded had come from set plays the previous season.

The previous fixture between the clubs was a 4-0 defeat but the board demanded results improved. It quickly became clear that our five-year plan of challenging for the league and AFC Cup wasn't my main priority. I called my agent that night and he told me to focus on winning games. From that moment on, I went away from implementing how I thought we needed to play to compete in future AFC Cup campaigns. I focused more on opposition weaknesses and our results improved.

Colum was putting in long hours to make his first big job a success.

I arrived at the stadium at 6.15am to get my tasks done, get an update from the physio, and meet the technical staff. I would meet the analyst, observe the players in the gym, and have chats with players individually. We trained at 8am and finished between 9.00am and 9.30am. We'd have lunch before meeting with staff to review the session. Afterwards, I'd fill in an individual practice report analysing players based on what I saw and staff feedback. We would then finalise the training plan for the next day.

I'd also have one-on-ones with players, do video work, and have discussions with staff about the starting team and plan for our next game. On other days, you'd have media, messages from the board, dealing with personal problems of players and staff, input on travelling for away games, and looking at potential transfer targets on Wyscout. The days were always busy and it was difficult switching off in the evening.

Hun Sen Cup

Visakha started their Hun Sen Cup campaign in the round of 16 against Tbong Khmum. Colum's team cruised to victory with a 4-1 first-leg win and an empathic 9-0 win in the second-leg. In the quarter-finals, they faced a much tougher test against reigning cup champions, Boeung Ket. The two teams couldn't be separated, drawing the first-leg 1-1, and the second-leg 3-3. The tie had to be settled on penalties with Visakha winning 4-3.

The games against Boeung Ket were frustrating because they were so clinical. They had the most prolific forward line in Cambodian Football in Chan Vathanka, Mat Norin, and Sieng Chantea. We controlled games which led teams to defend deep and counter which Boeung Ket did very well. We had the majority of the ball and chances and thankfully made it through. We knew we had a great chance of winning the cup!

Visakha faced second division team Prey Veng in the semi-final. Visakha dominated the game against a Prey Veng side that was on course for promotion to the topflight. The game finished 1-1 and Visakha prevailed 9-8 in a tense penalty shoot-out.

Prey Veng had a very exciting young team with pace all over the forward line. Their Goalkeeper Vireak Dara – who became Visakha's number 1 and the Cambodian National Team Goalkeeper – was 17 at the time, and had an unbelievable game. They went 1-0 up with a goal from Tola who won the golden boot. They sat on the edge of their box and tried to hold onto the lead. We had over 20 shots, and missed a penalty but eventually broke them down and managed to make our way to the final.

Visakha faced Nagaworld in the final – a good first division side – but Colum fancied their chances.

It was a tremendous feeling to be coaching in a cup final in my first season in charge. I was extremely confident going into the game and I knew the players were as well.

We knew Nagaworld would defend deep and look to hit us on the counter but we felt they lacked the pace needed to execute that game plan. Their players were good technically but individually they had a few players we could draw out of position. We identified a weakness on their right side and worked on exploiting it in training.

Colum tried to take the pressure off the players in the build-up.

This was the club's first major final, an opportunity to win their first-ever trophy, and a chance to qualify for the AFC Cup. I wanted to normalise our preparation for the game and not let the players get influenced too much by any noise from outside or pressure from within the club. The only thing we changed was staying in a hotel near the Olympic Stadium. We had to train at the stadium the night before so I didn't want the players stuck on a bus in traffic for hours the night before the game.

The team managed to pull off Colum's game plan in emphatic style.

I told the players to remain patient as we knew they'd sit back and try to frustrate us. We took the lead before half-time after a little bit of magic from our number 10, Keo Sokpheng. It wasn't a nervy game as they weren't troubling us. Shortly after half-time, we added a second with the goal coming down their right side as we had planned. The final was the most comfortable game in the latter stages of the competition.

Colum's side ran out 2-0 winners to become Hun Sen Cup Champions and secure the club's first major trophy in their history.

It was a strange feeling, almost like relief. I was so happy for the players; they received a lot of unfair criticism but I know how hard they trained every day. I was proud of where they had come from since the first day I walked in. We came a long way and winning the first trophy in the club's history was a proud moment.

Colum was sadly unable to share the moment with his family.

It was a shame that it was during the Covid-19 pandemic, as the stadium's capacity was limited to 10% but we still had around 5,000 in attendance. I know my family would've come from Ireland to watch the game if it wasn't for Covid. I had a video call with my brother on the pitch after the game which was nice. He watched it together with my uncles at home. I wish he could have been there. There was a party after, but I wasn't too interested; I had a beer and went home with my wife.

Colum was enjoying success on and off the pitch as his wife was enjoying life in Cambodia. Happy wife, happy life rings true for Colum.

Settling in and seeing Sinead happy with her school was great. She had a lot more friends in Cambodia than in China. Two of them even lived in our apartment block. The school was good and had a lot of foreign teachers, whereas she was alone in China while I was at work.

Season Review

Colum had doubted himself at the outset but managed to overcome it.

I was on the phone with Jim Magilton and didn't know what was going on initially. Senior football and millionaire owners who want to do this over five years. In the professional game, fans always question you. I'm quite strong mentally but self-doubt creeps in. I was only 30; can I do this? You need that self-belief and good people around you. What's the worst that can happen?

Dealing with the media was a big challenge for Colum initially.

I was getting interviews left, right, and centre. I'm confident talking to people about football. I was 30 when I got the job and I was getting battered by journalists and I didn't know what to say. Now I'm much more comfortable talking to the media.

The board and Colum didn't see eye to eye after their first defeat.

We had different views on the sporting direction of the club from the day of our first defeat and it was never going to be a smooth process. The CEO was the only person on the board that had an affiliation with football. He was a fan of the Premier League and was aware of Guardiola and Klopp having to make changes to the squads and structures of their clubs to continuously challenge. When the CEO was let go, things became more difficult.

Colum learnt a valuable lesson about trust and the power of winning.

I've learnt after speaking with Head Coaches at the top level and experiencing it myself: don't listen to what anyone tells you about long-term plans, just do everything you can to win the games, and work with people you trust.

The first season was a learning curve for Colum, finishing in fifth position in the league and winning the Hun Sen Cup.

It was a fantastic learning experience. I was delighted to end it with a trophy, as I know it's something many coaches go through their whole careers without achieving. Especially coming into a squad in which I hadn't signed any of the players. Overall, we implemented a professional environment and a clear playing philosophy in and out of possession, regardless of the system. But in football, you are only as good as your players, and I needed to overhaul the squad.

The lack of squad depth was clear to see against the league champions.

Midway through the season, we played an away game against my former club Svay Rieng. We were 2-1 up and playing well. We missed a big chance to make it 3-1 and then after half-time they brought on two of the starting front three for the Cambodian National team. Our boys were tiring as we pressed so aggressively and the pitch was heavy. I remember looking at our bench several times. I knew we lacked depth, but it was most evident in the big games.

Second Season

Colum was looking forward to his second season as Head Coach. He managed to recruit the players he needed to compete for the title.

I was excited to get the new season underway and was hoping to get a bit more responsibility for the recruitment of players. I wanted a total of 13 players which would be well within budget with the players we were releasing. I managed to bring in Marcus Haber, Thierry ChanthaBin, a French-Khmer player who had spent the previous seasons playing top tier in Malaysia and Thailand, and Charlie Machell who I worked with at Svay Rieng. When I spoke to them, I told them we would be right up there challenging for the league title.

We released a lot of players although not all that I wanted, unfortunately. But getting those three players in was key to our success that season. We also added a highly professional Goalkeeping Coach in Johann Noetzel. Goalkeeping quality in Cambodia is generally quite poor. They don't get exposed to good coaching from a young age so the basics aren't there, even for pros, so it was great to get Johann in.

Former West Brom and Crewe Alexandra player, Marcus Haber, proved to be a great signing for Visakha.

I spoke to a few people and they all told me what a great pro he is. I knew the players would benefit from watching how he goes about his work on and off the pitch. We changed shape from a 3-4-1-2 to a 3-4-2-1 to accommodate Marcus. He wasn't a prolific scorer throughout his career but he is a complete forward. He could run channels, drop into pockets and get on the half turn, hold it up, or go by players 1v1.

He had to adapt as his 6'4" frame and strength were a much bigger advantage in Cambodia than they had been in Canada and Europe. His aerial presence would get him a lot more goals. Playing two 10s off Marcus kept him in more threatening goal-scoring positions. It also allowed more players to get around him if we played directly to him and relieved some of the running he had to do defensively. He scored a lot of vital goals for us that season.

Colum also knew the league even better after one full season in charge.

After my first season, I got to know the league and opposition a lot better. Everything plays a factor, including the weather. For two away games, I asked the players to ignore our principles due to the pitch conditions, as we went a lot more direct. We won one of those games 5-1 against league champions Boeung Ket, which was their biggest ever home defeat. This was a big change from the season before when we lost 1-0 in our second game and the board called me in for that meeting.

The team was having a great season at the top of the table, after a long unbeaten run, but sadly this wasn't enough for Colum to keep his job.

It was disappointing and a big shock to get sacked. We had just come off a good away win against a top team and were on course to win the league and favourites to win the cup again. I also turned down a lucrative contract in another country to finish the job I had started here. To win three trophies out of four in my first two seasons would have been a dream start to life as a Head Coach. After I left, they finished third in the league and I was gutted for the players. They deserved to win it!

High Expectations

Colum feels clubs that invest a lot are more impatient.

If clubs are investing heavily, usually they want more involvement. This may even involve team selection and if you don't follow orders, then you could be gone whether you're winning or not. Speaking with coaches at clubs with lower expectations, they are given much more time to implement their ideas.

Colum, sadly, wasn't given the time to finish the league season.

I lost one game in 11 months and still got sacked. The club had three different Head Coaches within six months after I got sacked. Many players from my first season were playing in the second division in Cambodia. The club eventually released them after I had gone.

The club and I had very different views on the sporting policies and structures at the club. It's not my club and they have a way in which they want to work so there are no hard feelings. This is football. The board – on a personal level – was always very nice and welcoming, it was just from a sporting perspective where things differed between us. I left on good terms with everyone. I have been back to the stadium since and received a warm welcome. I'll always have a strong bond with the players.

The experience has taught Colum what to look for in the future.

I need a major say in the recruitment of players, as it's vital doing your due diligence. Some teams will sign a player based on a video from a cowboy agent sent directly to the owner or board who doesn't have any experience in this field. They will sign a player without knowing the player's previous injury record, if he was banned for ill-discipline, or was disruptive at former clubs. In Asia, your foreign players can make or break you. Some set the bar on and off the pitch. Others who have bags of ability, but haven't cut it in their own countries, arrive in Asia and cause disruption. Thankfully, I haven't had that yet and aim to keep avoiding it with good recruitment.

It was a great time for Colum to get into Cambodian football.

Cambodia's professional game is still in its infancy. Years ago, clubs were all playing at the Olympic Stadium. Now every club has to have its own stadium and there are owners throwing money here and there. We had a 10,000-seater stadium and state-of-the-art facilities. Salaries for the players are going up and I can see it becoming very competitive in the coming years.

Colum's Head Coach chance came much sooner than expected but you can't turn down a rare opportunity to break into the professional game.

There aren't many opportunities given to young coaches at home, unless you bring teams up. Initially, I wanted to get into the professional game as an Assistant to learn from someone. Then I moved to Cambodia and now suddenly I'm the Head Coach. That's not happening at home unless you played for a big club. I always tell myself how fortunate I am to be working in the game I've loved my whole life.

Chapter 18. Steve's Journey: Title Wins across South East Asia

Steve Darby grew up in Liverpool and was an avid fan of the great club at the end of the Shankly era. He loved playing football but claims a lack of ability was what led him down the coaching route at an early age.

Bahrain and Australia

Steve qualified as a Physical Education teacher but only lasted a term as a PE teacher in 1978. This was due to his college lecturer, Merv Beck, informing him of a player-coach role in Bahrain. The role involved working with a team and assisting the national team. The salary was four times his teaching wage but Steve would have coached for free, such was his passion for the game. He learnt a lot from the experience, including working with the Bahrain Head Coach, Jack Mansell.

I was 23 and loved every minute of the place. I am still in contact with some of my ex-players. I taught myself Arabic and also read the Quran. In general, I found the Bahrainis to be great people.

Bahrain was playing the United Arab Emirates when trouble broke out in the crowd.

They don't mess about there... in came the riot police with sticks and tear gas which was ok until the wind changed direction. I now know what tear gas does to your eyes and throat!

Steve went back to England and became the third-youngest to complete his full coaching badge at the age of 24. After this, he set off for his only offer, which was in Australia. Steve enjoyed Australia so much that he stayed for 17 years. He worked with Sydney Olympic, suffered his first sacking, and worked for the Australian Football Federation.

The highlight was being Youth Technical Director, but the lowlight was learning about football politics. Anyone who says football shouldn't be involved in politics is either naive or has no concept of politics and the financial influence in football.

Malaysia and Vietnam

Steve's friend, Ron Smith, asked if he wanted to spend six weeks coaching Johor FA in Malaysia in 1998. It was a great offer and opportunity so he went immediately. Steve impressed by winning promotion, the Malaysian Cup, and earned a further two-year deal. He led the team to the league title the following season.

I enjoyed my three years in Johor until I was sacked while we were third in the league. I had a great manager who was CEO off the pitch and I was CEO on it. Winning the Malaysia Cup from the second division has never been repeated. It was a great achievement and brings back memories of my captain Darren Stewart who sadly passed away at a young age.

Steve went on to Vietnam where he won the country's first gold medal at the South East Asian Games. This was a huge achievement for the women's national team and he fell in love with Vietnam. He has fond memories looking back.

I remember the pride on the players' faces. They loved playing for their country and this victory meant everything to them.

After winning gold, Steve returned to England to work in the youth setup at Sheffield Wednesday. He was working long hours and spent many freezing days on the pitch during the winter months.

Home United, Singapore

When Steve was in Sheffield, he got offered a great deal in Singapore. It only required working three hours a day in the sun. He was also told that he'd never become a first team coach in professional leagues in England. This was due to not having had a distinguished playing career which he agrees was true at the time. Moving to Singapore wasn't a hard decision for Steve to make.

I got paid four times the salary and 40 fewer hours of work a week!

Steve enjoyed a successful three-year spell in Singapore with Home United. They won the league, the FA Cup twice, and reached the AFC Cup semi-final. Steve says it was the people around him that made them successful in their double-winning season.

We had good players and great leaders on and off the pitch in Aide Iskander and Subramani. We also had quality foreigners in Sutee Suksomkit, Egmat Gonzales, and Peres. Our administrators were excellent. They never once interfered with my job until the end of my tenure and that's why I left. We had great support staff in Rosli Dollah and Francis Thomas.

The spirit of the Home United team was also a key factor in their success.

We were winning 6-0 and battering a team. They got a breakaway and I saw seven players chasing back at full pace to stop their attack. That was the moment I realised how much they cared.

Steve had to make some tough decisions during his time there.

The hardest part was having to release players as we had a strict salary cap. It's never easy not renewing a contract. It confirmed my belief that you had to treat players as people first and footballers second.

Travelling to play AFC Cup games in Syria and Libya was an experience for Steve and the Home United team.

Some of the away trips in the AFC were exciting such as Damascus and Tripoli. There were bullet holes in the dressing rooms in Tripoli. The Syrians did everything to upset us, especially how they treated us off the field. The trips to the Maldives were great – except for the Thai players, who got seasick on the water taxis.

Asian Adventure

After his spell in Singapore, Steve moved back to Malaysia where he spent three years at Perak. The team came second in the league, lost in the Malaysian Cup final, and qualified for the Asian Cup. Steve bravely gave a young keeper his debut in the Super Cup final victory.

The highlights were the Super Cup win versus Selangor in front of 100,000 people and giving an 18-year-old his debut in this game – Nasril Nourdin, the keeper.

While Steve was at the Asian Cup in Lebanon, he got a phone call from former England international, Peter Reid. He asked Steve to become his Assistant Coach with the Thailand National team, which he accepted. Steve spent three years working under Peter Reid, followed by Bryan Robson, the former England and Manchester United captain.

It was an education with two genuine football men who loved the game. They were highly professional and prepared well for every session. They also taught me the value of managing up.

The Thai national team played Liverpool in a friendly; it was an honour for Steve to play against his boyhood team.

It was the culmination of a dream. I am a Liverpool fan and would have given anything to play for or coach them but I wasn't good enough. To get a 1-1 draw was a fantastic feeling, especially as one of my favourite players scored for us, Sutee Suksomkit.

Following his spell in Thailand, Steve spent a year working for Everton in China, followed by another spell in Malaysia with Kelantan. He was then offered the chance to become Assistant Coach of Mumbai City in India for the inaugural season of the Indian Super League. He worked with Peter Reid once again and players such as Nicolas Anelka, Freddie Ljungberg, and Manuel Friedrich.

Mumbai City FC was a very professionally-run club where the players were treated properly. Anelka was not only a fantastic player but a super professional and also very humble… he was almost shy. The public and media image of Anelka is not the reality.

Laos World Cup Qualifiers

Steve was appointed Technical Director of the Laos Football Federation, and led their 2018 World Cup qualifying campaign.

A highlight was playing against Korea and seeing the gulf between a top nation and one that was struggling to survive economically. It was fascinating. Korea had two EPL players in Son Heung-min and Ki Sung-yueng and a couple more playing in the Bundesliga. All our players were amateur or semi-pro on a maximum salary of 200 USD a month. You can prepare all you want tactically, but if a player pushes past their marker and can't be caught, then everything falls apart. Set pieces were interesting versus Korea... we never got any! Their keeper didn't touch the ball until the 29th minute. I knew we would struggle near the end as fitness was going to be a factor, so I didn't make any subs until the 60th minute. But it made no difference… they scored four in the last 15 minutes as the lads were exhausted.

In another World Cup Qualifying game, Laos scored to make it 2-1 in the 83rd minute against Myanmar. Unfortunately, they couldn't hold on, with Myanmar equalising in the 87th minute.

It was frustrating as there is always the cynical part of the brain saying how did such a soft goal get allowed.

Steve got the nation's first World Cup qualifying points, which meant a lot to the people of Laos. He also led the team to its highest-ever FIFA ranking. After Steve left, four players were charged with match-fixing, and (years later) 45 Laos players got banned for life by FIFA.

I had been warned that two of our players were fixing. I couldn't drop them as they were easily in the best eleven. They trained hard and never let me down in official games. I did see a few mistakes in away friendlies that were dodgy. After I left, four players were suspended for life. Two I know, the other two shocked me and to this day I think one of them was set up. You have to remember that the bookies can also threaten or set up players who refuse to fix as a warning to others. Also, why should unpaid footballers not be corrupt when the police and politicians were far more corrupt? The culture of the nation dictates corruption.

What a journey it has been, spanning over 40 years of coaching abroad.

Being a pro in the game as either a player or coach is a great lifestyle. There are millions of people who love the game and it will give you the greatest moments of your life. You will meet wonderful people from all cultures and experience incredible situations. Such as experiencing tear gas in the Middle East, a crowd of 1,000 monks in Thailand, the Bohmos in Malaysia, or drinking Kava in Fiji.

So many wonderful stories and valuable experiences to learn from.

Chapter 19. Getting Jobs and Succeeding Worldwide

Getting jobs and succeeding around the world isn't easy. The coaches we've interviewed have developed successful academies, national projects, and won titles in multiple countries. Here's their advice on building credibility, getting jobs in professional football, and succeeding worldwide.

Credibility

To get yourself into a position to succeed you must first build credibility. You need people to trust in you and believe that you're the right person for the job. It's the key to getting in the door, staying there, and progressing to higher levels. Three layers of credibility include profile, performance, and reputation. All three interlink and impact one another.

1. Profile

Your profile is made up of what's on your CV, which can get you in the door but it takes more to stay there. Having a CV with many qualifications, job titles, responsibilities, and successes at renowned organisations helps you stand out. The coaches have developed their profiles in various ways.

Personal Profile

Your CV and application documents should be tailored to the organisation's requirements. Having values that match the organisation's, or how they see the game, makes you an attractive prospect. Scott's passion for developing young players made him a good fit for the Philippines who wanted a younger squad. A rare skillset that complements those in the organisation also helps you stand out as we discussed in chapter 4. If recruiters feel you're a good fit, it massively increases your chances of getting jobs.

Qualifications

Licences are essential as many associations require coaches to have a certain licence to lead teams in competitions. Scott knows the importance of getting the licences and revalidating them.

They're critical because you can't be permitted to coach without them.

Despite this, it's not always a deal-breaker for coaches as discussed in chapter 2. Regardless, it's best to meet the qualification requirements and keep your licences valid to increase your opportunities. Having qualifications may present opportunities, but you need to deliver when given the chance. An A licence coach may seem better than a B licence coach but that's not always the case in practice. Qualifications can help you stand out on paper but it takes a lot more to succeed in the game.

Experience

The location and level of your experiences are crucial. Scott believes owners will go for coaches who have worked in big clubs or leagues.

The coach that followed me at Buriram was with Real Madrid reserves and had worked with Jose Mourinho. That's massive. They'll go with someone that's worked at a high level.

Steve says you need to be realistic. Working at top professional academies in Europe doesn't mean you'll walk into a top job in Asia. Scott knows you need to build your profile first.

It's difficult getting into the top Asian leagues unless you come with something big on your CV. It can be a big club as an Assistant, good results in another league, or you start in a lower league and get promoted.

Colum believes knowing the players and league helped him get his first Head Coach role in Cambodia. Scott knows this is an important factor.

Clubs will go with someone that knows the league and club well.

Working at higher levels unlocks the door to better jobs. Scott, Simon, and Steve have all coached National Teams and big clubs in South East Asia. Scott reckons having experience at various levels makes his profile more appealing to owners.

It's my diverse background. I've worked at every level of football with credible teams. I've been in AFC Champions League elimination rounds, World Cup qualifiers, and won back-to-back promotions. Taking a team from nothing to something, working with academy teams and youth national teams. That diversity mixed with results helps.

Working at senior level in a good club or a federation creates a strong profile when looking for senior positions. Coaching at renowned academies will make your profile appealing to academy recruiters. Big organisations, well-known competitions, and working with respected coaches boosts your credibility. Having well-known people in your network also means you can get better references. Credible people who will put their name on the line to vouch for you strengthens your profile.

Job Success

A role involving big responsibility and success boosts a coach's profile. People focus on titles such as Head Coach or Director but titles mean different things across organisations. Titles may appeal to recruiters but the responsibilities and achievements are vital.

Being responsible for planning, delivering, and reflecting on sessions for a high-level and successful team boosts credibility. As does creating a pathway that sees players progress into the first team. Recruiting and managing staff in a team that exceeds expectations proves your qualities as a Director. Your roles and achievements show your suitability and what you'd be able to do for the organisation hiring you.

Great achievements make you stand out. Simon was the youngest National Team Head Coach in the world and led the Philippines to the semi-finals of the Suzuki Cup for the first time in their history. Scott got Buriram United into the quarter-finals of the AFC Champions League and they were ranked 7th best in Asia. He also got Ubon United back-to-back promotions to the topflight from the bottom league. Sam's Hong Kong FA was voted AFC Member Association of the year and he created programmes for over 4,000 players. Colum won league and cup titles in Cambodia and Steve Darby won titles in Malaysia and Singapore.

Success can be trophies, keeping an unfancied team up, or any achievement that meets or exceeds the owner's expectations. It can also be stats such as win percentage, number of first team academy graduates, or any other positive statistic that's valued by recruiters. These achievements show a level of competence that boosts a coach's credibility but it's only the starting point. If you have a great profile but your current performance and reputation in the game are poor, you won't last very long. Invest time in developing your performance and earning a positive reputation to make a lasting impression.

2. Performance

You can gain credibility by having a good profile and reputation in the game, but Colum doesn't believe it will last if you're not performing.

You would get found out very quickly if your standards weren't high or you think you're going to get by on reputation. The players will judge you on what they see, regardless of what you've done in the past.

You may have succeeded previously, but every new role presents different challenges that coaches don't always get right. To perform, coaches need to make the best of what they've got, to meet or exceed the objectives set. The coaches have highlighted the main factors required to perform and progress in the game.

Job Selection

Job selection is a critical factor in determining your success. Research the situation you're walking into. Find out why the previous coach left and if it's a good club to work for. It's also vital to know what stage the project is at and the resources you will have to meet the objectives set.

Scott had the budget, players, facilities, working environment, and owners he needed to succeed at Buriram United and Ubon United. Simon went into the Philippines National Team with a good core of players and exceeded expectations, which was a springboard for his career. Colum got his first Head Coach role at a club with one of the biggest budgets, which boosted his win percentage. This increased their chances of succeeding and attracting other clubs and federations.

Steve recommends finding an owner who has a long-term vision.

A sad reality is that "long-term" in club football in Asia is usually next week. Try to find intelligent owners who can see a job may take two years. The great football sides of the world have consistency of management at all levels.

Scott says your success all comes down to the control you're given.

Your measure of success in Asia is only based on one thing: it's the amount of control you have. You don't get control by shouting and screaming or saying, "You don't know anything about football. Leave this to me. You do your job." And I've heard people say that. That's a sure way to get yourself sacked.

The amount of control you have is dictated by the person who controls the club. If you don't have a relationship with that person, it's never going to work. The quicker you understand that, the better you'll be.

Get perspectives from people online, at the club, and inside the country, for an unbiased opinion. Visit the club, if you can, to meet the owners and see the day-to-day setup before deciding. Reaching out to a range of sources with inside knowledge and meeting them yourself can paint a clearer picture. Football can be a tough industry, so do everything you can to give yourself the best chance of succeeding.

Cultural Understanding

When arriving in a new country, Michael believes you have to understand the culture before finding the right approach.

You have to be very open-minded as a foreign coach coming to China. You've got fantastic experience but you're here to learn, respect, and understand the culture. Then you'll slowly implement some of your work and knowledge.

Michael found that – to succeed – you need to adapt your approach at times.

You might believe you know the best way of working. However, they are very insistent in their ways in China. Sometimes you need to know your priority. If the local staff's way of working is going to keep them, the players, and management happy, then we will keep it that way. The players might improve more the way you're working, but if it's going to upset a lot of people then you don't do it. The team's morale and the coaching staff's happiness are more important than your happiness.

Colum feels you need to learn about the country and its history. He found out all about Cambodia's history with the Khmer Rouge.

Try to engrain yourself in the culture as much as possible and show empathy for the country's history. In Cambodia, they had the genocide in the 70s.

Understanding a player's background and life story is crucial for Colum.

Some of the boys' families depend on them to make money. There's massive pressure on the players. We had some deep conversations with the boys. Some of them spoke English and others you did through a translator. You need much more empathy with the players here. They're not like footballers back home who would be more well-off.

Steve always felt it was important to make an effort to learn the language. It allows you to speak to the hearts of locals and gets them onside.

It's amazing how far a few keywords can get you. Even basic courtesy words such as please, thank you and good morning can break the ice. It also shows respect for the hosts as well as being useful day to day. In short-term contracts, fluency is not expected, but try learning five words a day and basic grammar to strike up conversations. Acceptance in the dressing room often helps performance and language and jokes are a vital part of that. When you can tell jokes in your second language you've made it!

Although you will often have a translator to overcome language barriers, Steve used key football phrases during sessions.

Football terms are universal like shoot, goal, and pass. It helps if you are working with an 18-year-old striker to know how to say "bend your run" or "arrive late" in his language. Even more important things to say are "well done" or "excellent" in that language. Immediate and personal praise is a wonderful motivator.

Steve also doesn't enforce foreign diets on local players. Players may rebel if you try and force them to stop eating staple foods like white rice.

It is naive to demand European diets for Asian players. Intelligent research can reveal local equivalents, which have the same nutritional value. Players may get sick if they are forced to eat alien food. Why would you expect players from poor economic backgrounds to buy expensive pasta, for example, when rice is far more accessible?

Following the right diet also impacts coaches, as Steve explains.

Try to understand the food as it is not funny when you are in bed for five days, have lost a load of weight, and are unable to work. Learn what you can eat and drink and never experiment on the day before a match. It is your responsibility to be fit to work, and diet is part of this.

Simon is well aware things are done differently abroad and won't always go to plan.

If you're someone that rides with the bumps and goes, "We had a few problems today, but we still did OK." If you're one of those coaches that can adapt, you'll do all right in South East Asia.

During his time in Asia, Sam found a common theme amongst the coaches who were successful abroad.

I worked with lots of people in different positions and countries. In Asia, there are a lot of countries that have foreign staff. They might be Dutch, Belgian, English, Italian, or Spanish. It's very interesting meeting them and hearing about their experiences – what they've struggled with and what's worked for them.

The common thread was the ones who felt they were having success had adapted to the culture. Ultimately, this is the number one thing that I've learned from working abroad. You must appreciate and understand the best way of working with the people that you have in front of you.

Building Relationships

Strong relationships with owners buys you time during tough moments and gives you the power you need to get things done. Steve highlights the importance of getting the hierarchy onboard.

The coach needs a good relationship with the "administration", which varies from nation to nation. In some nations, a club is run by a large administration. In others, one person is the "boss" and whether a coach likes it or not, that is where the wages are coming from. There are cultural differences that are perplexing at first. But the bottom line is establishing a strong relationship with the key person in the club will make the job more enjoyable and enable you to succeed.

Once the hierarchy is onboard, it's about getting the players onside, which Steve believes is critical for success.

You need the respect and support of the players, otherwise everything else is irrelevant.

Strong relationships get people to believe in what you are saying and trying to achieve. It also gets you jobs as Simon got the Philippines job after one of the players he coached recommended him. Good relationships and coaching create a positive narrative around a coach. Scott got the Muangthong United and Philippines jobs after two of his former Buriram players recommended him.

Your communication with players is important because owners always talk to players. Players shouldn't be making that decision, but owners ask experienced players. When players say good things about you, it works in your favour.

Colum went into a topflight club in Cambodia as an Assistant for four months and they won the league. He made a good impression on one of the foreign players who recommended Colum to his agent. His agent helped Colum become Head Coach at another top Cambodian club.

One of our foreign players at Svay Rieng spoke highly of me to his agent. His agent contacted me for the interview process which led to my first Head Coach job.

Colum builds relationships by connecting with the person first.

You are coaching people, not footballers, and every person is different. Find out what makes each player tick. It's something I've learnt massively over the last few years.

Being a good person helps you gain respect, as Michael explains.

Firstly, you need to gain their respect. You don't gain people's respect from your qualification and experience. You need to be a good person. You don't undermine them because you think you're better than them. You have to be very down-to-earth.

Michael feels that once players see that side of you, and recognise you can help them, the relationships will grow.

Players need to know that you're there to help them and that you're good at your job. Players who know you can help them are going to be more inclined to trust you.

Sam believes being genuine and delivering quality sessions is vital for building relationships.

It's a balance between making sure the training you deliver and the information you give the players is good quality. As well as the relationships off the pitch. They have to feel that you genuinely want to help. You're not only there for the money or the position. That you want to improve them, help football in their country, and you won't leave after one year. That takes time and is something you have to be conscious of.

Cederique also assesses the players to see what they respond best to.

You always find different profiles and attitudes in groups. You can be stricter with some players, and for others, you need to say, "After training let's speak one on one." Because if you shout at them in training, they will break down. This is the same around the world. They are people and we need to watch them individually.

Colum also highlighted the importance of team morale during difficult moments. He considers the players' input when making decisions.

We had external factors like Covid-19 and salary cuts affecting the players. You need to manage the group and speak to the senior players. Maybe you need to adapt your sessions. I gave the lads a day off as they'd trained well for three days. They were upbeat and came back flying in the next session.

It's not only people inside the club you need good relationships with but the media too. The media in some countries are only interested in results whereas others are interested in controversy, tactics, and style of play. Steve knows the importance of getting them onside.

In some countries, journalistic ethics are quite flexible. A vindictive journalist can ruin a playing or coaching career for ridiculous reasons. Giving "off the record" information early on, which is inconsequential, enables you to find the true journalists with ethics and the ones you can't trust.

Get to know the key media personnel early. Be honest with them and treat them fairly and equally. Don't lie to them with team selections. Give them stories to make their jobs easier. The media is the essential link to the fans. Help the media and, in return, they will usually help you. They are often an incredible source of knowledge about players which can be useful in the transfer market.

Quality of Work

The quality of your work is a huge factor in determining your success. You may have a reputation but a player's impression of you starts the moment they first meet you. They will be looking at initial impressions of how you greet people, how you behave, and the quality of your work on and off the pitch, as Colum explains.

It's your demeanor and sessions. Your first engagement with staff, players, and the board. It's how you conduct yourself around the place.

Colum says you need to maintain this no matter what's going on behind the scenes.

You'll have a meeting with the board and sometimes it won't go well. Despite that, you need to get into the office and come out and set the tone for the players. You need to be buzzing onto that football pitch. Have a little joke and ask how a player's family are.

Colum has found players at higher levels are more demanding.

The higher you go, the more players are on you. They expect more from you and your sessions.

You need to deliver if you're to succeed in the job and benefit from further opportunities. Colum impressed, which attracted one of the top teams in Cambodia – Visakha FC.

A couple of the Cambodian National Team players spoke to each other about the new coach. They said the sessions are good and he's a good guy. The Visakha CEO watched one of the sessions I was leading at the stadium. Overall, people were impressed with my work.

Having a clear and effective way of working gets players buying into what you're trying to achieve. This was important for Colum in Cambodia.

I instilled values and principles that we stuck to and a way of playing. It doesn't matter about systems. They're the key elements I wanted to keep in every session.

Another Irishman was impressing having just won the Cambodian League. Colum felt that helped his chances of getting his Head Coach job.

They knew that Conor Nestor was doing well as a young Irish Head Coach so we'll see if that works. I've got Conor to thank for that as well.

Simon knows from experience that people will hire you if your team plays well.

You can have a great game and the other team's owner looks at your setup and says, "This is a really good team. Their coach must be good. Why don't we bring him here?" You stick in people's minds when your team performs well.

Cederique has found the quality of your work is ultimately what people will judge you on.

In the beginning, people said, "You're not an ex-professional – it's difficult for you to build a career." For the last couple of years, nobody has told me this. You do good work and people will notice you. You'll build a reputation and they'll respect you. They'll forget about your playing background. Stay true to yourself and show with good work and attitude that you have quality. This is the most important thing.

Sam impressed by getting thousands of children on the pitch and co-creating documents at the Hong Kong FA. The hierarchy at the HKFA was impressed, which led to his promotion. Sam believes the legacy you leave behind is a huge indicator of your success at clubs and federations.

As a foreigner, you're there to do the best job you can and leave a legacy that is going to remain for years. Coach education is one way of doing that. If you have a strong coach education system, with good coach educators, that is where you could have a long-lasting impact. Imagine you've got 25 people on a C license, and you deliver four courses a year. That's 100 people whom you've influenced. You do that for years, and it's like the roots of a plant that filter down.

Steve believes in high standards and having good people around you.

You must work hard, set high personal standards, and continue to educate and improve. A wise coach listens to people they trust, as nobody gets it right all the time.

Michael impressed with his work ethic and got promoted to the first team in the Chinese topflight. He loves football and his passion for the game shines through in his work.

I've not had that playing experience, but the players and coaches see me as someone who's very passionate and always trying to get better. They see that I'm a very committed, professional, and determined individual. I ensure that whatever they need, I'm here to help them.

Michael met Thomas Tuchel when his Paris Saint-Germain side was facing Monaco in the French Cup Final in Shenzhen. Tuchel told him progressing in the game is all about being your best every day.

I asked Thomas Tuchel, did he think he'd be working at a top European club with the best players in the world. He said he never thought about it. He made sure that every day he was working to the best of his ability... so there were no regrets. He prepared to work the best he can, and he went on to win the Champions League with Chelsea. You have to be professional and work hard. By doing that, you ensure you're prepared when the opportunity comes.

One common theme in all stories is that the quality of work has to be high to make you stand out. It's important to keep developing, adding value to others, and succeeding on the job.

Improving Quality of Work

- Build strong relationships to increase buy-in to what you're trying to achieve.
- Access the best possible people, learning resources, and working environments.
- Get a high-level mentor you can observe, and who can observe you and provide feedback.
- Plan thoroughly and maximise the time spent on the grass delivering.
- Ask for feedback from coaches and players alongside reflecting on your performance.
- Develop an action plan from this feedback and reflections to improve your practice.
- Showcase your work in front of the right people. This can be going into higher-level environments or utilising online platforms.
- Open yourself up to critical feedback and challenging situations to improve yourself faster.
- Find ways to achieve and exceed the aims set out by your bosses. Success leads to opportunity!

Winning in Style

Playing football with a certain style is becoming more desirable for owners, especially for the best teams who expect to dominate games. What owners at all levels care about is the number of first team games they win and their league position. Colum lost only once in 11 months in Cambodia and Scott won 23 out of 29 games at Buriram United, losing only once. Scott feels this helped him get jobs.

First and foremost, it's your win percentage. My win percentage isn't bad. It was boosted massively by Buriram and Ubon.

Win percentages may not be a great stat for students of the game. It doesn't differentiate between draws and defeats or the context of the results and performances. Some owners only want to know if a coach will win games and a win percentage may be the only evidence they need.

Buriram United's performances in the Champions League and Ubon United doing the double over Muangthong increased Scott's profile.

The Buriram and Ubon results are there. The Japanese clubs were interested because they saw Ubon playing Muangthong. It's based on your results.

Scott was a consultant at Suphanburi FC who hired a coach working in the Maldives.

The former Suphanburi coach, Velizar Popov, had won the Maldivian league three years in a row and had a good win ratio. They knew it was a lesser league but he'd got a good record.

Winning games creates credit in the bank in Simon's eyes.

If you manage to win some games; you're going to get jobs. Success leads to jobs, that's just how it is. How they come about is often your network and social media.

Winning helps you get jobs and gives you the political power to get what you want from owners. It also impacts communities and gets the fans onside, as Steve discovered.

I was working in a country where I was appalled and upset about the poverty of the people who supported the team. A wise administrator asked me, did I think that I could change the poverty of this nation. All I could do was win games for their team, which was a great boost to the community's morale!

Luck

Luck is not something coaches like to speak of. But it's hard to argue the coaches haven't had huge strokes of luck throughout their journeys. The Philippines scored a 94th-minute equaliser to qualify for the Suzuki Cup, which kickstarted Simon's career.

Without that goal, I wouldn't be sitting here now. If Jimmy Younghusband doesn't put his head on that ball, we lose that game. I wouldn't have done the things I've done or have the CV I've got. It's down to that one goal or a referee's decision. The Gods were with us that day. We went on to the semis and now we're here. It could have been so different. Anyone that tells you luck isn't part of football hasn't had enough experience to understand it.

Scott realises how lucky he was to be at Leicester City which was Thai-owned, and led to his break in the Thai League. Sam found the Hong Kong FA job hours before the position closed. Michael also got promoted to the first team in China due to the Covid-19 pandemic.

I've had a succession of many lucky opportunities. If there wasn't a pandemic, maybe the reserve team would continue [it was scrapped because of Covid]. *If the foreign coaches stayed here in the off-season* [they went home and couldn't return due to Covid], *I wouldn't have had the opportunity to prove myself with the first team.*

Sometimes, you need a bit of luck, but you don't sit at home and wait for it to happen. You have to make sure that you work hard. Bosses want passionate people, who are proactive and show initiative in all cultures and countries.

Luck can play a big role but you don't twiddle your thumbs and wait for it. It doesn't come without all the other components that have made the coaches successful. You've got to be ready to perform if you're going to take advantage of any luck that comes your way.

3. Reputation

Your reputation is what people think and say about you, which is crucial in football. The more supporters you have, the easier it'll be to stand out, engage more people, and get jobs. You can be the best performer, but if people don't know you or aren't spreading positive messages, there won't be many opportunities coming your way.

How to develop a reputation:

- Get yourself into a position where you're being seen by more people in person, in the media, on television, and online.
- Build a clear identity through strong values, your appearance, positive actions, and what you say.
- Develop a large network with good relationships at work, locally, and worldwide by treating people well and adding value.
- Showcase good quality work that exceeds expectations and has a clear leadership and playing style.
- Develop your profile with qualifications, experiences at top organisations, working at high levels, and achieving success.

Word of mouth is the best form of advertising for coaches. If someone close to the decision-makers regards you highly, then it makes it much easier for them to hire you. If you are unknown or have a bad reputation, then it can be difficult to secure good jobs as Simon well knows.

You can go in there and tell everyone to f**k off when you lose, but you'll never get another job. If you go there – your team plays well but loses – and you say: "Congratulations, you played well." The owners think he's a nice guy and his team's good. When we lose our coach, maybe we can speak to him. You never know who's watching – go in and do the job!

It's important to keep your reputation intact when leaving clubs too. Scott got the Ubon United job after being recommended by the owner of his previous club. Leaving jobs on good terms increases the chances of people recommending you to other clubs. Having a strong network is also vital, as discussed in chapter 6. Develop a group of well-connected people who know your work and will recommend you to clubs. Cederique knows it's essential.

It's important to stay connected with people who know the quality of your work. You can be the best coach, but if you work in the forest nobody will know you or hire you. You need to put yourself out there.

Sometimes networking has a negative sound. But it's important to build a group of people, with good qualities, who you can call to discuss football and your career. If they know you are good and an opportunity pops up, you're only one call away.

Your reputation is what people will remember. It's what you say, how you behave, your appearance, your achievements, and how you work. People form impressions of you when they see you in real life, in the media, on television, and online. You can't please everyone, but clear values and principles create a strong identity that can make you more appealing to clubs who believe in your approach.

Simon was all over television and the media wearing a nice suit during high-profile Suzuki Cup games. The Philippines semi-finals against Indonesia were played in front of 90,000 fans in the stadium and millions watching on television. This provided a great opportunity to make Simon a well-known name in South East Asia. They didn't win but it raised his profile by publicising the great job he had done by getting to the semi-finals for the first time. This boosted his reputation and led to future jobs in the region.

The Philippines' 2-0 victory over Vietnam in the Suzuki Cup increased Simon's standing in the country which secured him a job there.

That made me known in Vietnam. When a club wanted a new coach, they thought, what about that Philippines guy – is he available? That's how it happened. I ended up getting a job in Vietnam on the back of that.

An owner in Indonesia took over a club and wanted to build a young squad. He knew Simon had a reputation for developing young players, so he hired him as Head Coach. Owners may be looking for different qualities but having a reputation can attract the right club.

Every social media post and interaction sends a message. Simon's social media following grew massively when he became Indonesia's Head Coach. His reach in the national media and on social media made it easier to grow his reputation as he was being seen by more people. Use the chapter 6 tips to grow your social profile as Steve believes it's vital.

In recent times, there has been massive growth in social media. This is a complex area and can have both positive and negative effects. Control of this medium is vitally important for coaches.

Treat everyone with respect as all your interactions form how people view you. Steve recommends treating people well as you never know when you'll meet them again. Players Steve has coached quickly rose into positions of power at clubs after they finished playing.

Treat all people how you would like to be treated – with honesty and respect – and you will enjoy the job. Footballers are the same around the world and dressing room laughs are universal. Share the passion for the game and win a few games as well. It really helps!

Developing strong relationships, delivering quality work, and having a clear identity builds a story around a coach. People you work with will spread positive messages and your reputation will grow. Assess your reputation (and your profile and performance) by asking people you trust. If they're straight shooters they can tell you directly or use an anonymous survey for a forthright response. You can ask how they would describe you, what they like, what they dislike, and why.

Also, do an online search to see what comes up from your posts, media reports, and what people are saying about you. Only do this if you don't face a barrage of unfair abuse online, and are in the right place mentally.

Be aware of your reputation, define it, and bring it to life. Look after it, as it only takes one incident to destroy it. Choose carefully what you want to be known for and find ways to grow your reputation in person, the media, and online. It's your brand and main selling point as a coach. A positive reputation can be the driving force behind a coach's career!

A strong profile, performance, and reputation increase your chances of getting jobs and succeeding. It's valuable to plan out how you will develop each area to land the positions you want. All the coaches had to pack their bags and leave home to find jobs. Some were in the same country and others had to move to the far side of the world. There's no right or wrong path.

The coaches have shown there are different ways to build credibility and a career out of the game. Find a path that suits you, follow it to the best of your ability, and you'll be amazed at where you end up!

Chapter 20. Simon's Journey: Title Contention in Indonesia

After leaving the Philippines, Simon McMenemy had a short spell in Vietnam before arriving in the Kalimantan jungle of Indonesia in 2011. Simon knew how passionate the fans are in the region, but he was about to learn a whole new side of Indonesian football.

Mitra Kukar

Simon and his wife arrived in Indonesia with only 20 dollars left in the bank. To make matters worse, his contract stated that if he lost three home games he would be sacked without compensation. He tried to negotiate its removal but failed. Right away, Simon knew the pressure in Indonesia was going to be extreme and he had to win.

Simon's first taste of an Indonesian derby came when his Mitra Kukar side faced Samarinda away from home.

It's about half an hour between the two cities. All the players and the bosses knew each other and it was the first time the derby had been played in the top league. There were 30,000 in the stadium and it was live on TV.

Simon's team was on the verge of victory before it all kicked off in the closing stages of the game.

We're 2-1 up with five minutes left and the Samarinda winger cuts inside and takes a shot at goal. Our defender turns his back and it hits him slightly above the elbow, putting it out for a corner. The referee gave the corner and the crowd went mental screaming handball. They were throwing things, invading the pitch, and the police were trying to force them back. It took about five minutes to get them off the pitch and regain control.

Further drama ensued as the referee changed his decision.

When we got back onto the pitch, the referee changed his mind and decided it was a penalty. So now we're going mental. I walked away from the bench and was off by the corner flag. Their fans started celebrating. The buzz changed in the stadium and everyone was happy because Samarinda are going to score a goal in the last minute... but our keeper saves it.

The late drama caused pandemonium in the stands and saw more fans invading the pitch.

The fans pile back onto the pitch, but this time they're coming on with flares. You couldn't see the centre circle. We were held in the dugouts surrounded by police officers with their guns, while this massive riot was going on. You can't see anything and *we're coughing because of the smoke. The referee is standing with us and I'm chatting with the other coach. The players are calm but the supporters are going batsh*t crazy. It was all kicking off.*

The referee blew the whistle to end what was an eventful first Indonesian derby for Simon.

It took seven minutes for the smoke to clear. By that time, the referee looked at his watch and went, "That's enough, you guys win." We shook hands and walked off the pitch with the fans still going mental.

It was a weird, crazy, and emotional game. The corner being changed into a penalty and getting saved, having all the fans coming at you and them being held, and finally winning the game and being back in the dressing room. It's an average day in Indonesia, sadly.

Simon and the team were exceeding expectations in the league but sadly that wasn't enough to keep his job. The owner was unhappy with one or two results which was all it took for him to relieve Simon of his duties.

Mitra Kukar had a lot of money to spend, so they went and signed Marcus Bent (former Premier League striker) plus three or four national team players. One of them was the national team captain who's quite a face in Indonesian football. We were fourth in the league and our target was fifth. This was the first time they'd been in the top league. We were doing well but the boss sacked me.

Persipura Away

Simon had already experienced Samarinda away, but nothing compares to trying to get three points at Persipura.

For Persipura — away — you have to fly from Jakarta to Makassar, which is two and a half hours and there are only two flights a day. You have a two-hour layover and then it's a three-and-a-half-hour flight to Jayapura. That's only for a league game. You're travelling for pretty much a day to get there. It's a long, long way.

Jayapura is that far away it's on the same island as Papua New Guinea.

It's almost a different culture. You're playing against Papuans who are big, strong, physical guys. Compared to your average under-five-foot-six Indonesian, it's a very different challenge going down there, even with a good team. They dominated the league for the best part of four years. Nobody really loses at home but they didn't lose at home for four years.

One of Indonesia's biggest clubs played Persipura away and didn't get the memo about the home team needing to win.

Persija went down there, beat them 1-0 and the fans kicked off because it was Persija. There were 30,000 home fans in the stadium. No away fans could go because no one's got the money to travel that far. Persija were held in the dressing room for three hours while everybody rioted. They set fire to the stadium and cars, attacked police officers, and there were injuries with at least one person reportedly dying.

It was decided the only way to get the players out safely was by sea.

The stadium is very close to the sea. It's a lovely setting. A boat was brought in because they thought that was the best way to get the players out. It was the only way to stop them from being attacked by the home fans.

The players had to go directly home without collecting their belongings from the hotel.

The players had training kits to change into but everything they brought to the game was what they flew back to Jakarta with. They got onto the boats and got taken straight to the airport. They were protected by police at the airport until they could fly back to Jakarta. Their belongings were forwarded on from the hotel.

Away days at Persipura are a tough mission for any team to handle.

To go there and win, you then have to deal with the aftermath of winning. Trying to get out of there alive is a whole new ball game. It's a difficult place to go. Persipura will always bring out all the fans and you'll get hit at full force by the power of their supporters. That was a scary incident!

Sadly, in October 2022, around 131 fans reportedly died after an Indonesian league game. Arema was defeated 3-2 at home by Persebaya and the Arema fans invaded the pitch after the final whistle. The police tried to force the Arema fans back into the stands when the disaster occurred. No Persebaya fans were allowed to attend the game due to the rivalry between the two teams. It's one of the world's worst-ever football stadium tragedies.

Pelita Bandung Raya

After Mitra Kukar, Simon had another spell in Indonesia the following season with Pelita Bandung Raya. The owner wanted to build the team around young local players and Simon had a reputation for developing young talent. It was between Simon and a Serbian coach for the job but Simon got the nod.

We held a trial day for 250 kids over one weekend. I picked 15 and then strengthened that with senior players and a few foreigners. We tried to teach these guys about the league and develop them but it was a tough ask.

They didn't have the best of starts to the season and the owner decided to bring in a Technical Director. The person chosen was Darko, the Serbian coach who Simon had won the job over.

We were sitting third from bottom after eight games, and the owner says, "I'm bringing in a Technical Director – it's Darko." They brought in a Technical Director above me who is the guy I got the job over. This guy came in and was constantly looking over my shoulder and saying, "I wouldn't do that. Do this. No, don't do that."

Whenever I went against him, he went to the boss. The boss came to me and was pleading, "Please Simon, be the bigger man. You know, he's trying to make an impression. Please try and work with him."

Simon took the job as the owner promised to give him time to develop their young team.

I had an agreement with the boss that I would take this job on with young players if he didn't sack me for the first year. If we got that first year's development, I believed we could build on it in year two. "I'm never going to sack you, Simon. Don't worry about that." I had it on paper that he'd give me a full year's salary if he did.

Then this Technical Director comes in and he's over my shoulder all the time. He's in the ear of the owner, "Simon's not the right guy. I would do things differently if I was the coach."

The situation reached boiling point as Simon confronted the Technical Director.

I'd had enough. I pulled him to one side and said, "Do you want this job? Is this why you're criticising every single thing I do?". He responded, "No, no, no. I only think about the players. I'm trying to help."

The pressure was piling up on Simon and the Technical Director finally got his wish.

The games go on and we get a couple of wins and a couple of losses. The pressure's on my shoulders and eventually, I get sacked. The Technical Director calls me to his house. In my head, I'm thinking, be the bigger man, walk in there and be sensible. I went in there and he sacked me.

I said, "So you're Head Coach now, I guess you got what you want?" He replied, "No, I don't want." Two days later, he takes over as Head Coach and I walked away with a full year's salary, which I was quite happy about.

Not everything turned out how the Technical Director had hoped as he got sacked soon after.

Darko got sacked five games later because he got worse results than I did.

Simon kept his cool as you don't want to develop a bad reputation or burn any bridges in the game.

You may want to fight with people when you've got every right to. But as a coach, your CV is important but your reputation is much more important. Being that guy who fights with people as opposed to the guy who people say, "I don't have a bad word to say about Simon. We sacked him but he's very professional." That's what I want to take with me.

I was trying to be the bigger man throughout, but I could have torn a few people's heads off at the time. My wife was trying to calm me down all the time. You learn a lot from those situations – it makes you a stronger person.

Bhayangkara

Simon decided to move back to the Philippines and spent two years with Loyola Meracalo Sparks, finishing second in the league and winning the PFF National Men's Club Championship. Simon enjoyed his second spell in the Philippines but he had unfinished business in Indonesia.

As Simon was about to fly to Jakarta, he was reading comments on his appointment as Head Coach of Bhayangkara FC.

A fan commented, "Why is this guy coming back? He's already been a loser twice." I got on the plane and I sat there thinking about it. He's right – I've been sacked twice. I was thinking to myself: this is it. I have got to go in and smash it because, if I don't succeed, I'm never going to get invited back to this part of the world again.

Simon kept hold of this comment and used it as motivation. On arrival, Simon saw positive signs and believed they were set up for a good season.

We had a lot of good young players, which is always a positive sign. You can mould the young players and then we had good foreigners who were well thought of in the league. There was no expectation on us as they had finished eighth the year before. The boss was hoping for a top-five finish but so long as we improved on last year, he would be happy. There was no pressure to win the league, which is always nice.

The club was a police-owned team and didn't have much of a fan base, which Simon didn't mind.

We didn't have any fans but the support from the police was brilliant right from the word go. It felt like there were a lot of people behind you, helping you and not pressuring you. It was a nice feeling to walk into a club and have that for once. It gives you motivation and belief.

It was a change for Simon as previous clubs didn't give him the same feeling.

All my previous experiences were going into bad situations. You notice good signs but I've seen the bad indicators as well. A Technical Director over your shoulder or a manager who doesn't leave you alone and is constantly talking about money. You're thinking, why do we stay at crappy hotels? Why is the manager always trying to scrimp and save money all the time? Why does he not back the team?

These little indicators give you an idea of what you're up against and how your season is going to go. With Bhayangkara it was the opposite. All positive from minute one and it got you into a positive frame of mind.

Simon knew what he was walking into because he had known the club's Technical Director for many years.

When I worked for Nike, I employed him to build an academy in Jakarta, so I'd known him for a long time. It was while I was working for Nike that I met him. He said, "Si, do you fancy coming back to Indonesia sometime? I'm about to get involved with a club team." I asked, "What team's that? He said, "A police team, but it's got good backing and good players." I told him, "I'd love to get back to Indonesia." And that's how it turned out.

The inside information he provided Simon with was accurate and hugely helpful.

He was always giving me good information about the club and the players. He said, "A lot of these players have played for the youth national team together and won stuff. They're a good group, so try and play to their strengths." He knows a lot, was very well-connected, and fed me really good information about the club. I knew a lot about the players and he gave me tips about how to handle the police. The police are a different culture within a football culture, which is tough.

I didn't need to do as much research as I had with other clubs. I felt more confident. I'd been there twice before and knew the country and league. I knew some of the downfalls but I had a good feeling about the club. I thought if I'm given the chance, I know this environment and I can succeed!

Simon knew the team was missing an identity, regularly changed players, and the foreign players would dominate the locals. He knew this needed to be addressed. When Simon saw the team on the field it was clear what he needed to do.

I watched a couple of training sessions before I took anything. This group of young players had known each other for a long time. They played short, sharp passes with good movement and I thought that's the way we're going to set the team up. They look really good doing that and if I get them doing it any other way they're going to struggle.

It gave me a clear picture of how to move forward. I was already coming in motivated and with a belief that I'd got lucky here. The signs are good – I've got a good feeling about this season!

Foreign Recruitment

Simon built the team around the local players and signed a marquee player to complement them. It's difficult for top-level players to adapt to life and football in Indonesia. Coaches spend time catering to their needs which isn't fair on the local players, who also need their coach's time and attention. It's also a big risk if they haven't played in a foreign country before. Simon experienced this when signing former Everton striker Marcus Bent at Mitra Kukar.

The league said you can sign a marquee player between $15,000 and $50,000 (USD) a month. It needs to be in that bracket above your average foreigner. Everyone's going out talking to Robin van Persie, and all these guys, and trying to bring them to Indonesia.

I had signed Marcus Bent previously, so I knew what it's like trying to live up to the expectations of a Premier League footballer. I said to the Boss, "Let's limit ourselves to $15 or $16,000 per month. We're not going to go over that. Let's try and find someone who's been in Asia before."

Simon identified a foreign player called Paulo Sergio. He had come through the Sporting Lisbon youth ranks with Cristiano Ronaldo and won the Singaporean League with Brunei DPMM. Simon called former Blackburn Rovers boss, Steve Kean, who worked with Paulo in Brunei. Steve said he should sign him.

We ended up signing Paulo Sergio who'd won the Singaporean league with Brunei. It was arguably a lower level than Indonesia but I convinced the boss that this is the guy we need.

This proved to be a clever move as other clubs opted for bigger names. Persib signed former Chelsea stars Michael Essien and Carlton Cole who could only lead them to a 13th place finish.

Simon also kept goalscoring machine Thiago, Otavio Dutra, and Lee Yoo-Joon, who was a great professional and one of the best holding midfielders in the league. The foreign players complemented the local players brilliantly which led to a great team dynamic.

New Season

Two weeks before the league started, the club suddenly moved from Surabaya to Jakarta. It's a 90 minute flight away which made life difficult for Simon. It meant he would be commuting back and forth to his wife who couldn't travel. She was heavily pregnant and was due to give birth at a Surabaya hospital.

The team got off to a good start, winning three of their first five league games. They continued to get better game by game and went on an 11-game unbeaten spell in the middle of the season. This included five away games which were key as Indonesian teams don't typically perform well away from home.

It made you believe that it didn't matter who we were playing against, we could go and get a result. That positivity was only with me to start with. But the more games we won, the more everyone started believing we were good enough and there was no one we can't beat.

Throughout the season, the team was playing attractive football and dominating games. Simon's vision for the team was coming to life. Despite being entertaining to watch, they only had 1,000 fans on a good day. Most of those fans were off-duty police officers who were told to be there.

Their fan base was much smaller than other teams with two of the big clubs bringing 35,000 fans to away games. This suited them as there was no difference between their home and away support. They weren't relying on huge home crowds like their opponents.

We won more away games than anybody else in the league. When we played Persib at home they had 35,000 away fans and we had 500. When we played them away, they had 45,000 fans so there wasn't a lot of difference. It was the same game home or away but only in a different stadium. It helped our mentality and confidence that we were always playing in front of away fans.

Indonesian players are so used to playing in front of home crowds of 40,000 that they get away with a lot. You'd see them faking, falling over, and diving a lot. You'd get that at home because 40,000 fans would shout at the referee. We had no fans there, so the referees aren't intimidated and would say stop diving. But our opponents play a certain way because of the influence of the fans.

Simon decided to replace star striker Thiago midway through the season. It was a big risk but proved to be a pivotal moment in the season.

Thiago was a lovely guy. The year before I arrived, he scored 25 goals in the league. The boss loved him but in the last game of the season, he broke his ankle. When I signed, they told me we were going to be without Thiago. We need to be able to score goals and win games without him. Thiago wasn't available until a quarter of the way through the season.

When he comes back, he knows that if he doesn't score goals, he's not going to get a new contract. He needs to prove himself. He starts making it all about him and every half-chance he shot. We've built this culture of passing the ball and trying to help each other and all the other players are up in arms.

Simon had to convince the owner a change was needed.

I had to try and convince the boss, halfway through the season, that we need to replace Thiago. We needed a different type of striker who fitted our style of play. Again, we talk about how you educate the bosses. I needed to show him and prove to him that this is the right decision. I wanted to replace him and in the end, I managed to do it. We loaned him out to my old club Madura (Pelita Bandung Raya was bought and renamed Madura United) and we signed Spasojevic.

Simon explained to Thiago that he would be better suited in a team that was built around him. Thiago was unhappy, but Simon firmly believed it was in the best interests of both parties.

The Run in

Bhayangkara was locked in a three-team title race with two teams who had much bigger budgets and fan bases. Being top of the table was a huge surprise for a club like Bhayangkara. Normally, the clubs with the biggest fan bases win the league but they were out of contention, which helped. No one expected them to challenge for the title and the underdog tag was working for them. The mid-season unbeaten run was pivotal as they only won twice and drew once during the final six games of the season.

With three games to go, Bhayangkara received a huge slice of luck after drawing 1-1 with Mitra Kukar. Momo Sissoko, the former Liverpool and Juventus midfielder, played when he was supposed to be suspended. The league awarded Bhayangkara the three points which left them one victory away from the title with only two games remaining. Simon was feeling the pressure during the run-in.

They think we're going to win the league. We've got to keep winning, we've got another game at the weekend, and we've got to win that as well. We might win the league! Jesus, what's going to happen if we win the league? I was on the golf course two or three times a week to help me put those pressures aside.

Bali United could go level on points with a win on the final day. But Bhayangkara had beaten them home and away which gave them the advantage on the head-to-head rule. Simon's team had the chance to win the title with a victory over his old side, Madura United.

There was bad blood in the run-up to the game with the Madura United fans being banned from the stadium. It turned into one of the nastiest encounters that Simon has ever been involved in.

The game had the most ferocious tackling I've ever seen. They went out to hurt us. They had three men sent off and should have had more. After the game, I was speaking to Peter Odemwingie (The ex-Premier League player) who got sent off in the game. He told me they were fired up and angry about the allegations that Bhayangkara was using political influence to win the league.

Simon says you're always under scrutiny in Indonesian football.

There's this constant undercurrent of suspicion in pretty much every game you play. They complained that because we're the police, their fans weren't allowed at that game. Their supporters brought flares to the previous game so the police were there to stop their fans from entering. They saw that as Bhayangkara stopping fans from getting near the stadium and trying to influence the game. No, it's the police doing their job. You're up against this constantly and it never stops.

Bhayangkara won the game 3-1 with Spasojevic bagging a hat trick. The team celebrated their title victory but the celebrations didn't last long.

Bali United had appealed the decision to award Bhayangkara three points after the Momo Sissoko incident. Their appeal was rejected a few days later and Bhayangkara lifted the trophy in their final home game of the season.

Making History

Simon created history, once again, by becoming the first British coach to win the Indonesian league title. He was also voted the best coach in Indonesia.

It was the highlight of my career so far. Everyone was crying on the pitch when we won the league. The boss was doing backflips. I had an emotional moment in the corner of the pitch.

The feeling at Bhayangkara was amazing, right from the moment Simon landed at the airport.

I was overcome by the crescendo of positivity that I felt from the minute my plane landed in Jakarta. When I landed, I saw a rainbow that ended on a group of lads playing football. There was just something the whole way through the season and I can't put my finger on it. There was a belief that something was going to happen.

It mainly came from our little Portuguese guy, Paulo Sergio, who's a religious guy. He said, "God's on our side this year." And he said that again and again and it kept being true. We kept getting last-minute goals.

Simon puts his success down to adapting to the culture in Indonesia.

Everybody knows football and there are a million better coaches in the world than me. But there aren't many coaches who know how to adapt to the culture, certainly in Indonesia. That's why I won the league and was the National Team Head Coach. That gives me confidence. I would do the job for free if people ask me nicely – I enjoy it that much.

The Indonesian players were brilliant and the team was full of belief.

I didn't think we'd win the league, but we were full of belief. You could see it going from player to player. Guys that were average the year before were now being talked about going to the national team. This feeling that was flowing through the team was fantastic. We were great off the pitch and we were great on the pitch.

A big part was also the foreign players they signed to complement the Indonesians.

Paulo Sergio won the league in my first year and we finished third and qualified for the Asian Cup in my second year. Paulo then left and went to Bali, won the league there, and then retired. For three out of four years, he won the league with three different teams. He was a diamond.

Paul Sergio gave Simon the perfect formula when it comes to signing foreign players.

Sometimes you get it right, and sometimes you get it wrong. That gave me a lot of boxes that foreigners need to tick, based on signing Paulo. He's the most perfect foreigner I've signed. When I look at foreigners in the future, has he got a good attitude? Is he going to be a role model? Is he going to do the right things off the pitch? Is he a good player?

Being a good player is not the number one priority. It helps but signing Messi doesn't mean he's going to fit into your squad. There's a lot more to bear in mind. I've learned a lot about signing foreigners. I've signed some bad ones and some good ones, but like anything… you learn.

Simon took a big risk replacing Thiago with Spasojevic, but it paid off.

That was a pivotal point in the season. If we kept Thiago, we wouldn't have won the league. Spasojevic came in and scored 15 goals in half a season and won us the title. It could have backfired massively if I hadn't got the right guy. But, for whatever reason, the gods were shining on us that season and it worked out.

It was a huge relief as Simon was feeling the pressure having already been sacked twice in Indonesia. It was an amazing feeling having proved everyone wrong and succeeded at the third attempt.

I proved something to other people but I also proved it to myself. When I stick to what I know and I'm positive – I can go in and succeed. If I hadn't been sacked twice in Indonesia, I wouldn't have come back and won the league. I learned a lot being sacked and did a lot of soul-searching. Did we do this right? Did we prepare right? Are those the right things in training? Did I treat them the right way?

I went through that, came out of it, and got another opportunity with a good squad. I put all that knowledge into our season. That experience shone through and we had a fantastic season. Getting sacked makes you question yourself. But winning the league gives you the belief that if I'm in a good situation, I can win stuff!

Simon combined the lessons from his previous two sackings to achieve the dreams of many coaches, by winning a league title in the professional game!

Some of our 25+ football coaching books

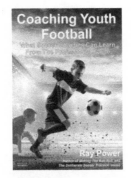

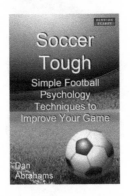

BennionKearny.com/**soccer**

CPSIA information can be obtained
at www.ICGtesting.com
Printed in the USA
BVHW042127230523
664790BV00004B/117